RECEIVED

MAR 1 8 1986

INTELLECTUALS IN POLITICS IN THE GREEK WORLD

INTELLECTUALS IN POLITICS IN THE GREEK WORLD

FROM EARLY TIMES TO THE HELLENISTIC AGE

FRANK LESLIE VATAI

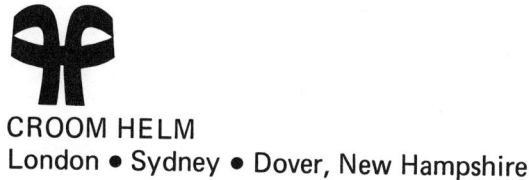

CROOM HELM
London • Sydney • Dover, New Hampshire

© 1984 Frank L. Vatai
Croom Helm Ltd, Provident House, Burrell Row,
Beckenham, Kent BR3 1AT
Croom Helm Australia Pty Ltd, First Floor,
139 King Street, Sydney, NSW 2001, Australia

British Library Cataloguing in Publication Data

Vatai, Frank Leslie
   Intellectuals in politics in the Greek world.
   1. Intellectuals – Greece – Political activity
   2. Greece – Politics and government – To 146 B.C.
   3. Greece – Politics and government – 146 B.C.-
   323 A.D.
   I. Title
   323.3'2   JC75.I/
   ISBN 0-7099-2613-8

Croom Helm, 51 Washington Street,
Dover, New Hampshire, 03820 USA

Library of Congress Cataloging in Publication Data

Vatai, Frank Leslie.
   Intellectuals in politics in the Greek world.

   Bibliography: p. 168
   Includes index.
   1. Greece – Politics and government – To 146 B.C.
2. Intellectuals – Greece – Political activity. 3. Elite
(Social sciences) – Greece. I. Title.
DF82.V38   1984   305.5'52'0938   84-15589
ISBN 0-7099-2613-8 (U.S.)

Typeset by Columns of Reading
Printed and bound in Great Britain by
Biddles Ltd, Guildford and King's Lynn

CONTENTS

Acknowledgements	vii
1. Introduction	1
The Issue	1
An Emerging Pattern	6
Sources	12
2. Pythagoras and the Pre-Socratics	30
From the Seven Sages to Pythagoras	30
Pythagoras and Pythagoreanism	36
Archytas and Empedocles	60
3. Plato and the Academy	63
Plato	63
Dion and the Academy	83
4. From Polis to Monarchy	99
Isocrates and Panhellenism	99
Aristotle and Alexander	112
The Hellenistic World	116
5. Epilogue	130
Notes	133
Bibliography	168
Index	180

To my mother and father,
Laszlo and Irene

ACKNOWLEDGEMENTS

The publication of a first book gives its author the opportunity of looking back and acknowledging debts. Louis Gottschalk and William Bossenbrook first awakened my interest in history, and Finley A. Hooper led me to the study of Greece and Rome. My dissertation committee, Thomas W. Africa, Gerald Kadish, Saul Levin and W. Warren Wagar, made many valuable criticisms of form and content. Professors Africa and Levin in particular have been very generous with their time and advice. Jacques Kornberg read and commented on parts of my first chapter. All have played a role in the formation of this book, but I alone am responsible for any remaining errors or misinterpretations. I thank them all, along with my parents to whom this book is respectfully dedicated.

The 'philosopher', on the other hand, is the *reaction*: he desires the *old* virtue. He sees the grounds of decay in the decay of institutions, he desires *old* institutions; – he sees the decay in the decay of authority: he seeks new authorities (travels abroad, into foreign literatures, into exotic religions –); he desires the ideal *polis* after the concept *'polis'* has had its day (approximately as the Jews held firm as a 'people' after they had fallen into slavery). They are interested in all tyrants: they want to restore virtue by *force majeure*.

F. Nietzsche, *The Will to Power*
No. 427 (Kaufmann)

1 INTRODUCTION

The Issue

This book is an exploration of the role of intellectuals in the politics of the classical and Hellenistic periods. Political theory is not discussed except to illuminate the similarities and the differences between what philosophers said about politics and how they behaved in the political arena. The difference between these two attitudes can be broadly termed the difference between theory and practice. The question as to whether intellectuals ever assumed so important a position in society that their very utterances could be considered as political events can, in general terms, be answered in the negative. Kings and tyrants established themselves in powerful positions where they were likened to gods and their word was law; intellectuals, with the possible exception of Pythagoras, were never allowed such a dominant status, save in the eyes of their followers. For some, like Plato, this was a bitter disappointment; others, such as Aristotle, may have felt that the Athenians paid too much attention to resident intellectuals such as himself. The *demos* had its reasons, however, for Aristotle and his followers maintained close Macedonian links.

The word 'intellectual' cannot be defined with any precision.[1] In general, sociologists provide working definitions that are valid for whatever point they are trying to make. Naturally, resemblances exist between the various definitions and sociologists and historians are usually gracious about quoting other definitions, especially if these fill out an area in which the scholar's own definition is weak. Historical and cultural differences also make any single blanket definition virtually an impossibility.[2] To add to the difficulties, there is the particularly eclectic nature of the term 'intellectual'. Ray Nichols, in his recent study of Julien Benda, notes the ambiguous nature of what an intellectual is and what counts as an intellectual action:

> The discourse is *reflexive*: in strange mirrors we see (and make) our faces, and experience sudden shocks of recognition. Nowhere is this more true than with the intellectual ... Perplexity over diverse practices, social and conceptual, and their relations — the problem of the intellectual lies here. Efforts to grapple with it in turn reveal

themselves as contributions to it or re-presentations of it, and they become part of their own subject matter, part of their own problem – social expressions as well as social analyses.[3]

Efforts to turn the mirror into a window are tenuous at best. Of the many discussions and definitions of intellectuals, those of Max Weber and Edward Shils provide the best vantage point from which to commence our survey of Greek intellectuals.

Weber tells us that by 'intellectuals' he understands 'a group of men who by virtue of their peculiarities have special access to certain achievements considered to be "culture" values, and who, therefore, usurp the leadership of a culture community'.[4] This definition should be augmented by Shils's observation that

> there is in society a minority of persons who, more than the ordinary run of their fellow men, are inquiring, and desirous of being in frequent communion with symbols which are more general than the immediate concrete situation of everyday life and remote in their reference in both time and space. In this minority, there is a need to externalize this quest in oral and written discourse ... This interior need to penetrate beyond the screen of immediate concrete experience marks the existence of the intellectuals in every society.[5]

This minority quite naturally view themselves as an elite. They are almost as naturally drawn towards each other. In any society, it is given to few individuals that their personal visions remain private truths, for a prophet requires an audience. If the masses serve no other function, they can at least be used as a yardstick to measure the difference between the chosen few and the unenlightened many. Among the Greeks, this self-image of a privileged elite was further strengthened by the fact that many philosophers and their epigoni came from the aristocracy. This is especially true with the Pythagoreans and members of the Academy. It is also the case that members of this aristocracy turned to the philosophical schools when their own positions within society were threatened by the 'new education' or the accelerated commercialism of the late sixth, fifth and fourth centuries. In the philosophical schools, the politically declining aristocracy found a new cohesiveness; bound together by their feelings of natural and acquired superiority they could again turn outwards towards society and attempt to reclaim their 'rightful place'. Florian Znaniecki notes that 'in order to be qualified as a scientist [intellectual] whom his circle needs, a person must be regarded as a "self" endowed with certain desirable characteristics and lacking certain undesirable characteristics'.[6] These desirable characteristics for the Greeks included good breeding, a sense of loss over what they regarded as their true role in society and a romantic sense of themselves as that segment of society *engagé* with a rapidly deteriorating world. Unlike the modern world where knowledge gives social status, the opposite was the case for much of the period under discussion. For most Greek intellectuals social status was the prerequisite to true knowledge and goodness.[7] In the words of Aristotle,

> a man's own goodness is nearer to him than that of a grandfather, so that it would be the good man who is well-born. Some [writers] have indeed said this, fancying that they refute the claims of noble birth by means of this argument. As Euripides says, good birth is not an attribute of those whose ancestors were good long ago but of whoever is simply good in himself. But that is not so. Those who give pre-eminence to ancient goodness make the correct analysis. The reason for this is that good birth is excellence of stock, and excellence is to be found in good men. And a good stock is one which has produced many good men. Such a thing occurs when the stock has had a good origin, for an origin has the power to produce many offspring like itself.[8]

Goodness is biologically determined. M.T.W. Arnheim points out that 'this naturalistic argument is Aristotle's way of reconciling the traditional aristocratic outlook with the more fashionable views that each individual should be judged on his own merits'.[9] Arnheim goes on to remind us that not even Euripides could bring himself to accept the latter view.

Karl Mannheim speaks of the perennial attempts of intellectuals to lift the conflict of interests to a spiritual plane.[10] He sees in the intellectuals a coherent group able to rise above the petty egoism of the conflicting parties, simultaneously penetrating the ranks of society and compelling it to accept their demands. Such altruism is today possible, he thinks, due to 'participation in a common educational heritage' that acts to dispel differences of birth, status, wealth and so on.[11] His idea of an unattached intelligentsia must be viewed sceptically, however, and, for the Greeks, the idea must be rejected altogether. Greek intellectuals were united through the educational programmes of a Pythagoras, Plato, Aristotle, or Zeno, but it was a union of 'members of a leisure class who reflected the views of a defunct aristocracy and disdained labor and commerce'.[12] Such individuals were very much part of the conflicting factions of the time. There is a sense in which Mannheim is correct, if we define the conflict of interests to include the social and political interests of the intellectuals: many aristocrats, faced with a decline in their political and military fortunes, decide to wage their battle for power with the rest of society on a new plane, a spiritual one. Their new weapons become the cultural symbols. They monopolise the interpretation of such symbols and newly rearmed re-enter the political fray.

The relationship between values and interests works both ways. Alvin W. Gouldner writes:

> The New Class believes its high culture represents the greatest achievements of the human race, the deepest ancient wisdom and the most advanced modern scientific knowledge. It believes that these contribute to the welfare and wealth of the race, and that they should receive correspondingly greater rewards. The New Class believes that the world should be governed by those possessing superior competence, wisdom and science — that is themselves. The Platonic Complex, the dream of the philosopher king with which Western philosophy begins, is the deepest wish-fulfilling fantasy of the New Class.[13]

The New Class to which he refers encompasses both the technical intelligentsia and the intellectuals. The quotation describes the situation of that section of the New Class called the 'humanistic intellectuals'. Gouldner's words describe the contemporary situation in 1979, but they are equally valid for any period in history when intellectuals feel that their power is not commensurate with their self-image as they judge it. Since intellectuals have always had a very high opinion of their value, the tensions that exist between this status group and the rest of society exist today as they existed in the fourth century when Plato wrote, 'that the ills of the human race would never end until either those who are sincerely and truly lovers of wisdom come into political power, or the rulers of our cities, by the grace of God, learn true philosophy'.[14]

In so far as tension between intellectuals and power is a perennial problem, it is of interest to examine the character of Greek intellectuals and their relations with society, their role as social beings.[15] In general, the Greeks treated their philosophical elites with a mixture of indifference and humour.[16] Finding such an attitude unacceptable, Greek intellectuals attempted to position themselves within society in such a way that they could no longer be ignored or scoffed at. This jockeying for political influence took the two forms that Plato had mentioned: intellectuals attempted direct political rule; or working through an existing ruler, the philosophers tried to rule the state by controlling him. The first method does not presume any single political system and so philosophically minded activists were both tyrannicides and tyrants, setting up or supporting governments ruled by the one, the few or the many. In the majority of cases, however, direct intervention was not possible or advisable and philosophers followed Aristotle's advice and became advisers to rulers.[17] Since it was judged easier to gain ascendancy over one individual than over a group, philosophers came to be a regular fixture at the courts of tyrants or kings. A modern example is Henry Kissinger, who managed to sidestep both Congress and Richard Nixon's executive staff in order to maximise his influence with the President. The *amour propre* of this man has been well summed up by Michael Howard:

> Kissinger's memoirs make it clear that he knew very well what he was doing there. He was the Merlin at this Round Table; the wise man drawing on deep wells of ancient magic to help this naive, rumbustious good-hearted people among whom his lot had been cast; rescuing them from the disasters into which their good intentions had already led them, setting them on a path that would avoid future catastrophe, and teaching them the skills by which their noble endeavors could be turned to good effect.[18]

Few Greek intellectuals achieved Kissinger's success or shared his survivor instincts. Their failure was due in part to the fierce rivalry among competing intellectual groups, particularly in the fourth century. It is always necessary to be aware of interpersonal relations among intellectuals. There was fierce competition for a favoured place in the retinue of the mighty. Rival blue-prints for a new society or rival arguments for the justification of the old order were common occurrences. Further, Greeks of all political persuasion loved a contest and found it natural to pit rival schools and philosophers against each other; the energies that might have gone outward into society were thereby deflected into inter-scholastic squabbles. This, however, is not a state of affairs limited to Greeks.

An Emerging Pattern

While discussing problems in psychic research, William James notes that

> the peculiarity of the case is just that there are so many sources of possible deception in most of the observations that the whole lot of them *may* be worthless ... I am also constantly baffled as to what to think of this or that particular story, for the sources of error in any one observation are seldom fully knowable.[19]

On an equally melancholy note, E.N. Tigerstedt concludes an admirable summary of the problem of writing a life of Plato: 'Many, if not most, of the ancient writers had no interest in telling the truth, if ever they knew it.'[20] Tigerstedt succinctly analyses the difficulties facing the historian of antiquity. The historian

> cannot simply disregard the sources, yet he can still less trust them unreservedly. Even a statement that looks probable may simply be due to a plausible invention. Nor are the earliest sources necessarily the more reliable, as the example of Aristoxenus proves. On the other hand, the tendentious character of a source does not in itself make it absolutely unreliable. Much of what Aristoxenus told about Plato might have been true, though he interpreted it to Plato's disadvantage.[21]

The situation holds true not only for a life of Plato, but for all the philosophers with which this thesis concerns itself: the sources are often late, ill-informed, and with various personal and academic axes to grind. Tigerstedt's solution to the problem has been to concentrate his attention on the image of Sparta in antiquity or on the various ancient and modern interpretations of Plato. This is a valid approach in itself and is equally useful for trying to arrive at some conclusions about what actually did take place. For behind the image lies some reality, and even if the historian cannot penetrate the image, at least the image contains elements of truth in the same way as comedy contains elements of the reality that it caricatures. An attempt at reconstructing the roles that philosophers played or aspired to in politics can be made, both because the importance of the subject requires such an attempt, and because the sources, though bad, are not completely chaotic. However tentative, a reconstruction is possible through disciplining the historical imagination.

In discussing the manner in which he has constructed a historical model out of the Homeric poems, M.I. Finley emphasises an important methodological rule: 'No argument may legitimately be drawn from a single line or passage or usage. Only the patterns, the persistent statements have any standing.'[22] This rule has served Finley well, and the controversial thesis of *The World of Odysseus* has stood the test of time. Since he was working from the Homeric poems and, to a lesser extent, myths and oral traditions, the lack of hard, documentary evidence dictated his methodological rule. This principle of patterns can be applied to my own reconstruction where hard, documentary evidence is often lacking or sometimes buried under a welter of hagiography, polemic and fiction.

By itself, a pattern is not enough. In separate articles D.R. Stuart and Janet Fairweather have pointed out that Greek biographers were prone to make persistent errors in such matters as the derivation of biographical material from an author's writings.[23] When the works in question include dialogues or poetry, scepticism is called for. Other examples, such as *topoi* concerning witticism, the circumstances of a philosopher's death, and so on, require that the pattern principle be reinforced by additional controls.

Finley suggests comparative analysis: 'A behaviour pattern which can be shown, by comparative study, to have existed in one or another society outside the one under consideration.'[24] Reaching beyond the sources, there is a presumption that given a similar set of circumstances, men with similar attitudes and value systems will act in a more or less similar manner. Thus, how intellectuals in one period of time behave throws light on the behaviour patterns of intellectuals from a different period of time or from a different culture. Weber has argued similarly:

> The general psychological orientation of the intellectuals in China, India, and Hellas is, in the first place, in no way fundamentally different. As mysticism flowered in ancient China so Pythagorean esoterics and Orphism did in Hellas. The devaluation of the world as a place of suffering and transitoriness is familiar to Hellenic pessimism ... These are representations appropriate to any cultivated intellectual strata. The differences of development were located in interests ... established by political circumstances.[25]

The historian works from the known to the less known. Periods better documented than the classical or the Hellenistic can be used to arrive at informed estimates of how Greek intellectuals behaved.

Working from the less known to the even less known, W.K.C. Guthrie likens Pythagoras to Confucius and minimises the Greek's personal ambition while emphasising his personal zeal for reforming society according to his moral ideas.[26] Bertrand Russell's description of Pythagoras as a cross between Einstein and Mary Baker Eddy is well known.[27] The Pythagoreans have always been liable to such comparison. Analogies have been made with the Calvinists at Geneva, the Freemasons of the eighteenth century, Chinese thought reformers and Catholic monks.[28] George Thomson and Kurt von Fritz demonstrate the dangers of using comparative methods to justify conclusions already reached. Thomson attempts to locate the Pythagoreans according to Marx's conception of the historical dialectic; he considers them to be a commercial theocracy of the type and in the same line of development as the Calvinist elders of Geneva.[29] Von Fritz wished to minimise the role of the Pythagoreans as a group in politics and finds a natural parallel with the Freemasons of the eighteenth century who, though influenced by Masonic theory, 'certainly did not govern, compose, or write poetry in their quality as Masons, much less because they were Masons'.[30]

Weber's thesis that the general psychological orientation of intellectuals differs in no fundamental way from period to period can be illustrated by comparing Isocrates to Comte. Isocrates wrote letters to Dionysius, Jason and other rulers: his behaviour, and his faith in what he had to say, can be compared with the activities of Auguste Comte who sent covering letters with his book, *System of Positive Polity*, to Tsar Nicholas of Russia and the Turkish sultan.[31] A comparison of Isocrates' declamations with Fichte's *Addresses to the German Nation* is enlightening from the point of view of underlining the evangelical fervour of both individuals. A comparison of Isocrates' Panhellenic ideal with the crusading ideals of the Hildebrandine Papacy is rewarding for understanding the attitudes and public stance of Isocrates and his followers.

What applies to individuals works with elite groups as well. One of the most important of the nineteenth century elites was the Saint-Simonians. As Frank Manuel points out, this group

> accentuated the final phase of the tradition of their master and elevated to pre-eminence the *artists* — their generic name for what he had called the Platonic capacity — a category that extends far beyond painters, poets, and musicians and embraces all moral teachers, whatever may be their instruments of instruction ...

The man of moral capacity set goals and inspired his brethren with the desire to achieve them.[32]

The premises of the Saint-Simonians were at variance with those of the Academy or the Pythagoreans. The self-image of the various groups, however, bears comparison, as does the manner in which they set about trying to achieve their goals.[33] It is useful to note the position of Saint Simon within the movement and the way in which the movement altered following the master's death. Such a self-righteous group, convinced of the probity of its motives and the truth of its goals, easily falls into eccentricity and becomes prey for satirists. What would an Epicrates or an Antiphanes have made of the followers of Enfantin who wore their vests buttoned in the back to enforce dependence on one's fellow man?[34]

Although many Saint-Simonians came from the upper classes, Saint Simon's own falling out with Napoleon and the Saint-Simonians' obsessions with technology and progress blunted the aristocratic element in their thinking. The elites proposed by English intellectuals of the nineteenth century were frankly aristocratic in nature. Ben Knights has pointed out that Matthew Arnold 'like Coleridge ... proposes an ideal cultural system, and then performs a dialectical conjuring trick by which the ideal is found to be latent in the *status quo* ... We are dealing with reactions to what were seen as mechanistic accounts of the human spirit, the most prevalent of which was liberal nationalism.'[35] Coleridge, who formulated the notion of an intellectual elite or clerisy, openly acknowledged his debt to Pythagoras and Plato. In a conversation towards the end of his life, Coleridge ruminated as follows:

> All harmony is founded on a relation to rest – a relative rest. Take a metallic plate and strew sand on it; sound an harmonic chord over the sand, and the grains will whirl about in circles and other geometrical figures, all, as it were, depending on some point of sand relatively at rest. Sound a discord, and every grain will wisk about without any order at all, in no figures, and with no points of rest.
>
> The clerisy of a nation, that is, its learned men, whether poets, or philosophers, or scholars, are these points of relative rest. There could be no order, no harmony of the whole without them.[36]

To go back to Weber's assertion, intellectuals do behave in a consistent enough manner that analogies between a better and a less well-known period are possible. The psychological orientation of such individuals, whether it be seen as an indignation to changes in society that it cannot control, or whether it manifests itself in a zeal to reform society to higher truths, does form a consistent behaviour pattern. The English clerisies never got off the ground; Saint-Simonianism, though not without influence in the mid-nineteenth century, never became more than a trial balloon which, in the words of Louis Reybaud, 'swells up before the eyes of an astonished crowd, rises, grows smaller and smaller, and is lost in space'; but the Pythagoreans held political sway in part of southern Italy for a considerable period of time and the Academy and other philosophical schools were a potent political force in the fourth century.[37] The reason for the differences lies in the second part of Weber's statement: 'The differences of development were located in interests ... established by political circumstances.'[38]

It is not only individuals or elite groups that can be fleshed out by means of historical analogy. Sometimes a historical situation can be made clearer by means of historical comparisons. The anti-intellectual fervour that gripped America in the fifties, caused partly by fear of the unknown Soviet menace and partly by the fact that many Americans had not forgiven the intelligentsia its left-wing cosmopolitanism of the thirties, has a parallel in fourth-century Greece where Demosthenes and other local patriots found the intellectuals' support of a united Greece under the aegis of Philip intolerable.[39] Demosthenes' nephew, Demochares, briefly succeeded where Joseph McCarthy ultimately failed, but in both societies anti-intellectualism became a political issue.

A final example of this type of clarifying historical parallel is supplied by Napoleon's relations with the ideologues. George Grote compared the French emperor with the tyrant Dionysius I, an effective piece of attitude structuring given the average Englishman's view of the emperor. Both Napoleon and Dionysius maintained a love-hate relationship with the intellectuals. Dionysius' joy at receiving first prize for a tragedy he composed was as sincere as the young general's sentiments upon being elected a member of the French *Institut*. Bonaparte solemnly asserts: 'Les vraies conquêtes, les seules qui ne donnent aucun regret, sont celles que l'on fait sur l'ignorance.'[40] In this spirit Napoleon acknowledged that long before he can consider himself the equal of such distinguished men, he is to be considered their pupil. And yet three years later, while entrenching himself in power, Napoleon's tune had changed and had become threatening: 'Ils sont douze ou quinze metaphysiciens bons à jeter à l'eau. C'est une vermine que j'ai sur mes habits ... Je ne le souffrirai pas.'[41] Dionysius gave the Spartan captain

Pollis specific instructions along these lines, if some stories are to be believed.[42]

At a certain stage of his career, prior to the *coup d'état* of 18 Brumaire, Napoleon had need of the support of the ideologues and their *Institut*. He cultivated them and received their assurances that his actions were entirely justifiable. Paul Gautier describes the mood of many of the ideologues: 'On crut tenir une sorte de philosophe grand général, grand politique; un Marc-Aurèle. La philosophie était donc au pouvoir, et naturellement les "philosophes" et leur amis pensèrent gouverner à leur tour.'[43] Intellectuals commonly serve a legitimising function and Napoleon's use of them prior to 18 Brumaire is similar to the way in which Philip consistently manipulated intellectual opinion in his favour as evidenced by the intellectuals' support of Philip during the Sacred War. Philip's assassination does not allow the comparison with Bonaparte to come full circle, but Alexander, whose megalomania exceeded that of Napoleon, felt that he could dispense with their support. Intellectuals were not a vital element in his plans for the future.

Besides using historical analogies to throw light on the Greek experience with intellectuals, models taken from the social sciences also serve to clarify the past. A historian would not be taking full advantage of the resources at his command if he failed to make use of the ideal types of Max Weber; Georg Simmel's subtle discussion of the role of secrecy in society and the nature of a secret society; Vilfredo Pareto's analysis of elites; Ferdinand Tonnies's distinction between *Gemeinschaft* and *Gesellschaft*; A.F.C. Wallace's studies of revivalistic movements from the point of view of cultural anthropology; Edward Shils's models of intellectuals and authority; or the speculations of Carl Jung as to the complementary and compensatory nature of the 'rational' and the 'irrational' within an individual or a group.

Weber, who discusses at length the problems and procedures of comparing models with concrete cases, notes that 'where relationships of the kind as abstractly described in the construct ... have been observed or are assumed to exist in reality to some degree, we can make the *particularity* of this empirical relationship pragmatically clear and understandable to ourselves by reference to an *ideal* type.'[44] In other words, an ideal type can be used as a description of the empirical world, should the ideal world and the particular world coincide. Weber argues correctly that every historian, consciously or unconsciously, uses such a *modus operandi* when assessing a given case. Further, upon being asked to defend his interpretation of the facts, he is forced to be explicit about his comparative procedures.[45] Of course, historical cases also hone the social science models; this, however, is the task of the sociologist.

Sources

While both comparative history and sociological insights can aid our investigation of the Greek intelligentsia, the persistent problem of shaky sources must be confronted. Four short ancient surveys of Greek philosophers in politics are extant in the following works: the *De oratore* of Cicero, the *Reply to Colotes* of Plutarch, The *Deipnosophistae* of Athenaeus and the *Mithridatic Wars* of Appian. None of the four sources display any objectivity or value neutrality. Intellectuals as politicians were a contentious issue, and arguments for their effectiveness and accomplishments or their villainy and counter-productivity were made in the heat of debate. The historian must be on his guard for rhetorical hyperbole. Two of the surveys are hostile to the philosopher-politicians, and two of the writers defend the intellectuals' activities.

Philosophers in their capacity as teachers of rhetoric were defended by Cicero in *De oratore*.[46] Cicero wishes to demonstrate that those individuals become the greatest orators and statemen who have acquired learning and the further ability to express it in words. Cicero mixes eloquent politicians and philosophers and their students in equal amounts, and the passage is of great interest as added testimony that Aristotle had Isocrates in mind when he took up the study of rhetoric 'and linked the scientific study of facts with practice in style'.[47] Plutarch's defence of philosophers occurs in his *Reply to Colotes*, where he attacks the Epicureans for their views on law and religion.[48] 'But what has proceeded from Epicurus' philosophy and maxims?' asks Plutarch rhetorically and he contrasts the Epicurean disdain of politics with the noble endeavours of a number of eminent philosophers.[49]

The views of Cicero and Plutarch are challenged by a valuable passage in Athenaeus where, in the context of an anti-Platonic diatribe, followers of Plato are brought to task for being despots and scoundrels.[50] Much of this material comes from Demochares, the nephew of Demosthenes. In his capacity as advocate for the politician Sophocles, Demochares delivered a scathing denunciation of philosophers as a threat to Athenian democracy.[51] Philosophers, he maintains, have always either become tyrants or, at the very least, supported them. In pleading his case, Demochares naturally weighted the evidence against the philosophers, just as Plutarch used only positive examples to glorify the same class of individuals. In neither case need the material be rejected. Special pleading dictated the selection of examples, but one can work with and through the open biases of Plutarch and Demochares (or Theopompus for the Macedonian material in Athenaeus) to achieve a useful and informed synthesis of the political activism of assorted philosophers, with special reference to the fourth century, the peak of their political activity. The picture that emerges of some intellectuals favouring democracy and others autocracy is consonant with what we know of the activities of intellectuals in better documented times. Nor should the fact that men of similar intellectual disposition hold differing political views be surprising. Heidegger and Sartre were both existentialists. The German communist Kurt Eisner told a friend while discussing socialist revolution that 'at such critical moments it would be the Kantians, and not the Prussian Hegelians, who would act, and if necessary, die for social justice'.[52] When Eduard Bernstein finally turned against Marx and Engels, he testified: 'And in this mind, I at the time resorted to the spirit of the great Konigsberg philosopher, the critique of pure reason, against the cant which sought to get a hold on the working class movement and to which the Hegelian dialectic offers a refuge.'[53]

The final anti-philosopher survey is found in Appian. Enraged by the conduct of the Epicurean politician Ariston, Appian engages in a highly discriminatory attack on philosophers in politics.[54] Appian tells us nothing new, but he points out that the activities of a few philosophers soured the image of the remainder in the eyes of many. The attraction of philosophers to politics came to be viewed as motivated not by high ideals or a love of truth, but by poverty or lack of occupation combined with envy of those in power.

Any discussion of source problems must take into consideration two particular kinds of sources to which the historian is indebted for narrative material, anecdotes and letters. Since much of this book relies on often dubious sources, some words of justification are required. We know that many anecdotes are undoubtedly false, but others simply cannot be proven either way.[55] In Diogenes Laertius, for example, we read that Plato mounted the platform during the trial of Socrates to speak on Socrates' behalf.[56] Before he could engage in a defence of his master, the judges shouted him down. There are a number of reasons for treating this anecdote with scepticism. The source is late: Justus of Tiberias was a Jewish historian who lived during the reigns of Nero and the Flavians.[57] He was Josephus' rival and wrote a *History of the Jewish*

Wars. Josephus replied to Justus in his *Vita*, bitterly condemning him but conceding that his antagonist 'was a clever demagogue and ... not unversed in Greek culture, and presuming on these attainments even undertook to write a history of these attainments'.[58] Tiberias was a hellenised Palestinian *polis* and Justus was a member of the ruling tetrarchy and familiar with the Hellenic tradition. In the emotion-laden climate that led to the Jewish Wars he could sympathise with the effort of Plato to stem the tide of Athenian irrationalism that culminated in the execution of Socrates. Where this anecdote belongs in the corpus of Justus' writings cannot be known.

The anecdote clearly belongs in the pro-Platonic tradition that tries to combat the charge of political inactivity on Plato's part by showing that, given the political climate of the day, reasonable counsel was an impossibility and retreat from an active life was the only alternative for an honourable man. The story of a famous student attempting to defend his beloved mentor is not without parallel: Isocrates attempted to defend Theramanes. From another angle, Alice Swift Riginos speculates that the story may be patterned after the anecdote in Zenophon's *Memorabilia*: young Glaucon, Plato's brother, wished to speak before the public and make a name for himself, but he was laughed off the platform because of his youth and inexperience.[59] Finally, the story is at variance with Plato's own account in the *Apology*, where the episode is not mentioned. The issue, however, is far from being decided.

To take the last point first, why would Plato mention such an unpleasant episode, even had it occurred; the episode would take away from the high seriousness of Socrates's speech. A more fundamental objection is that Plato's dialogues, like a poet's verses, must be used with the greatest caution. As Fairweather notes: 'Anyone, then, who is attempting to derive biographical information from an ancient author's works will ignore at his peril the factor of the poetic, rhetorical, or philosophical *persona*. It seems, unfortunately, that some ancient scholars were not above ignoring such subtle considerations completely.'[60] On the question of basic themes in philosophers' lives, *topoi* must be kept in mind, but so must the fact that philosophers in Greece were very conscious of themselves as such and were prone to behave in highly stylised ways. There was a strong element of imitation in their behaviour. They viewed themselves as teaching correct behaviour, following the examples of their teachers and hoping themselves to become exemplars. Since such a philosophy was taught by example, ironic or even absurd anecdotes were introduced by the biographers to illustrate the results of what happens when a philosopher follows his own precepts too strictly. Plato's entire Sicilian venture can be seen in such a light and certainly the tale of Plato's slavery fits this mould. In fact, the story of Plato defending Socrates with such poor results can be seen as an anti-Platonic anecdote illustrating the futility of the philosopher's ventures into the practical life. Certainly, this account is older than Justus, who probably recorded rather than invented the story.

A historian finally decides against the anecdote; the lack of external evidence militates against Plato's having delivered such a speech, for, had he done so, it would have been noticed, as was his willingness to defend Chabrias.[61] In sum, this anecdote is typical of many: it is biased, although a bias does not mean an untruth; it comes from a late source, although the anecdote probably had an earlier genesis; and it follows certain well-worn themes, although, again, this does not necessarily make the story untrue.

The anecdotes about Plato have been collected by Riginos; Ingemar Düring performed a similar service for the biographical tradition concerning Aristotle.[62] Naturally, anecdotes of a pro- and anti-Aristotelian tradition abound. Aristotle attracted the venom of the anti-Macedonian party at Athens and Demochares attacked the philosopher in a famous speech, accusing him of betraying Stagira to the Macedonians. Further, said Demochares, Aristotle tried to profit from the destruction of Olynthos by denouncing the wealthiest citizens of that *polis*. As proof, Demochares adduced certain letters. Indeed Aristotle was a noted letter writer and Artemon collected and edited his correspondence.[63] Although the collection has been lost, there can be no doubt that Aristotle was in close correspondence with Antipater, so that the mention of 'certain letters' was a clever psychological ploy on Demochares' part. The specific allegations are heavily distorted by partisanship and, though there may be a grain of truth in them, historians have rejected Demochares' slanders. Aristotle's involvement in political affairs, however, is beyond dispute. He was, as Aristocles notes, envied as well as hated for his friendship with kings.[64] He was also the recipient of an honorific decree issued by the Amphictionic League in 329-328 BC and was possibly given equal honours by the Stagirites and the Athenians.[65] Naturally, the Athenian decree would have been granted while the Macedonian presence was supreme, for if the anecdotes, both pro and con, agree on anything, it is that Aristotle was consistently loyal to the Macedonians and, especially, to Antipater.[66] In so far as he desired to aid Athens, Aristotle did so on the assumption that Macedonian rule was a reality that had to be accepted. Such realism spawned an anecdotal tradition highly critical of the philosopher and rival philosophers, particularly Isocrates, Epicurus, and their followers, added their own anti-Aristotelian biases.[67] Nevertheless, the anecdotal tradition does present a plausible and consistent picture of Aristotle as a politically involved individual which can be utilised by the historian.

To understand this anecdotal tradition better, one must turn to the Hellenistic world of the third century BC when many of the anecdotes were first collected. Arnaldo Momigliano correctly brings out the tone of the writings of such individuals as Hermippus and Satyrus:

> The educated man of the Hellenistic world was curious about the lives of famous people. He wanted to know what a king or a poet or a philosopher was like and how he behaved in his off duty moments. When the information was not directly available, it had to be supplied by guesswork: the unscrupulous biographers added invention to their ingredients. Fundamentally it was a Greek curiosity about Greek men – the more so because so many Greek men now lived among barbarians.[68]

During the sixth and fifth centuries, Greeks were relatively indifferent to the private lives of their poets and philosophers.[69] Such an attitude reflected the lack of a proper vehicle in which to discuss biographical details.[70] This factor must be modified by the scanty nature of our evidence, but it nevertheless remains true that biography became a precise notion only in the Hellenistic age.[71]

What kinds of material did writers in Alexandria and other intellectual centers have at hand to satisfy the curiosity of their audience; and did the readers of the *bioi* expect the stories they were told to be of a purely factual nature? Hellenistic readers supposed the stories to be true, but they were uncritical. Above all, they wished to be entertained and possibly edified as well. Hermippus wrote a work on how philosophers met their deaths, and although his stories inspire little confidence, this does not mean that all the tales are necessarily false.[72] The quotable tag that Pherecydes gave 'someone passing by' prior to the sixth-century philosopher's death should be treated on a par with other stories about Pherecydes.[73] However, the death of Menedemus which Hermippus details can be taken more seriously because more is known of Menedemus, whose life had been told by Antigonus of Carystus and Heracleides Lembus. Antigonus also discussed Menedemus' death and, though the two versions differ, it can be seen that Menedemus died feeling betrayed and bitter. What we have of Hermippus indicates a taste for the bizarre which, however, may mean no more than that he contented himself with chronicling the unusual aspects of his subjects' lives. Stories of other people's degradation, as with their deaths, have always been of interest to readers, and Hermippus wrote to entertain. What A.A. Long has written about Timon of Phlius applied equally to Hermippus and his peers:

> Timon's *Silloi* could satisfy the biographers on all these counts [witticism, anecdotes, and eccentricities], combining as they do, the doxographical, the satirical, and the anecdotal. Fantasy apart, Timon does not seem to have invented any of his pictures of the philosophers. His *Silloi* are a doxographical pastiche, rather than a travesty of philosophers' lives, but this made them no less welcome to Diogenes Laertius and his predecessors.[74]

In the fourth century AD, Jerome had linked Hermippus' name with Antigonus of Carystus, Satyrus and Aristoxenus as Greek predecessors to Suetonius.[75] Three of the four individuals had Peripatetic links and Hermippus was known as both a Callimachean and a Peripatetic.[76] He, therefore, had two rather impressive traditions to fall back on, although he seems to have been more indebted to the material found in the *Pinakes* and on oral tradition than to rigid Peripatetic doctrine.[77] A work on a subject such as *Lives of Those who Passed from Philosophy to Tyranny and Despotic Rule* might have a strong Peripatetic tone if it illustrated various virtues and vices of the philosophers concerned. Unfortunately, the scanty remains make it impossible to evaluate much of this work. One of the fragments deals with the Academic philosopher Chaeron whose 'Platonic communism' had been excoriated by Demochares.[78] The other fragment concerns the Stoic Persaeus' activities in Corinth.[79]

The relationship between Peripatetic doctrines and biographical writing is no longer as clear cut as was thought prior to the studies of Rudolf Pfeiffer and Momigliano. The latter notes:

> The type of life we call Peripatetic is the result of a sort of compromise. The basic interest in discovering a variety of human characters has a philosophic root, but the wealth of strange details, of piquant anecdotes, was ultimately meant to satisfy the curiosity of the common reader.[80]

This emphasis on the strange and the sensational in the sphere of human action has a parallel in paradoxography which chronicled the strange and the fantastic in the natural world.[81] The audience placed a premium on simplified, easy to remember statements about the doctrines of philosophers rather than hard analysis; nor were they particularly concerned with the external details of the philosopher's lives. Their concern was to acquaint themselves with the philosophers' personalities and descriptions of their manner of living and the best way to isolate such details was through anecdotes.

Antigonus of Carystus seems the most promising of the third-century biographers, because he wrote of his contemporaries or near contemporaries, Arcesilaus, Lycon, Crates, Pyrrho, Zeno and his teacher, Menedemus.[82] Like Aristoxenus, Antigonus was a man of wide-ranging interests and he enjoyed the patronage of the Attalids.[83] The Attalids also patronised the philosophical schools at Athens where they attempted to establish their influence. Many stories, as well as the political activities of Menedemus with Antigonus Gonatas, are recounted by Antigonus of Carystus and we have no reason to doubt his authority.

The Hellenistic biographers were used by Diogenes Laertius. Arguments concerning how Diogenes used his sources and what sources he used have been going on since the nineteenth century. As with Plutarch, the answers given to these questions have been numerous, and no one view has ever monopolised the field.[84] In contrast to Plutarch, few modern scholars have been generous in their praise of Diogenes Laertius. The poems he composed in honour of the various philosophers are neither profound nor clever and even Jørgen Mejer, who attempts a sympathetic evaluation, concludes that 'Diogenes' epigrams demonstrate that he did have some kind of personality, not a great mind but enough to know what he was doing even if he didn't do it very well'.[85] Very little is known of Diogenes, who lived in the second or the earlier half of the third century AD, and his work has no formal connections with any of the contemporary schools of learning. The way in which he treated the lives, however, shows him to be in sympathy with the Hellenistic sources he uses. Like the Alexandrian biographers and Antigonus of Carystus, he is not primarily concerned with constructing an accurate chronology of the philosophers' lives. The often quoted statement by Plutarch in his *Life of Alexander* is relevant to Diogenes' purpose as well:

> For it is not Histories that I am writing but lives; and in the most illustrious deeds there is not always a manifestation of virtue or vice, nay a slight thing like a phrase or a jest often makes a greater revelation of character than battles where thousands fall, or the greatest armaments or sieges of cities.[86]

This attitude has bearing on the political role of various philosophers, for Hellenistic biographers were interested in how philosophers oriented themselves towards power. Anecdotes about Zeno and Antigonus Gonatas serve the purpose of showing that the virtues of Zeno were such that his head was not turned when the Macedonian king desired his intellectual company and promised him influence at court. In drawing out the connection between the two men, Diogenes appends letters they sent each other and tells us that Zeno, although declining the offer, sent Persaeus and Philonides in his place.[87] There is no reason to doubt such evidence, or other passages where the relationship between monarchs and the heads of the philosophical schools are discussed. Diogenes was a conscientious compiler of earlier sources.

A few words should be said about Philostratus, a late second and early third century AD Sophist and an important member of the Second Sophistic.[88] As the name implies, this movement honoured Sophists, preferring them to ethereal philosophers.[89] It also honoured the worthies of the 'First Sophistic'; all the more so as 'the second century shows a predilection for antiquity and archaism'.[90] Philostratus wrote anecdotal biographies of these early Sophists and provides some useful information about Isocrates, Critias and others. We learn that the Academic Dias of Ephesus was utilised by Philip to persuade Greeks to accompany him on his expedition, 'since it was no dishonour to endure slavery abroad in order to secure freedom at home'.[91] Philostratus' real value, however, lies in his biographies of his contemporaries.

Finally, Plutarch took an interest in philosophers in politics. In his *Reply to Colotes*, he had castigated the Epicureans for their political quietism. Additionally, in *The Contradictions of the Stoics*, Plutarch took Zeno, Cleanthes and Chrysippus to task for treating public affairs in a strictly theoretical manner.[92] Who of the Epicurean and Stoic sages ever travelled in their country's interest, served on an embassy or expended a sum of money on public gifts, asks Plutarch, who had done all these things.[93] Plutarch was quite adamant that philosophers should become politically involved and wrote an essay with the title *That a Philosopher Ought to Converse Especially with Men in Power*. In the essay, Plutarch justifies his political activism:

> Certainly the teachings of the philosopher, if they take hold of one person in private station who enjoys abstention from affairs and circumscribes himself by his bodily comforts ... do not spread out to others, but merely create calmness and quiet in that one man, then dry up and disappear. But if these teachings take possession of

a ruler, a statesman, and a man of action and fill him with love of honour, through one he benefits many.[94]

This theoretical statement is given both a fictional and a biographical backdrop. In two fictional works, the *Banquet of the Seven Sages* and the *Sign of Socrates*, philosophers and rulers converge and one of the lessons to be drawn from both stories is that power needs the educative influence of philosophy to complement it.[95] Neither Periander nor Epaminondas treat philosophers with anything other than respect in spite of disagreements that come up between the parties. In reality, this may even have been the case with Epaminondas, though it is doubtful that he deferred to his philosophical friends in any important political matter.

In the *Banquet of the Seven Sages*, Solon and Mnesiphilus are among the luminaries. These individuals also found their way into Plutarch's biographies. Plutarch constructed a philosophical succession that ran from Solon to Themistocles with the long-lived Mnesiphilus connecting the two statesmen.[96] Solon was considered *sophos* because of his interest in practical wisdom and his concern to apply morals to politics.[97] Similarly, Themistocles was known for an ability to apply practical solutions to complex problems. Born too late, he never joined Solon as one of the *Seven Sages*, but Mnesiphilus bridged the two and so it became possible for later writers to see an intellectual link between Themistocles and Solon. The succession literature aimed to establish an intellectual genealogy of a group of intellectuals going back to a famous founder, someone along the lines of Socrates, Plato or Isocrates.[98] Plutarch, who wrote a work *On The First Philosophers and Their Successors*, actively contributed to this genre and was familiar with the works of Solon and others.[99]

As a school, this triad (Solon-Mnesiphilus-Themistocles) need not be taken seriously, but Plutarch wished to demonstrate that behind every successful statesman stood a wise teacher. Thus he paired Mnesiphilus with Themistocles, Plato and Speusippus with Dion, Sphaerus with Cleomenes, Anaxagoras and Damon with Pericles, Aristotle with Alexander, Ecdemus and Megalophanes with Philopoemen, and so on. To take one example, Anaxagoras taught Pericles to value philosophy and disdain pandering to the mob: the result was his serene and graceful speeches.[100] The sage also taught Pericles to rise above the petty superstitions that spring 'from an ignorant wonder at the common phenomena of the heavens'.[101] In the *Life of Nicias*, the enlightened Dion and Pericles are contrasted with Nicias, whose ignorance of the natural causes of the lunar eclipse and his absorption in sacrifices and divination cost the Athenians so dearly.[102] Additionally, Pericles had the advantage of Damon's advice. The latter 'trained Pericles for his political contests, much as a masseur or trainer prepares an athlete'.[103]

The relationship between a philosopher and a politician does not consist primarily in the former directly influencing the policies of the latter. As Alan Wardman has shown, the relationship was more oblique.[104] In Wardman's view of the behaviour pattern, philosophers improve the politician's character and free him from superstition. They impart to him a love of freedom and a hatred of flattery. When reverses are encountered, philosophers can be called upon for consolation and to renew the spirit. What Plutarch has in mind when he describes these things is his contemporary situation. Wardman notes that 'the effect of the *Lives* is to emphasize that philosophy is respectable, that philosophers are upright men with the same interest as [good] government ... Plutarch was probably in harmony with a new trend which preached the necessity for philosophers and men of power to act on the same side'.[105]

Plutarch, who had defended the Academy against the Epicureans, strove in his biographies of Dion, Lycurgus and Numa to show that this school has the most to offer receptive men of power. Plutarch often quotes from Plato's works; and at the beginning of the *Life of Dion* he notes that wisdom and justice must be united with power and good fortune.[106] Similar sentiments are echoed in the *Life of Numa* and in the *Comparison of Demosthenes with Cicero*.[107] Plato epitomised Plutarch's conception of how a sage should behave at court and, if the philosopher ultimately failed in his quest to reform Syracuse, he is at least given credit for pinpointing Dion's arrogance as an important cause of that failure. The contrast to the Stoic Sphaerus is obvious. Although admiring the manliness of Cleomenes, Sphaerus 'increased the fires of his high ambition'.[108] Opposed to this, the 'Platonic' legislators, Numa and Lycurgus, helped relieve the 'inflamed' conditions of their respective cities.[109]

Legendary characters such as Numa and Lycurgus could be used by Plutarch as *exempla* of the combination of philosophy with power where 'by some divine good fortune royal power is united with a philosophical mind'.[110] For those *Lives* which are not clearly mythical, Plutarch's assertions concerning philosophers at court should be taken on par with any other 'fact' that he has to relate about antiquity. Plutarch may exaggerate certain situations or individuals and enlarge on their importance, but to deny that such events took place without specific proof to the contrary is to call the entire Plutarchean corpus into question and that is unacceptable.

The Pythagoreans present a series of difficult problems. In general, modern attempts to discuss the Pythagoreans fall into two streams of thought. A minimalist school maintains that only evidence up until Plato may be utilised to construct what we know of Pythagoras and his early followers. An exception is made with Aristotle whose work *On Pythagoras* survives only in fragments. Aristotle also mentioned the Pythagoreans a few times in his surviving works.[111] Applying this rigid standard of source utilisation to the role that Pythagoras and his followers played in politics would produce extremely meagre results.[112] We would know only that the Pythagoreans banded together in a society where they practised a distinctive and extraordinary way of life. Pythagoras emerges as a man of predominantly religious importance, little concerned with philosophic problems; and these sources indicate no concern with political problems at all.[113]

If, however, other sources are allowed to come into play and form the narrative, a political reconstruction of the Pythagoreans is possible. The sources in question are Aristoxenus, Dicaearchus and Timaeus, whose views are embedded in the writings of Porphyry and Iamblichus, often through the medium of Apollonius and Nicomachus, the latter two being writers of the second century AD.[114] Diodorus Siculus and Justin-Trogus also contain important earlier material. Much depends upon how successfully the fourth-century BC writers can be extracted from the later sources. The importance of this operation depends in turn on how much reliance is given to Dicaearchus, Aristoxenus and Timaeus as valid sources for the Pythagorean religious and political sect.

The modern history of the 'source critical problem' began with an important article by Rohde and reached an apex with Kurt von Fritz's book, *Pythagorean Politics in Southern Italy*. Relying heavily on previous studies by A. Rostagni and A. Delatte, von Fritz evaluated the later sources and reconstructed the historical narratives of Aristoxenus, Dicaearchus and Timaeus.[115] In the process, he established the chronology of Pythagoras' life and sorted out the problems of the break-up of the Pythagorean brotherhoods.[116] Even critics who do not trust the reliability of the fourth-century sources attest to von Fritz's success in isolating them.[117] Having traced the primary sources, it remains to assess their trustworthiness.

Aristoxenus was a controversial figure in antiquity and his personality continues to exercise modern commentators. Ingemar Düring writes: 'Seething with hatred and malignity, he collected every derogatory piece of information [on Socrates] he could get hold of, and by this means created a tradition which was to have unfortunate consequences in the future.'[118] Attempting to analyse this 'fatal influence', Düring lays the blame on 'Pythagorean fanaticism, personal aversion, and the conceit of a musician'.[119] J.A. Philip, too, finds in Aristoxenus an 'aggressive and disgruntled man, hostile to the philosophical and intellectual tendencies of his time'.[120] But Aristoxenus has not been without his admirers and Arnaldo Momigliano has a favourable estimate of him as a sensitive individual who, exposed to a number of schools and individuals, formed no complete and binding loyalties. Quite the contrary, his life experiences developed his capacity to observe humanity and to unify what he saw within a biographical framework. Momigliano concludes: 'He has the tone of a man who has seen too much to take a narrow view of human attitude . . . He was the man to produce a new blend [of biography] : learned, yet worldly; attentive to ideas, yet gossipy.'[121] Momigliano is not as upset as some by Aristoxenus' attacks on Socrates; in fact, he relishes the picture, though appreciative of the fact that it contains 'an element of malice'.

Aristoxenus' account of the Pythagoreans encompasses three books: a life of Pythagoras; a description of the Pythagorean way of life; and a book on Pythagorean maxims.[122] To be sure, Aristoxenus had his biases. He preferred Aristotle to Plato and Pythagoras to both. He was concerned about the reputation of the Pythagoreans in the fourth century and how they had become the butt of the comics' jokes. He indulged in a certain amount of rehabilitation, such as the assertion that Pythagoras, far from being a vegetarian, was in fact fond of the meat of tender young kids, suckling pigs and cockerels.[123] The point was to make Pythagoreanism less ridiculous to a fourth-century audience. This rationalising bias must be kept in mind, but it must not obscure other tendencies in Aristoxenus' work. A native of Tarentum, he was familiar with the Pythagorean tradition. His father was acquainted with Archytas and he himself says he knew the last of the Pythagoreans.[124] Dionysius the Younger told him the story of Damon and Phintias, an important anecdote, and one we have no reason to disbelieve.[125] Aristoxenus prized such tales and made them a regular feature of his writings. Because of the nature of his sources, these anecdotes concerning Pythagoras and Archytas and other philosophers should be taken seriously and cannot be dismissed. Likewise, the story of Polyarchus, the envoy of the Younger Dionysius in Tarentum, is revealing both of the political and intellectual situation in Magna Graecia and of the relationships that philosophers maintained with each other.[126] In another context, it is Aristoxenus who tells the story of Plato's disastrous public lecture on the Good.[127] Aristoxenus heard the anecdote from Aristotle who seemed to enjoy telling the story.

Dicaearchus was a Peripatetic contemporary of Aristoxenus and the two men knew each other.[128] Although differing on certain key events such as the catastrophe that overwhelmed the Pythagorean Order, both writers agree that Pythagoras and his followers were an active political force in southern Italy.[129] It served Dicaearchus' purpose to make Pythagoras a man of affairs and, like Aristoxenus, he engaged in a lot of debunking, but he also relied on popular tradition and von Fritz's evaluation of Dicaearchus is that he is a reliable source and a good supplement to the account we have of Aristoxenus.[130]

Delatte, Rostagni and von Fritz have all demonstrated that Timaeus was an important source for all later treatments of Pythagoras, most especially those of Diodorus Siculus, Justin, Diogenes Laertius and Apollonius of Tyana. Timaeus incorporated his remarks on the Pythagoreans into a larger work on the Greek west. Von Fritz notes that 'he has the enormous advantage that he deals with the Pythagoreans within the framework of a general history of Southern Italy, so that he has to correlate and check in all directions'.[131] True, Timaeus had a weakness for historical coincidences, but von Fritz's model is valid and, unless proven wrong, Timaeus' assertions should be taken seriously.[132] The fact that Timaeus visited the archives at Delphi for Crotoniate oaths and treaties deposited there may not have impressed Polybius, but the modern historian can be more charitable.[133]

To Timaeus we owe much of what is known concerning the training of future members of the sect as well as the most comprehensive recording of Pythagoras' own thoughts. For the former, Timaeus is an important addition to the works of Aristotle and Aristoxenus. For the latter, where he records Pythagoras' four speeches upon arriving at Croton, Timaeus is either following or elaborating on a similar tradition to that used by Dicaearchus. Since Dicaearchus and Timaeus disagree as to whom Pythagoras first addressed, it is not necessary to assume mere elaboration.

The authority of these four speeches has been either contemptuously dismissed as a later addition by Timaeus or Iamblichus, or passionately defended as an important but neglected source. Rostagni and especially Cornelia de Vogel have argued at length for the validity of Pythagoras' sermons.[134] It is now agreed that the major source is Timaeus. Dicaearchus also notes that Pythagoras gave four speeches, but he fails to report the contents of them. Diodorus and Justin-Trogus refer to speeches Pythagoras made upon arriving at Croton and, like Iamblichus, these writers rely on Timaeus.[135] The question is, does Timaeus rely on Dicaearchus exclusively, merely filling in Dicaearchus' framework and, if not, what independent sources had Timaeus to draw on.[136] It seems likely that he had access to Dicaearchus' well-known works. However, Antisthenes refers to Pythagoras' four speeches as examples of *polutropia*.[137] Rostagni deduced from this that a tradition independent of Dicaearchus existed in the fourth century and that this formed the basis of a rhetorical speech by Gorgias who, in any event, was aware of the Italian traditions.[138] Further proof of awareness of the speeches in the fourth century can be found in Aristophanes' *Ecclesiazusae* (446 ff.) where the comedian, according to Rostagni, parodies Pythagoras' address to the women.[139] De Vogel accepts Rostagni's proofs, but rejects Gorgian authorship for the speeches. Her arguments against Rostagni appear conclusive and it is probable that the speeches were known in Athens in the fourth century at a time when many Pythagoreans had fled southern Italy because of the threat of conquest by Dionysius the Elder.[140] If the tradition was known in Athens, it must have been alive in Magna Graecia and Timaeus would have had ample opportunity to record it. Thus the speeches could represent a genuine tradition or at least mirror early Pythagorean thinking. De Vogel's defiant conclusion cannot be dismissed: 'I wish to underline that we are concerned here with an historical fact, just as trustworthy and well-founded as anything else we may claim to know about Pythagoreans.'[141]

The sources concerning Plato's political activities are not markedly better than the sources about the Pythagoreans whom Plato admired. If one momentarily sets aside the Platonic *Epistles*, it is difficult to establish whether Plato had any political contacts at all with the Younger Dionysius in Sicily.[142] Ephorus, who is one of the major sources for this period of Sicilian history, has nothing to say about Plato in Diodorus' account.[143] However, Diodorus' narrative is not complete at this point. In D.S., 15.7.1, Plato is at the court of Dionysius the Elder, but Diodorus' account of Dion in Book Sixteen shows omissions. The account of Dion breaks off at 16.20.6 and the thread is only resumed in 16.31.7. It could be plausibly argued that it is only a chance factor that we have no specific mention of Plato and Dionysius the Younger in Ephorus or Theopompus; there are many omissions in Diodorus.

The other important tradition comes from Timaeus. Nepos, who used Timaeus extensively in his *Life of Dion*, has two statements about Plato that are not to be found in the *Epistles*.[144] The first concerns Plato's invitation to Sicily by the Elder Dionysius and the second is about the philosopher's sale into slavery. Both these statements, however, refer to Plato's first — and better attested — trip to the west. Although we know that many of Plato's students wrote biographies of their master, and these include such notables as Aristotle, Speusippus, Hermodorus and Heracleides Ponticus, almost nothing remains of these efforts and the historian in search of Sicilian material draws a blank.[145] Aristotle has many historical references scattered throughout his writings, but no mention of political activity on Plato's part. However, there is a fragment from Aristotle's student, Aristoxenus, where he says that Plato's venture in Sicily was no more successful than Nicias'.[146] Aristoxenus was surely informed on such matters and it brings up the further point that, if the whole episode is spurious, how could the Academy have managed to deceive everyone on so recent an event?

Speusippus' propaganda that Plato was the son of Apollo may not instil much confidence in that writer, but, taken with Timonides' letters to Speusippus, we can see an underlying motive to Speusippus' actions — the glorification of Plato and the Academy.[147] That Plato's nephew should want a first-hand account of the Sicilian venture is entirely understandable. Speusippus was an ambitious man who did not hesitate either to upgrade the Academy's image by deifying the founder, or to thrust the school into the politics and controversies of the day, as witnessed by his letter to Philip. Plutarch uses Timonides on a number of occasions and there is an unmistakable eye-witness quality to much of what Timonides writes and one, further, that inspires confidence. It is possible, as Guthrie speculates, that Plutarch got some of the information concerning Plato's activities in Sicily from Timonides.[148]

The lack of primary material other than the Platonic *Epistles* puts a tremendous burden on that source. If the crucial letters are authentic, then Plato is hardly likely to make up a story of his failures in Sicily. The same argument holds true if we presume that not Plato but someone close to him wrote *Epistles Seven* and *Eight*. There may be an effort to whitewash the Academy of the failures of Dion and Callippus, but the individual that really mattered to the Academy was Plato and according to the letters Plato went to Sicily three times.

The authenticity of the letters has been hotly debated in modern times if not in antiquity, where the letters were taken for granted as being authentic. The more critical methods of modern scholarship leave the ancients behind, however, at the cost of a considerable diversity of view. The earlier treatment of the letters has been chronicled by Paul Friedländer and E. Tigerstedt.[149] Although Renaissance thinkers such as More and Campanella had followed the Greeks in assuming the letters to be genuine, academic scholarship of the nineteenth century dismissed the *Epistles* as forgeries, as indeed it dismissed the *Laws* and *Parmenides*. With the active support of Eduard Meyer and the conversion of Ulrich von Wilamowitz to the authenticity of the *Seventh Epistle*, the tide began to turn and the situation is as M.I. Finley expresses it:

> Nevertheless, despite the air of unreality that pervades the tale, despite some serious inaccuracies in matters of fact which appear in the two letters, despite the silence of Aristotle and Diodorus, most modern historians accept the saga, but a dogged minority continues to insist on the discrepancies and improbabilities, concluding that the saga is largely, perhaps wholly, fictitious (apart from the early, private visit by Plato in 387).[150]

As seen from Finley's use of the word 'saga' he leans towards the 'dogged minority'. His uncharitable estimate of a recent work by von Fritz (more than 150 pages of special pleading and circular argument) also shows his disinclination to accept the *Seventh Epistle*. Von Fritz's 'special pleading' is that the *Seventh Epistle* is genuine.[151]

A few general rules in discussing authenticity prevail.[152] One cannot argue from the authenticity or spuriousness of one letter to the authenticity or spuriousness of an entire collection. It is not acceptable to argue that an individual such as Plato could not have written such a letter, interpreting 'could' in either an ethical or a logical sense. After a century of stylistic analysis, I believe G.J.D. Aalders is correct in pointing out (as against H. Thesleff): 'Opinions of scholars with a good knowledge of Greek differ widely; so long as no convincing stylometric evidence emerges, it does not seem right to me to condemn this letter on the grounds of stylistic arguments.'[153] Nor can any definite conclusions be reached by comparing the contents of the *Epistles* with the corpus of Plato's known works. As with stylistic analysis, leading scholars using the same techniques can come to differing conclusions concerning the *Epistles*. This was the case with Norman Gulley and Aalders in the *Entretiens* devoted to pseudo-epigraphica.[154] Gulley felt all the *Epistles* were forgeries; while Aalders found the *Seventh Epistle* genuine, the *Eighth Epistle* probably genuine and a number of the other *Epistles* written either by Plato himself or by a contemporary. Even those who accept the *Seventh Epistle* differ as to reasons why. Konrad Gaiser argues for the authenticity of the letter, using as his basis of reasoning Plato's esoteric philosophy. Von Fritz also argues for the genuineness of the letter, but reaches conclusions contrary to those of Gaiser and the Tübingen School.[155]

The ultimate question boils down to whether we accept this letter – or any letter or anecdote – as false until and unless it can be proven true, or whether we accept a document's genuineness unless we can prove it to be a forgery or full of factual nonsense. The first view is maintained by Lionel Pearson and J.R. Hamilton who argue against the authenticity of the letters Plutarch quotes in his biography of Alexander. 'The onus of proof lies in the person who would assert the authenticity of any of the letters,' writes Hamilton.[156] On the other hand, already in the nineteenth century, August Boeckh had maintained that only forgery and not authenticity can be proved conclusively.[157] From the point of view of source criticism, a document can be proven false more effectively than its validity upheld, given the absence of any external evidence. The strength of the attestation is an important positive consideration. Yet, even so, if nothing prevents us from accepting a letter as written by Plato, then there is no need to reject it. If the letter can be shown to have been written by a contemporary of Plato, its contents for the historian will be of almost equal value.[158] My thesis accepts *Epistles Three*, *Four*, *Six*, *Seven* and *Eight* to be genuine. The *Seventh Epistle* is the crucial source for any reconstruction of Plato's political activity.

Epistle Six was written by Plato to Hermias, the tyrant of Atarneus, and the Academics, Erastus and Corsicus. We are better informed about this episode of the Academy in politics than of the others. A treaty between Erythrai and Hermias has been partly preserved in an inscription that makes reference to Hermias and his companions.[159] These companions can only have been Erastus and Corsicus. Didymus' commentary on Demosthenes' *Philippics* preserves a number of favourable and unfavourable judgements on Hermias.[160] A hostile source is Theopompus, who both as a Chian and as a student of Isocrates had reason to dislike Hermias and his friends.[161] In attempting to discredit Hermias, Theopompus tried to negate the influence of Aristotle at the court of Philip. Finally, Aristotle and Callisthenes wrote favourably of the tyrant who had treated them so well.

Letters are important for understanding philosophers at the Macedonian court as well. Though spurious, *Epistle Five* was probably written in the generation after Plato's death, possibly by Speusippus.[162]

Speusippus' letter to Philip has been generally accepted as genuine since the important edition and commentary by E. Beckermann and J. Sykutris.[163] The intellectual opponents of the Academy kept up a correspondence as well. We know from Didymus that Theopompus wrote to Philip, as did his teacher, Isocrates.[164] Isocrates' *Epistles* can be accepted as genuine. I agree with Georges Mathieu who, after surveying the historiography of the letters, concludes, 'Là encore il ne nous semble pas que les adversaires de l'authenticité, à qui incombe la preuve de leurs doutes, aient abonti à des resultats qui nous forcent à nous écarter de la tradition manuscrite.'[165]

If utilised in a judicious manner the sources allow the historian the possibility of a historical reconstruction. Such a reconstruction can be given added depth by the use of comparative material and sociological insights. These methods in turn reinforce those behaviour patterns that can be found in the relevant sources. A recent note by William M. Calder has successfully put such a methodology in a correct perspective by showing that what may seem at first sight to be no more than a literary *topos* can in fact contain historical truths about the biographies of a number of individuals.[166] In a similar manner, stories of intellectuals who were politically active can be treated as valid biographical material and utilised accordingly.

2 PYTHAGORAS AND THE PRE-SOCRATICS

From the Seven Sages to Pythagoras

It would seem a natural thing to begin a book on politically active Greek intellectuals with a study of the Seven Sages. But as the ancients themselves realised, they were not philosophers as the term came to be known, but rather 'shrewd men with a turn for legislation'.[1] The lists varied; Hermippus of Smyrna gives us 17 names from which various people chose their seven.[2] Dicaearchus on the other end of the scale notes the four non-variable members of the group: Thales, Bias, Pittacus and Solon.[3] Of these, Thales and Solon are of interest to us; the former for obvious reasons, whereas Solon is more problematical. No one will deny that he was an intelligent politician, but whether he brought ideas to politics, or whether his ideas were formed in the process of governing, cannot be ascertained. What makes Solon important is his reputation as a lawgiver.

The reason writers could include Pittacus of Mytilene and Periander of Corinth among the Seven Sages was that in the sixth century there was no dispute among Greeks that both were *sophoi*. All seven possessed a practical mastery of a given subject, particularly politics, and, as H. Fränkel puts it, 'the Seven, therefore, were clever men rather than sages: their distinction was that in the storms of an unsettled period they knew how to build high the fabric of their own success'.[4] Solon and Pittacus left their mark in Athens and Mytilene. As ephor Chilon transformed the duties of his office and redirected Spartan foreign policy.[5] Periander pursued a successful public life and Cleobulus was a victorious Lindian general in Lycia.[6] Bias, whose pessimism impressed Heraclitus, made a name for himself as a judge.[7] A later period found Periander too cruel to be awarded the status of a sage and Cleobulus too little known. Chilon was rejected by those with anti-Spartan biases.[8] Their replacements were individuals such as Epimenides, Pythagoras and Pherecydes, men of a different turn of mind from those of the 'realist generation' they had replaced.[9] The earlier sages had formulated their pithy warnings and proverbs during the fierce struggles for wealth and power of the sixth century.

The patron god of such thinkers was Apollo, whose temple at Delphi contained a number of maxims of the type associated with the Seven

Sages.[10] As Plato put it, Apollo is 'the god who sits in the centre, on the navel of the earth, and he is the interpreter of religion to all mankind'.[11] The god's ministers were called *exegetai* and were usually chosen or elected from noble families who interpreted the will of Delphi. In identifying the Seven Sages with the god, the Greeks connected their works with divine law and order. In fact, a case could be made that Apollo was the patron saint of many of the philosophers as they immersed themselves in the politics of their day.[12] Many identified themselves or came to be identified with Apollo: one has only to think of Thales, Pythagoras and Plato. Intellectuals used this Olympic connection as both a crutch and a lever and attempted to legislate for a given population while at the same time placing themselves above criticism.

As will be shown, the intellectuals' peak activity as political activists coincided with the decline of the *polis*. Spurned by the *demos*, who mistrusted intellectuals, and largely ignored by kings and tyrants, save as courtiers and publicists, the philosophers found their major niche in the transitional stage from the Hellenic to the Hellenistic world. Hoisting themselves, often reluctantly, into the tumultuous times, intellectuals tried to impose order on the surrounding chaos. From Thales to the followers of Plato and Zeno, they failed and were swallowed up by the whirlpool of history. For most philosophers, not even their memories elicited respect, for many Greeks came to associate the efforts of the philosophers with the decline and fall of autonomous *polis* life. The followers of such philosophers as Pythagoras, Plato and Aristotle, on the other hand, revered the memory of their masters.

Often this meant calumniating rival philosophers and schools. The Pythagorean Aristoxenus has few good words to say about Plato and abusive rhetoric flowed briskly between the Isocrateans and the Peripatetics. Muddying the water even further, the image of philosophers as men of action as opposed to men of contemplation or vice versa varied according to the fashion of the day.[13] Revisionism, after all, is the meat of history. Contemporary with each other, Dicaearchus and Theophrastus represented opposite points of view in this matter.[14] Theophrastus held to the view that philosophers were primarily interested in *sophia*. Dicaearchus celebrated the life of action. To back up his claims with examples, he wrote *Lives of the Philosophers*, a work that demonstrates how the present is reflected in and is formed by the past. The earliest thinkers thus became the norm by which all subsequent philosophers are judged.[15] The image of the earliest of the philosophers, Thales, became a battleground between the two tendencies. Diogenes Laertius in his bland, indiscriminate way is testimony to this:

Thales is also credited with having given excellent advice on political matters. For instance, when Croesus sent to Miletus offering terms of alliance, he frustrated the plan; and this proved the salvation of the city when Cyrus obtained the victory. Heracleides makes Thales himself say that he had always lived in solitude as a private individual and kept aloof from State affairs.[16]

Heracleides was a follower of Plato and an inveterate champion of the Platonic ideal, the domain where truth and reality shine. The ideal is not to be found in the world of becoming and passing away, mingled as it is in darkness.[17] Plato accordingly depicts Thales studying the stars so intently that he fell into a well and was chided by a Thracian maidservant. Plato observes that 'anyone who gives his life to philosophy is open to such mockery'.[18] He speaks from experience. For his part, Dicaearchus probably embellished earlier traditions concerning the practical wisdom of the Milesian philosopher. As one of the permanent Seven Sages, Thales was treated with respect in the popular tradition. Part of this tradition was the anecdote concerning Thales' profitable monopolisation of the oil-mills.[19]

It is obvious that what we see of the pre-Socratics we see through a glass darkly. The historical evidence is slight. It is, as Jaeger says in an expansive mood, 'a plastic material almost waxy soft for the expression of the changing wish pictures of philosophical ethics'.[20] To get from the image to the reality is realistically impossible. Comparative analyses will shed some additional light, but it will not change the complexion of the glass.

In his Shearman Lectures of 1948, Ervin Schrödinger devotes a chapter to the Ionian Enlightenment.[21] Trying to explain the sixth-century movement, he remarks on the fact that the region's many small, autonomous *poleis*, as opposed to large, powerful states or empires, contributed to the development of free, sober, intelligent thought.[22] Surprisingly, he adds: 'In either case they seemed to have been ruled or governed quite frequently by *the best brains*, which has at all times been a rather exceptional event.'[23] This is a rather exceptional statement and G.L. Huxley, who quotes it approvingly, adduces Miletus as an example. According to Huxley, Miletus was governed by men who, like Thales, turned easily from responsible government to bold ratiocination and made their city an adornment to Greece.[24] The political and social history of Miletus, however, was hardly the paradigm of rational, level-headed behaviour. Under Thrasybulus, Miletus prospered economically and managed to hold Lydia at bay, but the dictator's rule at home was less than responsible. The overthrow of the tyranny threw the city into a state of *stasis* between the rich and the artisan middle classes. The atrocities the two sides committed are chronicled by Heracleides.[25] The conservative landowners held aloof from the struggle and the Parians finally had to arbitrate the bitter civil war.

The poet Phocylides summed up the lessons in the preceding history: 'Many things are best for the man in the middle. In the city I want to be a man of the centre.'[26] Thales was also a believer in the advantages of equilibrium. According to Herodotus, Thales advised the Ionians to unite politically. There should be a single deliberative chamber and it should be in Teos, strategically located in the middle of Ionia.[27] The unification would be in the form of an *isopoliteia*, the various Ionian *poleis* being treated as so many *demoi*. An anecdote that many Greeks held to be true (albeit not Herodotus who tells us the story) states that, as an engineer, Thales had been employed by Croesus in the king's disastrous campaign against the Persians and was successful in diverting a river for fording.[28] With regard to the unification of Ionia, the philosopher attempted a piece of social engineering on behalf of the increasingly beleaguered Greeks, but humanity proved harder to mould than nature. Thales was the first of a long line of intellectuals who were, in the words of A.R. Burn, 'to make the bitter discovery that men would not change their manner of life and the conduct of their society merely because of an exposition according to reason'.[29]

Other Milesian philosophers involved themselves in political activity. Anaximander's interest in geography had a practical side to it. Alban D. Winspear finds in this proof of the influence of the rising mercantile life and the interests that it dictated.[30] S.C. Humphreys, pairing Anaximander with the geographer Hecataeus, notes that geographical lore has to be linked with a practical political consideration of the feasibility of Greek resistance against Persia.[31] Anaximander also conducted a colony to Apollonia on the Pontus.[32] In Miletus a statue bearing his name has been found. If the statue is of the philosopher Anaximander, then there may be something to John Burnet's speculation that 'it was not ... for his theories of the Boundless that Anaximander received this honour; he was a Statesman and an inventor like Thales and Hekataios'.[33]

Both Thales and Anaximander were Milesian aristocrats with a strong sense of loyalty to their city. Xenophanes and Heraclitus, though aristocrats, did not play an active role in politics. Xenophanes retreated from Colophon when the city was captured by the Persians; Heraclitus retreated into himself to become a prophet and religious thinker.[34] The activists, the exile and the prophet: all three of these postures were dictated by the turbulent political events of the sixth and early fifth century in Asia Minor. All three postures were adopted by the most important of our philosophers, Pythagoras of Samos.

Before turning to Pythagoras, a few words need to be said about the Athenian, Solon. Humphreys has summarised important aspects of his career:

> It was Solon who provided the ideal model of the intellectual as sage. He first appears to us as a rebel using poetry in a new way, for a direct appeal to the citizenry calling for action disapproved by the ruling group. There was evidently no precedent for the use of poetry in a political context in the *agora*; Solon pretended to be a herald gone mad. His appeal was successful; Athens won control of Salamis and the power of his verse won such respect that he was later invited to mediate between nobles and *demos* in a revolutionary crisis and make new laws for the city.[35]

Solon's purpose was to convince his hearers in the most vivid manner possible of the correctness of his views. His posing as irrational gave way as he spoke to rational argument, for Solon wished to convince by force of logic. He was certainly less a 'rebel' than an innovative and independent thinker who endeavoured to work within the system. Solon was, as A.W.H. Adkins notes, an 'advanced thinker', albeit an 'advanced thinker' of the sixth century.[36] Later intellectuals were to substitute philosophy for poetry, and aristocrats, not the *demos*, were the primary targets of Solon's successors. Quite often it was the democracy that came under attack. However, Solon was not forgotten. Plato habitually compared him with Lycurgus and in the *Phaedrus* adds Darius to the list as one who has won 'immortality among his people as a speech writer; ... a peer of the gods while still living, and do not people of later ages hold the same opinion of him when they contemplate his writings?'[37] The emphasis of this passage (and the reason Darius was included) is on power; that is, orators and kings who have acquired immense power.

Aristotle's account of Solon in *The Constitution of Athens* is also very positive; he defends Solon against the oligarchs and radical democrats of the fourth century who had created their own traditions as to Solon's worth.[38] By this time an image of Solon had been moulded to fit every faction's taste and further verbal swords had been crossed by the various factions and their historians as to whose interpretation of Solon was to be the commonly accepted one. A similar debate raged over Theseus and Cleisthenes.[39] It served Aristotle's purposes to portray Solon and not Theseus as the real founder of democracy.[40] Although his political philosophy colours his narrative, every historian has his biases and Aristotle's account is at least as valuable as the Atthidographers. Additionally, he quotes Solon's poetry extensively and was genuinely concerned with defending his personal integrity. Earlier, Aristotle had come to Solon's defence against the charge that he had created radical democracy: 'Solon, for his part appears to bestow only the minimum of power upon the people, the function of electing the magistrates and of calling them to account.'[41] Such limited democracy also found favour with Isocrates who wished a return to it. He wistfully notes that Solon above all others proved himself to be a 'friend of the people'.[42] Summarising the success of Solon, Isocrates notes:

> For when he was placed at the head of the people, he gave them laws, set their affairs in order, and constituted the government of the city so wisely that even now Athens is well satisfied with the polity which was organized by him.[43]

Since neither Plato nor Aristotle lacked a sense of criticism towards their predecessors, Solon's positive image is all the more impressive. His achievements as a lawgiver survived the politician and, since most intellectuals were interested in making and leaving a similar mark on their society, they looked back to Solon as one who was altogether successful in his endeavours and whose success required no compromise of principles.

While in office Solon formed a friendship with the Cretan seer, Epimenides of Phaestus.[44] Plutarch tells us that Epimenides helped Solon in many ways. The purifier of Athens from the Cylonian curse was a man to be reckoned with. Using his religious authority, the Cretan helped smooth over public opinion, allowing Solon to pass his legislation more easily. What we know of Epimenides indicates a hermit-like individual who was said to have slept for decades in the cave of Zeus and to have been a brother to Minos.[45] He was alleged to have been reborn many times, to have heard voices from heaven and in Crete was worshipped as a god.[46] The point is that in Athens both the purifier and the lawgiver were required. The fact that the two men got along increased the chances for a successful resolution of Athens' social and economic problems. Since Epimenides dealt with religious matters,

Solon could be remembered in the light of a pious rationalism freed from any mystical undertones. These two tendencies, the mystical and the poetic or philosophical, were to merge in Plato, but, above all, in Pythagoras.

Pythagoras and Pythagoreanism

Pythagoras was a Greek from Samos who emigrated to the western Greek *polis* of Croton around 530. For over half a century the society he founded became linked with the political history of Magna Graecia. In bald terms the question may be put as follows: what was the role of Pythagoras and the society he founded in the Crotoniate Empire that emerged subsequent to the destruction of Sybaris by Croton in 509? As it stands, however, the question is unsatisfactory for a number of reasons. We do not know to what extent Croton 'ruled over' a number of Greek cities in Italy and whether we are justified in using the term 'Crotoniate Empire'. Neither can we be certain to what extent the Pythagoreans constituted a brotherhood and whether this brotherhood was politically active in the first half of the fifth century. Finally, the role of Pythagoras is unclear.

The political machinations of Pythagoras and his followers can be partially reconstructed from the accounts of Timaeus, Aristoxenus and Dicaearchus. While the earlier scraps of evidence we have show Pythagoras — not unnaturally — in a purely religious light, the new generation of fourth-century writers could afford to take in a wider view of the topic and treat of political matters as well. This is especially the case with Timaeus who used treaties and oaths as evidence as part of his general history of the Greek West. Dicaearchus and Aristoxenus were students of Aristotle, learned men who availed themselves of the oral traditions that had grown up around the sect. They did not sufficiently distinguish between Pythagoras and his followers because of the Greek practice of identifying particular clubs with their leading members.[47] As a result, the person and actions of Pythagoras have become obscure and the necessity of linking the man with all the major events that affected the society has resulted in chronological confusion.

Another difficulty has been accurately pinpointed by E.L. Minar:

> It is a paradox sadly prejudicial to just historical judgement that throughout the early history of the Society, when it was powerful and struggled successfully, with the obstacles placed in its path to

dominance, we are told almost nothing of the means or the incidents of its acquisition and maintenance of power, but are only allowed to see the successive 'persecutions' to which it was subjected. The revolutions which they instituted or instigated were less spectacular but more effective than those of their opponents, but it is very difficult to discover anything definite about their actual technique.[48]

Still, these sources reveal enough about other aspects of the Pythagorean society to allow us to make reasonable conjectures. The sources dictate that our narrative revolves around the war with Sybaris and the two rebellions against the society.

The Samian background of Pythagoras' life is extremely sketchy. In so far as Pythagoras was over 40 when he moved to Italy in 530, Ionian influence on the philosopher cannot be discounted; neither can the neighbouring Near Eastern cultures be ignored. Pythagoras was a strong, individualistic personality who never allowed himself to be dominated by any one current of thought or feeling, be it western or eastern Greek or Near Eastern. He collected what was useful for his purposes and synthesised it into an array of religious and philosophical thinking. As an important trading centre and imperial power, Samos was an ideal place from which to view the world of the sixth century.[49] Moreover, Pythagoras actively sought out knowledge of the older cultures by travelling. A few probable facts can be related about the first 40 years of Pythagoras' life which cast a light — however dim — upon the philosopher's later activities in Magna Graecia.

After much scholarly discussion concerning the date of Pythagoras' birth, removal to Croton, death and so on, there now seems to be a consensus that Pythagoras was born about 570.[50] He was the son of Mnesarchus, who was either a gem engraver or a rich merchant or quite probably both.[51] Mnesarchus did not come from an alienated stratum of Samian society, for Polycrates carried out a number of building programmes and naval expansions to extend his influence among the merchants and artisans. The middle class had already set up a tyrant named Demoteles as early as 604 and throughout the first half of the sixth century, with or without the aid of a tyrant, the merchants and artisans engaged in a ruthless power struggle with the local aristocracy, the *geomoroi*.[52] Pythagoras thus grew up in a period of strife, a period when the old order of the aristocracy was breaking down and the new class of merchants and artisans was clamouring for political power.[53] Pythagoras, like the Milesians, did not grow up in an atmosphere where value systems were taken for granted.

Paralleling this prolonged internal bickering and re-evaluation was the external tension with Persia. Describing Polycrates' attempts at thalassocracy, A. Andrewes astutely points out that 'the position of Samos, close against the Persian mainland, was such that he could develop a strong naval power only as Persia's dependent or as the leader of resistance to Persia ... All Persia's enemies became Polycrates' friends.'[54] Besides the difference between Greek and Greek — Samos had a longstanding conflict with Lesbos and, more recently, with Miletus — and between Greeks of differing classes, Pythagoras' attitudes were also formed by the differences between Greek and barbarian. This does not mean the one-sided sense of superiority of Greeks to barbarians which later came to be the norm and can be seen already in Thucydides, but rather a veneration of the older Near Eastern cultures and, especially, Egypt.[55]

The ancient land which Herodotus considers 'the most learned of any nation of which I have had experience' held a special appeal to Pythagoras who, as the earliest sources agree, was a man much concerned with the absorption of knowledge.[56] The story in Diogenes Laertius, 8.3, may well be true that Polycrates gave Pythagoras a letter of introduction to his then ally, Pharaoh Amasis. Our earliest evidence of Pythagoras in Egypt is from Isocrates. Praising the Egyptians, he introduces 'Pythagoras of Samos, who went to Egypt, and having become their pupil was the first to introduce philosophy in general to Greece, and showed a more conspicuous zeal than other men; for he reckoned that even if this led to no reward from heaven, among men at least it would bring him the highest reputation'.[57] What Pythagoras learned in Egypt cannot be known with certainty. Herodotus maintains that from Egypt 'some Greeks' adopted the immortality of the soul and its transmigration in a three-thousand-year cycle.[58] While the Egyptians did not believe in metempsychosis (such as is attributed to Pythagoras), there were elements in the Egyptian view of the power of the 'justified' deceased, especially the ability to change forms, which might have at least triggered Pythagoras' speculations.[59] What he must have noticed during his visit to the Nile, and what indeed struck Herodotus, was the high status of the priestly class and the highlighting of this status through special dress and bodily attentions.[60] The awe the priests inspired among the rest of the population by the number of taboos they kept would also not have gone unnoticed for, although a priest's life in Greece may have had some restriction, there was no comparable parallel in Hellas.

Less likely, but not impossible, are contacts with Persia and

Babylon.[61] Pythagoreans, according to Aristoxenus, prohibited the sacrifice of a white cock because these were sacred to the god Men.[62] This prohibition had its origin in Asia Minor. The tradition that Pythagoras wore white clothing, a golden crown and, in particular, trousers may show Persian influence. If Pythagoras indeed dressed in white, this indicates a closer contact with the Near East than would be achieved by viewing it, however closely, from Samos.[63] It has been noted that the famous Pythagorean theorem had already been solved arithmetically in Babylon and Pythagoras' mathematical interests may have drawn him there.[64] According to Porphyry, a similar interest led him to the Phoenicians. Curiosity of another kind would have led him to seek out the descendants of Mochus who were prophets in Sidon.[65] Further afield, he is said to have visited the Brahmins in India and the Druids of Gaul.[66] Josephus links Pythagoras and Plato with the Mosaic corpus.[67] Nor, if our sources are to be believed, did Pythagoras miss Arabia or the enlightenment of the Thracians.[68] Although the unreliability of our sources make it possible to debunk any investigative trips Pythagoras made to the Near East and to point out that much of what he was reported to have learned from the older civilisations could have been picked up at home in Samos, it is unlikely that someone with Pythagoras' well-chronicled curiosity would have been content to get information second hand. He was at least as curious as Herodotus. Even before his arrival in Croton, Pythagoras had the reputation of a polymath and a sage.[69] Heraclitus, who was otherwise unmoved by the reputation of Pythagoras, grants that his learning was prodigious and that he 'practised scientific enquiry beyond all other men'.[70]

There were also important movements in the Greek world that affected Pythagoras — the most important being the Ionian philosophy of the Milesian school. His attitudes as to the nature of matter and the universe were very much affected by the thinking of Thales, Anaximander and his contemporary, Anaximenes, although their exclusively monistic way of thinking would have left him unsatisfied.[71]

Samos during Pythagoras' years was one of the most important centres of Greek civilisation. Painfully aware that he lacked any constitutional underpinning to his position, Polycrates attempted to buy off the Samians with prosperity. The lack of internal justification was to be compensated by external show. The court was brilliant and reflected the tyrant's sensuous nature. Two lyric poets, Ibycus and Anacreon, served Polycrates well. Ibycus, if a choral ode found in Egypt is his, praises the beauty of the 'captivating youth Polycrates' and implies that Agamemnon's fleet was no worthier than the tyrant's.[72] As for the hedonistic Anacreon, when he sang 'The love god with his golden curls/ puts a bright ball in my hand/ shows a girl in her fancy shoes,/ and suggests that I take her,'[73] no responsive chord was struck in the grim soul of Mnesarchus' son. Disdaining another of Anacreon's pleas, 'to hang garlands of celery across our foreheads, and call a festival to Dionysos', Pythagoras turned his back on the court and on Samos and headed west.[74]

Aristoxenus has Pythagoras leave Samos because the tyranny of Polycrates was unduly severe.[75] But Aristoxenus is at great pains to link the philosopher with a spirit of freedom and concord which he says Pythagoras instilled among the inhabitants of Italy and Sicily: a concord which lasted for many generations.[76] Political disagreements with the tyrant are indeed possible, although Guthrie is quite correct when he comments: 'The experiences of the present century make one disinclined to agree with Minar when he writes "This [Pythagoras' departure] of course shows that a specifically political difference existed between Pythagoras and the democratically disposed tyrant".'[77] More probable would be the revulsion a person of Pythagoras' puritanical sensibilities would have felt towards Polycrates' entourage. There is also something to George Grote's commonsensical observation that the two men simply could not abide each other and parted ways.[78] A letter of introduction got the philosopher out of the tyrant's hair the first time, but in 540 Pythagoras left with nothing more than a store of ideas and a method for teaching them.

This pedagogy may help to give an additional reason for Pythagoras' departure. As well it gives important clues to the philosopher's *modus operandi* and personality. Aristoxenus relates that, when Pythagoras came back from his travels in the Near East and Egypt, he tried to set up a school in Samos.[79] The curriculum included arithmetic and geometry, but it had little appeal to the fun-loving Samians. Pythagoras had a flair for publicity, however, and he convinced a young man, a noted athlete with prestige among the population, to be his student. The youth was poor and Pythagoras agreed to give the boy three obols for every geometrical figure he mastered. The boy agreed; he learned quickly and became captivated by the subject and the teacher. At this point Pythagoras feigned poverty and stated that he could no longer pay him his wages. The student came up with the right solution however: in the future he would provide Pythagoras with three obols for every figure learned. It remained for the wily sage to remind the student — also called Pythagoras — that it would now be improper for his attention to be distracted by the gymnasium and other such stupid and vain pursuits.

The way in which Pythagoras manipulated the relationship with his pupil is impressive. There were three changes of direction. The student's attitude towards mathematics changed from doing a task in order to receive money to doing it for its own sake. The authority structure of the teacher-pupil relationship, which must have been very weak at the beginning, was transformed into a master-disciple relationship at the end. The third change of direction was that of the obols. All this manipulation was done very deliberately by Pythagoras and, indeed, if we consider a fourth directional change, that from Samos to Croton, young Pythagoras may have followed his master.[80]

Although he labours to show that Pythagoras' school of philosophy was a success at Samos, Aristoxenus is forced to admit at one point that no one came to the classes.[81] Pythagoras made little impression in Samian circles. Samos was near enough to Miletus for philosophy to have lost its novelty; it was also Ionian enough in spirit to look askance at the total dedication to philosophy and, especially, its exponent that Pythagoras demanded. This negative attitude played a role in Pythagoras' departure. Note also the aggressive way in which Pythagoras went after disciples. Like Socrates, he was found around the gymnasium. No shrinking violet, the activist attitude of this fisher of men was one of the things that impressed the more reticent Plato.

Herodotus says that, according to his informants from Pontus, another associate of Pythagoras was a Thracian called Salmoxis, who may have been his slave. What is of prime interest to us in the Salmoxis story is the following statement from Herodotus:

> He accordingly prepared a men's hall, and in it entertained the chief men of the country [Thrace], and, while feasting them, used to teach them that neither he himself nor his guests should die, nor their children after them, but that they would come to a place where they should live forever in the enjoyment of good things.[82]

Herodotus goes on to relate Salmoxis' ruse in the underground chamber. The sentence prior to the one just quoted gives the information that Salmoxis had lived in the household of Pythagoras. The underground chamber has all the marks of a Greek's or Hellenized Thracian's rationalisation of a resurrection myth. Probably the connection between Salmoxis and Pythagoras was introduced by the Greeks in order to take credit for the doctrine of the afterlife.[83] The fact that Pythagoras was involved meant that he must have been thinking along similar lines. He may have been doing his thinking out loud in such a hall as Herodotus describes.[84]

Pythagoras' interest in Croton may have been whetted by stories he had heard from sailors on the docks. Also, the court physician in Samos was the well-known Democedes and it may have been from him that Pythagoras learned of Croton.[85] Finally, Pythagoras was aware that Croton was noted for its worship of Apollo. Another southern Italian city with an Apollo cult was Metapontum and it is no accident that Pythagoras spent most of his time in these two cities.[86] In addition, Jean Bayet has observed that coins of fifth-century Metapontum have representations of Apollo on one side and Heracles on the other.[87] Unlike Apollo, whose worship by the Greeks was concentrated in Croton and Metapontum, Heracles was revered throughout the Greek west.[88] Under the tutelage of Pythagoras, the Pythagoreans considered the cult of Heracles to be of special importance and they cultivated the legend of a Crotoniate Heracles.[89] Pythagoras was at pains to incorporate both divinities into his thinking and his success can be seen when Milo, an aristocrat and a Pythagorean, donned the garb of Heracles. Marcel Detienne, who considers the Heraclean connection to be of particular importance, comments that Milo 'ne cède pas à une fantasie vestimentaire, il incarne des vertus exemplaires que le pythagorisme veut faire triompher sur les vices dont les Sybarites offraient l'exemple le plus achevé ... On peut reconnaître ... une sorte de combat du *ponos* contre la *truphé* des Sybarites'.[90] The fact that Pythagoras' views could be accommodated to and indeed thrive in a situation of almost continuous conflict goes a fair way to explaining his success.

A few preliminary remarks about the history of the wars between the cities prior to the arrival of Pythagoras help explain his success in the west. The first is the destruction of Siris. The war between Sybaris, Metapontum and Croton on the one hand and Siris on the other was due mainly to commercial and possibly to ethnic rivalry between the cities.[91] When Siris was destroyed around 540, 50 youths who had sought sanctuary by clasping the statue of Athena were pried from the statue and slain on the altar of the goddess, along with her priest.[92] When a plague broke out, religious pollution was blamed and the Crotoniates and others went to Delphi for the appropriate remedies. They were told by the priestess to erect an image to the dead youths and the offended goddess. What had begun as a commercial war had turned into a religious issue due to the excessive zeal of the Crotoniates and the others.

Religion was also important during the wars between Croton and

Locri. Although the Locrians were unable to procure Spartan assistance, the latter sent images of the Dioskouroi along with their best wishes; these images were reported to have materialised in battle. Apollo was promised one-ninth of the booty as opposed to the tenth that the Crotoniates offered, thereby securing his services. Finally, joining the Dioskouroi was the Homeric hero, Ajax, who wounded the Crotoniate general, Leonymos.[93] Later, legend had it that Leonymos was healed by the same hero on the sacred island of Leuke, but not before seeing Achilles and Helen. The Locrians won the battle by the Sagras river despite being heavily outnumbered. Of the outcome of the battle, the Greeks of that and later times were to say 'too good to be true', meaning an event had happened contrary to one's expectations.[94] Again, the traditions reveal a strong religious element in the thinking of the people who took part in it.

Croton was a well-situated city commercially and militarily. The defeat at Sagras had been a setback for the Crotoniates, but it was not disastrous. Justin says the demoralised citizens gave themselves up to luxurious living, caring neither for the exercise of valour nor the profession of arms, as had been the case previously.[95] Apparently, in the absence of imperialistic opportunities or designs, the people of Croton decided to enter into a period of isolation.[96] There was demoralisation of a sort. No Crotoniate won first prize at the Olympia between 548 and 532. Since Croton had always prided itself on its Olympic victors, this was a sure sign of listlessness. Fear also set in: perhaps the goddess had not forgiven the outrage at Siris. Among the aristocrats, there was fear that their hegemony at Croton was coming to an end. In particular, they viewed with alarm the vigorous tyranny of Telys at Sybaris.

Sybaris was then at the height of her power and controlled the valleys of the Krathis and Sybaris and the coastlines on both sides of the narrow Peninsula. She formed alliances with the Achaean cities in southern Italy, as her alliance coins attest.[97] Further, Sybaris maintained close ties with Miletus and the latter used Sybarite-controlled ports, particularly Laos, to extend trade to the Etruscans. Sybaris was not well located to be a great commercial centre, but in spite of such disadvantages the city flourished; the commons prospered and found a leader in Telys.[98] Socially, Sybarite stories had a great run in the ancient world. Whether Timaeus in the telling of them is a 'Man with a Muck-Rake' or in his stories exhibits 'as much here of regret as of moral indignation', it is obvious that Sybaris was a prosperous imperial city.[99] With victorious Locri to the south and the vigorous Sybarites to the north, the aristocratic ruling elite of Croton had reason to feel threatened.

Their fears became justified with the accession of Telys as tyrant of Sybaris. His policies at home and abroad were consistently anti-aristocratic. At first he had hoped to influence the course of affairs at Croton by marrying his daughter to Philip, an Olympic winner and reputedly the handsomest man of his time.[100] The aristocratic party at Croton got wind of this ploy and exiled Philip. Telys then resorted to provocation. He banished five hundred of the wealthiest citizens of Sybaris and confiscated their estates.[101] The exiles sought refuge at Croton, whereupon Telys delivered an ultimatum to the Crotoniates either to give up the refugees or face war. At Croton, an assembly of the people was called and the masses favoured returning the aristocrats. However, 'when Pythagoras the philosopher advised that they grant safety to the suppliants, they changed their opinion and accepted the war on behalf of the safety of the suppliants'.[102] Obviously, Pythagoras had acquired considerable influence among the Crotoniates. Iamblichus gives a slightly different twist to this episode: 'Because one of the Sybarite ambassadors had previously ordered the murders of some of Pythagoras' disciples in Sybaris, Pythagoras advised the members of his own circle that Telys' demands should be rejected, and that the Crotoniates not act with discord on this question.'[103] His lieutenants would then have ensured that the master's will be carried out by the people.

Croton was a city in stress after the battle of Sagras. The wars in the Greek West yielded to none in their ferocity, for commercial rivalry mingled with regional differences. To the victors, whether Sybaris after defeating Siris or Locri after the battle of the Sagras river, victory meant territorial advance, a commercial boom and a period of artistic upsurge. The vanquished could look forward to the destruction of their city and the demoralisation of the remaining citizens. Part of the reason that stories of Sybarite vice were so exaggerated was as a justification for the savagery of her subsequent defeat.[104] Sybaris' *hubris* was more than compensated by her fall and a series of unfavourable portents foretold the Sybarite defeat at the Traeis river.[105] Before its victory over Sybaris, Croton was prey to similar feelings of woe. Had Athena forgiven the Crotoniates their sacrilege at Siris? Were the gods and the heroes still against them? Could they summon divine assistance for their own side?

The aristocrats of Croton were disillusioned on two other fronts. Traditionally, the prestige of Greek aristocrats was due to their performance in war.[106] Primarily an agricultural society, Croton was still ruled by her *aristoi*, although with decreasing confidence. Prey to their recently aggrandised neighbours, the self-image of the Crotoniate elite was at a low ebb and further difficulties presented themselves in the attitude of the *demos* within the city. The situation within Croton was becoming similar to that of Samos in the time of the tyrants. Closer to home, tyranny was again becoming an issue in Magna Graecia. In all cases, a rising commercial class had come to feel that the aristocracy was standing in the way of political power.[107] 'Before the times of Theognis, Pindar, and Pythagoras there was no need for the ruling classes to think of justifying or consolidating its position,' notes Minar, 'but when that was threatened by a group that would loosen its hold on the reins of political power, the philosophy of aristocracy would begin to take shape.'[108]

Before Pythagoras, how had the aristocrats of Croton reacted to this situation of enhanced stress? According to Justin, they became demoralised and began acting hedonistically like their neighbours to the north. Perhaps military defeat by Locri was followed by an aping of the victor's way, but, as A.F.C. Wallace points out, such 'regressive' behaviour only increases or at best maintains the stress level of a society.[109] It also introduces an element of guilt into the mental make-up of the aristocracy and they may have turned to religion. The sixth century was a period of high religious fervour and the west had always been welcome ground to new religious cults. The cult of Dionysus was followed by that of Orpheus. Although Orphism may have attracted primarily the lower classes, it was not limited to them.[110] To aristocrats who felt spurned by the gods, it offered the hope of reunion. However, Orphism was first and foremost an other-worldly religion which did not encourage elitist thinking and the aristocrats of Croton and elsewhere were not willing to give up this world and the prominent position they had inherited in it. The search of many aristocrats for a new way of life continued.

Pythagoras had come to Croton with a reputation as a sage. It is highly probable that he brought with him some disciples who were kept busy publicising the master's presence. His first public speeches were a series of orations which Iamblichus has preserved most fully for us, while Diodorus and Justin provide epitomes of the speeches.[111] 'Every day he praised virtue and summed up the wrongs of luxury and the fate of states that had been ruined by that plague,' says Timaeus, 'and he induced so great a zeal for sobriety among the masses that it seemed incredible that some of them should live in luxury.'[112] Diodorus, also following Timaeus, is even more ecstatic:

Not only in eloquence of speech did he show himself great, but he also displayed a character of soul which was temperate and constituted a marvelous model of a life of modesty for the youth to emulate. Whoever associated with him he converted from their ways of extravagance and luxury, whereas all men, because of their wealth, were giving themselves over without restraint to indulgence and an ignoble dissipation of body and soul.[113]

Just as the kernel of Jesus' philosophy was compressed in or typified by the Sermon on the Mount, Pythagoras' speeches, as recorded by Timaeus and Dicaearchus, are our best example of Pythagoras 'fishing for men'. Two themes stand out in these addresses: the emphasis on purity, on turning aside from luxury, licentiousness and all the other evil things in life, for 'it is impossible that he who begins his course from a bad impulse, should run well to the end'; and the emphasis on tradition, 'to follow the steps of those that preceded them', for the finishing line is in the past.[114] Refusing to identify with the community as it existed, the philosopher identified himself with the way the community should be. Pythagoras articulated many new assumptions and novel syntheses to the Crotoniates, but he strove always to put new wine in old and even discarded bottles.[115]

In the course of these meetings, Pythagoras' fame and influence grew and the people began to consider him as divine. Capitalising on this awe, Pythagoras created a distance between himself and the rest of the population: 'It is generally agreed that by these injunctions he brought it about that nobody uttered his name, but that all called him divine.'[116] According to Aristotle, the Crotoniates came to identify Pythagoras with the Hyperborean Apollo.[117] A prophet had emerged in Croton who preached that the trouble and stresses the citizens were facing were due to the breaking of certain rules. Further, playing on the conscious or half-conscious assumptions of the Crotoniates that the gods had deserted them, he promised that through correct behaviour the gods and especially Apollo would take a renewed interest in their concerns. Apollo had seen to it that they were born, Pythagoras reminded his audience; 'they owed a lot to this god and must prove themselves worthy of him'.[118] A perpetuation of their extravagant ways of living, on the other hand, would result in a further lapse of their fortunes; and this could all too easily occur, said Pythagoras, for human nature is normally evil.

What the philosopher indicated in his speeches, and what later Pythagoreans stated explicitly, is that we must all be conscious of the evil within us and, further, we must realise that we are continuously being observed by the scrutinising gods.[119] 'What is said most truly?' the Pythagoreans asked themselves and made ready with the reply: 'that men are wicked'.[120] While this notion primarily implies sexual wickedness, any undue passion is to be held at arm's length. According to Aristoxenus, the sect taught that men 'have a variety of impulses and desires and other emotions. Therefore they need the kind of supervising authority which engenders control and order.'[121] Much of the doctrine builds upon Orphism but surpasses it. As Minar succinctly states: 'in Pythagoreanism the body is evil, in Orphism only wretched'.[122] The depth to which asceticism pervades the thinking of Pythagoras and his followers can be measured from another saying of the *symbolla*: 'Pleasure is in all circumstances bad; for we came here to be punished and we ought to be punished.'[123] Such words did not fall on barren ground. In E.R. Dodds's analysis:

> These beliefs promoted in their adherents a horror of the body and a revulsion against the life of the senses which were quite new in Greece ... By Greek minds these beliefs were reinterpreted in a moral sense; and when that was done, the world of bodily experience inevitably appeared as a place of darkness and penance, the flesh became an 'alien tunic'.[124]

There is some justification for concluding that we are in the presence of what Minar calls a 'depravity religion', although Dodds's concept of 'Puritan psychology' is more apt.[125]

This internal wickedness was reflected in and complemented by external vice, *truphé*. Detienne, following Santo Mazzarino, has observed:

> La 'mollesse' que fustige Pythagore, dont il veut purger la cité de Crotone, c'est la *truphé* qui caractérise les crises politiques du VIe siècle: un mal qui est à la fois économique, moral et politique. Sur le plan économique, c'est l'invasion des produits orientaux de luxe, des vêtements, parfums, objects précieux, l'accroissement des dépenses somptuaires, dans les milieux aristocratiques. Sur le plan politique, c'est le déséquilibre provoqué par l'inégalité, entre les citoyens, c'est la discorde, l'injustice, la ruine de la cité.[126]

Somewhat over 40, at the height of his intellectual powers, Pythagoras was an impressive person physically — something which would not have hurt him in Croton. His voice was pleasing, his cadence noble, and his person graceful.[127] An individual of commanding presence and diction and a polymath who synthesised as many of the intellectual currents of his day as possible, there is, none the less, more to Pythagoras. There is something lacking, for example, in de Vogel's picture of Pythagoras.

> People saw a leader before them whose moral preaching was grounded in a profound view of the world order and a well-thought-out explanation of all things; a man who for the Greek possessed the nobility of the thinker, and who at the same time devoted himself with his whole person to the tasks of realizing his theoretical views of life.[128]

Although de Vogel follows Empedocles closely, her Pythagoras would feel more home in a Dutch Reformed church than on the emotionally charged, semi-archaic terrain of southern Italy. Erwin Rhode's assessment of Pythagoras is more astute and can serve as an introduction to an analysis of the charismatic religious thinker:

> The new and potent feature which he introduced was the force of personality which was able to give life and body to the ideal. What was apparently lacking in similar movements in ancient Greece was now provided by a great man who for his followers was a pattern and an example, a leader inspiring imitation and emulation. His personality became a centre to which a whole community was attracted by a sort of inward necessity. Before very long this founder of a community appeared to his followers as a superman, unique and incomparable among all other men.[129]

What Rhode describes is the relationship between a charismatic leader and his disciples. The classic definition of charisma was given by Max Weber who maintained that it is

> a certain quality of an individual personality by virtue of which he is considered extraordinary and treated as endowed with supernatural, superhuman, or at least specifically exceptional powers or qualities. Those are such as are not accessible to the ordinary person, but are regarded as of divine origin or as exemplary, and on the basis of them the individual concerned is treated as a leader.[130]

The exceptional powers that Pythagoras possessed were intelligence, dignity and persuasiveness and his followers believed in the transmigration of his soul from the origins of things.[131] To them, he was the Hyperborean Apollo. There were many tales of his charismatic endowments. At the same hour of the same day he was reportedly seen in both Metapontum and Tauromenium.[132] When in Olympia, Pythagoras supposedly revealed that one of his thighs was of gold.[133] Even nature took notice of the man who regarded all living things as akin. Among the stories told are the following: as Pythagoras crossed the Sagras river, the river hailed him in an audible voice crying, 'Greetings, Pythagoras'; a wild bear was converted to vegetarianism and an ox came to regard the eating of beans as taboo; a white eagle allowed itself to be stroked by the master; an unrepentant snake, however, was driven out of Sybaris — no doubt contaminated by the lifestyle there.[134] As Weber points out, almost all prophets required charismatic authentication to establish their authority, 'which in practice meant magic'.[135] Weber cites Jesus as an example and, like Jesus, Pythagoras considered himself far more than a magician.

Pythagoras strove to make his opinion felt among a broad spectrum of the population, but he knew that in order to be most effective a smaller, more tightly knit group of religious *virtuosi* was needed. As Timaeus notes:

> And first, preaching in the famous city of Croton he won many disciples, so that he is said to have had six hundred people not only moved to accept the philosophy he taught, but living in what is called the common life, according to his command. And these were the 'philosophers', but the many were auditors, whom they call *akousmatikoi*. In one public meeting, the first which he held after stepping alone upon the shore of Italy, more than two thousand were won over by his discourse.[136]

The end result was that at some point after Pythagoras' public addresses, three hundred of the young men 'bound to each other by oath like a brotherhood, lived segregated from the rest of the citizens and brought the city under their control'.[137] Isocrates attests to this as well: Pythagoras 'so greatly surpassed all others in reputation that all the younger men desired to be his pupils, and their elders were more pleased to see their sons staying in his company than attending to their private affairs. And these reports we cannot disbelieve.'[138]

Pythagoreans never constituted a large segment of society; even within the aristocracy they were in the minority. At Croton, of the thousand who were in the Council only three hundred were Pythagoreans and at other cities this proportion would have been even less. What made the sect so formidable was not their economic and social power base, although these things were important, but the inner dynamic of the clubs which revolved around friendship, secrecy and the sharing of all things in common.

Friendship came to constitute an extremely significant part of a Pythagorean life. Other Greeks had friends, *philoi*, as well, and aristocratic Greeks often banded together in a *hetaireia* or a *synhedron*.[139] Yet competing or potentially competing with his association with like-minded aristocrats were ties with his *genos* as well. Additionally, 'the ties that held the *hetaireia* together were primarily personal ones, and ... it was therefore not easy for a new man to take over the leadership of the group'.[140] Sometimes these personal ties were the results of political opportunism and were often of a transitory nature. Some were erotic bonds and others were simply friendships.[141] Not so the Pythagoreans, who had more continuity than their non-philosophical counterparts and did not disband in order to regroup whenever the political horizons shifted. If forced to retreat, as during the brief tyranny of Clinias, the Pythagoreans returned in the same form and with the same membership as before.

One story that illustrates this is the friendship between Damon and Phintias. The story has good authority, for Aristoxenus claimed to have heard the tale from the Younger Dionysius himself in Corinth where the exiled tyrant was spending his last years teaching grammar.[142] Phintias had formed a plot against Dionysius the Younger, but was apprehended. The punishment was death. Phintias took the verdict calmly, for self-discipline was an important Pythagorean trait. However, he did ask Dionysius for some time in which to put his domestic affairs in order and said that his friend, Damon, another Pythagorean with whom he lived, would stand as surety for his death. To everyone's astonishment, Damon was willing to do this. While Phintias was away, Damon was baited by the court's wags, but at the appointed hour Phintias duly appeared. Impressed with such loyalty, Dionysius forgave Phintias, embraced and kissed the two men and begged that he be included in their friendship. This request probably tested the nerves of the two Pythagoreans more than anything else that day and they replied that they would have nothing to do with him. The story has a plausible Dionysian ring to it – with the rebuffed tyrant left wondering why it was that philosophers never cared for him.

W. Burkert, after a thorough review of the early evidence, comes to the conclusion that the Pythagoreans formed a brotherhood 'in accordance with the ancient custom of colleagues bound together in a cult'.[143] It was a religious association, a *thiasos*, dedicated to the Muses and, after Pythagoras' death, to the memory of its founder.[144] Any society, religious or political, bound together by a cult, will have some esoteric aspects in matters such as passwords or the behaviour of members within the group. For the Pythagoreans silence was the important *askesis* and the purpose of such training has been well brought out in Georg Simmel's classic study of secrecy:

> Certain association must not penetrate into the masses; those who know form a community in order to guarantee mutual secrecy to one another. If they were a sum of unconnected individuals, the secret would soon be lost; but association offers each of them psychological support against the temptation of disclosure. Association counter-balances the isolating and individualizing effect of the secret.[145]

Pythagoreans, we are told, held all things in common. Timaeus writes: 'When the young men came to Pythagoras and wished to spend their time with him, he did not immediately consent, but said that the property of people who converse together should be common as well.'[146] Another fragment notes that the Pythagoreans were the first to remark that the possessions of friends are held in common and that 'friendship is equality'.[147] Besides sacrificing their lives if necessary, Pythagoreans in need aided each other financially. Clinias the Tarentine subsidised Prorus the Cyrenaean after the latter had lost his money – due, significantly, to political upheavals.[148] Any Greek who wished to maintain himself as a political entity in his community needed a certain minimum of wealth. If Pythagoreans were willing to share their wealth in order that others of their order be maintained in positions of power, this would go a fair way toward explaining their success in politics, even after they had lost the goodwill of the rest of the population, including members of their own family. Timaeus says that their relatives bore it ill that 'they gave over their estates to be common property among themselves and deprived others of them'.[149] Pythagoreans considered their sect to be an extended family and would have agreed with Jesus' admonition: 'Whoever does the will of my father in heaven is my brother and sister and mother.'[150]

Between the Sybarites and the Crotoniates, war would eventually have broken out. Given the firm and uncompromising nature of Pythagorean friendships, an important cause of the war between Sybaris and Croton was the fact that Telys had certain Pythagoreans in Sybaris murdered.[151] The war had thus become a war of revenge. Further, among the aristocrats who had sought exile at Croton, some, at least, had Pythagorean sympathies. To give them up was to hand them over to certain execution. Finally, Sybaris and Croton were commercial rivals and both cities wanted land in order to expand.[152] Telys seemed intent on fomenting social disorder in Croton and, in fact, the political systems of the two cities were at variance. In order to stop the imperialistic Sybarites and fulfil her own ambitions, Croton went to war.

But there is something more to the role of the philosophers in this episode: the philosophical order left its mark by making the keynote of the conflict a holy war. Intellectuals in Croton had achieved a prominent position in government and they strove constantly to translate their ethic of religious salvation through philosophy into the public sector. Bringing ethics into politics, they invested political behaviour with moralistic reasoning. Having a monopoly on correct behaviour, they naturally looked down on the behaviour of lesser men. But the Pythagoreans also projected their own fascination with sin into the Sybarites. 'Evils befalling the individual are divinely appointed inflictions and the consequences of sin, from which the individual hopes to be freed by "piety" [behaviour acceptable to a god] which will bring them individual salvation.'[153] The Pythagoreans had a conscience that was burdened with sin; and their nerves were frayed from constant vigilance against uncleanliness of any form.

On at least three grounds the citizens of Sybaris were 'sinners' in the eyes of the Pythagoreans: their high valuation of the external things of life, exemplified best by their exuberant clothing; their veneration of food – James Beard would be the Sybarite idea of a saint; and the frank sensuality of Sybarite society.[154] The differences between Sybarite and Pythagorean ideas of youth and the role they were to play in society can be assessed from Timaeus' description of Sybarite boys: 'It was customary also among the Sybarites for the boys, until they reached the age of young manhood, to wear purple cloaks and have their hair tied up in braids secured by gold ornaments.'[155] This, combined with their intolerably easy-going manner towards such luxuries and an arrogance which extended to those who did not or could not enjoy life as they did, made Sybarites objects of hatred to the Pythagoreans.[156]

Sybaris became the 'justified execution' of the Pythagoreans. Against those whom they regarded as being beyond the pale, the philosophers developed and justified an intense hatred. Hippasos is the best example of a renegade Pythagorean whom orthodox Pythagoreans refused to associate with and, in fact, wished dead.[157] Intellectuals often couch their feelings and desire for war in the term 'crusade', and the Pythagoreans were no different: 'One must not fight with words, but with deeds; and war becomes lawful and indeed holy if one fights as man to man.'[158] Pythagoreans figured prominently in the war; the Pythagorean athlete Milo led the charge, followed closely by other ascetic 'Nazirites' and the rest of the Crotoniate population. Milo wore the garb of Heracles and provided an example of heroism in practice along with a reminder to his army of Croton's roots.[159] No Sybarite ventured to face him. The result was the total victory of Croton in spite of being heavily outnumbered. After a siege Sybaris was captured and the Traeis river was diverted from its course to flow over the city.[160] Whatever remained of Sybaris was put under Crotoniate control.[161]

Although the Pythagoreans had played a crucial role in the downfall of Sybaris, it is important to note that their power hardly survived this initial success. A major revolt led by Cylon and Ninon broke out in 509. Iamblichus, following Timaeus, describes the causes of the rebellion and gives us significant facts about the nature of Pythagorean dominance in Croton:

> Since his young pupils came from parents who were superior in reputation and estate, it so happened that as they grew up not only did they take a leading place in their own families but joined together to govern the city. They formed a brotherhood which was indeed large (over 300) but a small minority in the city which was not governed according to their ways and principles. However, while they remained confined to their original territory and Pythagoras was with them, the mode of government which had lasted since the foundation of the city remained in force although the state of affairs was uncomfortable and opportunity was sought for a change. But when they reduced Sybaris and Pythagoras departed, and they arranged for the newly won land not to be divided out in lots as the majority desired, the concealed hatred broke out, and the people sided against them. The opposition was led by those who in blood and friendship were closest to the Pythagoreans.[162]

Two important points to note are the disgruntlement of certain aristocrats, 'who in blood and association were closest to the Pythagoreans', and the dismay of the *demos* at not being able to participate in the spoils of war. The result was that Cylon allied himself with the common people and, in a situation not unique to Croton, made a play for tyranny. According to Aristoxenus, Cylon was a rejected Pythagorean; a convenient explanation to Pythagoreans and their supporters, but one that we have no reasons to disbelieve.[163] Cylon's animus against them was certainly marked and of a personal as well as of a political nature. The other anti-Pythagorean leader, Ninon, represented the lower classes.[164] The strategy they pursued against the Pythagoreans was two-fold, a combination of envy and hatred against the Pythagoreans, who were not governed by the same customs and practices as the rest of the population. The elite took its cue from Pythagoras, who drew an ever smaller and tighter circle around himself and no longer deigned to address the masses. This sect constituted a highly disciplined and monolithic group within the body politic and had powers far in excess of their numbers. Ninon played on this theme when in addressing the people he harangued that it was disgraceful 'that those who overcame 300,000 at the Traeis River should be defeated within the city itself by a force one three-hundredth as large'.[165]

The exclusiveness and efficacy of the society was aggravated by the secrecy with which the Pythagoreans conducted their affairs. In the tradition of demagogues, Ninon produced a 'document' that he claimed was authentic and proceded to read it to the masses.[166] Whether this *hieros logos* was in fact a contemporary document, much less whether it was authentic Pythagorean literature to be distributed internally within the society and which fell into the hands of Ninon, cannot be known. Timaeus may have had access to a book which later Pythagorean sympathisers were at great pains to destroy. What can be conjectured is that the document parodied Pythagorean tenets but did not falsify them. After all, Aristotle relates that among the secret doctrines of the Pythagoreans was the distinction of three kinds of reasonable creatures: God, man and beings like Pythagoras.[167] By emphasising such views, Ninon shrewdly played on the resentment of the populace. Everybody knew what Pythagoreans thought of each other, but that others were considered unmentionable and of no account confirmed the people's worst fears.[168] For those who needed concrete images, the document noted that cattle was the Pythagorean designation of the masses. The document also claimed that the Pythagoreans desired to subvert the institutions of the city by their taboo on beans.[169] This action, claimed

Ninon, masked the reality that beans were used in the ballot and that Pythagoreans 'fought against beans because they are lords of the vote and of election by lot'.[170] The whole tenor of the document and of Ninon's speech is that Pythagoreanism was a conspiracy against the common people.

Those who saw a conspiracy were strengthened by the refusal of the Pythagoreans to divide the land of the conquered Sybarites.[171] This should be seen as part of the larger picture of a struggle between the aristocrats and the *demos*. The refusal upset the common people and caused popular leaders like Ninon to attack the philosophers. Certain aristocrats, like Cylon, who may have represented the manufacturing and commercial interest of the community, were also displeased by what they saw as the continued political domination of the large landholders.[172] At first the discontented tried to break the Pythagoreans' power by democratic means. The Council was urged to throw open the public offices and assemblies and, importantly, officials were to be responsible for their actions to representatives chosen by lot from the citizen body.[173] The Council made some concessions, but the Pythagoreans refused any compromise to the ancestral constitution as they saw it.[174] It is important to note that the Pythagoreans were working within the system. The masses concluded that the only way to deal with such people was through force and leading Pythagoreans were attacked and killed as they were about to sacrifice to the Muses.[175] Democedes and some younger Pythagoreans managed to escape. The laws and decrees of the Pythagoreans were overturned and Democedes was charged with inciting the youth to tyranny. Another battle followed in which the Pythagoreans were defeated and Democedes killed. Timaeus, who quotes records and Delphic oaths in his narrative at this point, says that the victorious democrats annulled debts and divided up the land.[176]

Pythagoras' role in all this is not known with any certainty. According to Dicaearchus, Pythagoras wound up in Metapontum. Aristotle says that he left for Metapontum prior to the outbreak of troubles in Croton. Before being accepted at Metapontum, Pythagoras was rejected by Caulonia, Locri and Tarentum.[177] Exiled leaders are not desired commodities and at Metapontum the ethical reformer died of hunger in a temple where he was forced to take refuge.[178]

What is perhaps most significant in this episode is something we have almost no information about, namely, how the Pythagoreans returned to power. That landowning aristocrats would have behaved in such a tunnel-visioned manner concerning the distribution of land is not unusual; neither is the reaction of the people against the nobility. Popular demagogues such as Cylon and Ninon arose in many another Greek *polis* to wrest power from the oligarchy. In most places they were successful — as at Croton. But the philosophers returned as uncomprising as ever and, when early in the fifth century they suffered another setback during the shortlived tyranny of Clinias, they came back a third time.[179] Again, we lack details.

Aristoxenus, who downplays Pythagorean misrule, notes that, although the Cylonians continued to make trouble, the high principles of the Pythagoreans prevailed and the *poleis* preferred to be administered by them.[180] We do not know the form of control, but the Pythagoreans had exported their influence to other Italian cities. There may be some truth to Aristoxenus' contention that the sect was held in esteem in some of the other cities at this time, an evaluation that did not hold true by the 440s. Much of their success, however, can be attributed to the superior organisational ability of the Pythagoreans. Those qualities that made the intellectuals formidable when in power — single mindedness, internal cohesion, politics conceived of as an ethical duty — served them when out of power. The nobles at Croton, who had shown such anxiety about the coming times and had fastened on Pythagoras as a guide and teacher, had made a good choice. Those sections of the aristocracy who became reborn Pythagoreans no longer suffered from feelings of vertigo in a world that they felt had left them behind.[181] For the power of the philosophers to be broken, a calamity of major proportions was necessary and such an event took place between 450 and 440.

Between 510 and 460 Pythagoreanism stood at the centre of Greco-Italian society.[182] Little is known as to what went on during these crucial years. Externally, friendly relations between the powerful Sicilian tyrant, Gelon, and the Crotoniates enabled the Pythagoreans to expand in peace. According to Eusebius and Pausanias, a Crotoniate athlete, Astylus, won three consecutive Olympic victories and in at least the last two of them had himself announced as a Syracusan to flatter Gelon.[183] The fact that the Crotoniates erected a portrait of Astylus in the sanctuary of Lakinian Hera indicates that they approved of the act, which must certainly have pleased the tyrant.[184] Gelon's successor, Hiero, took a greater interest in the affairs of Magna Graecia and went so far as to aid Croton's traditional enemy, Sybaris. The Crotoniates showed their displeasure at this reversal of policy by decreeing that Astylus' house be turned into a prison and destroying his portrait in the sanctuary. Fortunately for Croton, Syracusan tyranny was not to last much longer.[185]

Internally, the extent of Pythagorean rule will always be unclear. That many of their members actively engaged in politics is certain; that Pythagoreans preferred their own counsel to those of others can be safely presumed, as can the fact that they kept themselves informed of each other's activities and involved themselves in the furtherance of their order's advancement. The order's rules were not slackened; admittance was just as difficult as before. Since admission to a philosophic and religious elite meant a commission to exercise both divine and political authority over other men, a situation inevitably arose where many felt themselves called, but not all were chosen. Pythagoreanism became the idiom in which the elite competed for power and authority.[186] Significantly, it was the rejected Pythagorean candidate, Cylon, who led the first rebellion against the philosophers.

Very little can be known as to the nature of the Crotoniate expansion. Alliance coins, that is, Crotoniate coins with the first letter of the 'alliance' city on the reverse side, tell us something about Crotoniate influence.[187] Her hegemony reached as far north as Elea where Zeno and Parmenides picked up their differing opinions of Pythagoreanism. The southern boundaries were fixed at Rhegium. The *poleis* and the territory in between were somehow politically or economically dependent on Croton. Dunbabin suggests that Croton exercised at least as much control over these cities as Corinth did over her north-western colonies with whom also a special coinage was issued.[188] U. Kahrstedt in a famous article attempted to chart the rise and fall of this 'empire' by studying the alliance coins of Croton. Although his chronological conclusions have not been proven in full, Crotoniate hegemony over the south Italian cities can be validly gauged by whether the cities used alliance coins, or whether they reverted to independent coinage.

What was the role of the Pythagoreans in this imperial venture? Following Nicomachus, Porphyry reports that Pythagoras freed various cities 'through his disciples in each of them'.[189] Interestingly, most of the Pythagorean societies that Iamblichus mentions stood at the periphery of the Crotoniate empire. Pythagoreans operated actively in Rhegium and Posedonia. In Tarentum there was a powerful Pythagorean component which under Archytas held a dominant political position. Pythagoras, ever peripatetic, visited members in Metapontum and Tauromenium; he was alleged to have died in Metapontum. Minar speculates that if Crotoniate expansion had not been halted due to internal difficulties, the 'reactionary international' would have incorporated all these cities.[190] More concretely, he adds that no independent Pythagorean society is known to have been in power at the same time as the Crotoniate.[191] The activities of the Pythagorean clubs within the empire were subservient to those of the mother city and we do not hear much of them although their members were in close contact with the group at Croton. Kahrstedt's assessment of the situation is somewhat too optimistically stated, given the nature of our evidence; nevertheless, it is a plausible assessment and one which has influenced von Fritz, Minar and the others who have had to attempt reconstructions of the period.[192] Kahrstedt notes:

> Die Behauptung, 'die Pythagoreer' als solche hätten die grossgriechischen Städte beherrscht, wäre ebenso verkehrt wie etwa: 'die Tyrannen' beherrschen um 550 die griechischen Staaten. Vor allem aber wäre unklar, wie ein Schlag die ganze Herrlichkeit zu Boden werfen konnte. Ganz anders, wenn man sich vorstellt, dass die Pythagoreer nur in Kroton, das ja auch immer als ihr Sitz schlechtin erscheint, zur Macht gelangt sind, und dass das durch sie organisirte und disciplinirte Kroton mächtig ausgreift, ähnlich wie in weit grösserem Massstabe der Getenstaat des Burebista oder das Medina Mohammeds nach einer ähnlichen religiösen Reform getan haben.[193]

We know from a passage from Polybius that the local *synhedria* were indissolubly linked with the Crotoniates. Following the burning of Milo's house in Croton, where Pythagoreans from all over southern Italy were assembled, similar incidents took place throughout Magna Graecia and many of the leading citizens were murdered.[194] Aristoxenus' account states that the Pythagoreans now ceased all political activity due to the depletion of manpower and the general indifference of the other *poleis* to the Pythagoreans' fate.[195] Von Fritz surmises that this indicates that Croton was not the only city with Pythagorean leadership, since in the face of such adversity the least the Crotoniates could expect was to have their allies come to their aid.[196] Again we are handicapped by our inability to isolate the obligations that Pythagoreans of various cities had towards Croton.

The massacre may have been felt as far away was mainland Greece where around 450 Damon was ostracised. According to Plutarch and Plato (but not supported by Aristotle), Damon was Pericles' mentor and close associate.[197] He was a teacher of music and a music theorist with strong Pythagorean leanings; it was alleged by his enemies that this was all pretence and that in reality Damon was a clever sophist who used his skills to further Pericles' ends.[198] He was associated with Pericles as a trainer with an athlete, says Plutarch, and Aristotle claims that Damon gave the Athenian politician many of his ideas, including the notion that jurors should be paid.[199]

The anti-Periclean tradition liked to represent Pericles as surrounded by a coterie of intellectuals, many of whom were of non-Athenian origin and some of whom, in conservative eyes, engaged in professions that disqualified them from public trust.[200] As it proved difficult to attack Pericles directly during his lifetime, his enemies had to content themselves with indirect attacks and levelled charges of impiety against Aspasia, Phidias and Anaxagoras.[201] When the Pythagorean débâcle occured in Magna Graecia, it was Damon's turn to be attacked. J.S. Morrison speculates that Damon 'may have fallen a temporary victim to the unpopularity which Pythagoreans inspired in democratic circles and which had such violent results in the West'.[202] The tradition that Pericles was manipulated by some nefarious 'brain-trust' need not be taken any more seriously than the stories of Themistocles' reliance on Mnesiphilus. No doubt the sophisticated politician enjoyed the company of intellectuals and valued the spontaneity of creative individuals as a welcome complement to his own studied deliberateness.

Pythagorean political influence was limited to the Greek west, where, severely weakened, the brotherhood nevertheless remained in the political picture. The events are unusually difficult to reconstruct with any probability at this point. Minar is probably correct in assuming that after the affair at Milo's home, Croton and southern Italy were in a state of *stasis* and that the Pythagoreans' 'retirement was gradual and reluctant'.[203] Indeed, according to Timaeus, the remnants of the society were invited back by the Crotoniates some time around 420.[204] About 60 battle-ready Pythagoreans returned through the good offices of the Achaeans, who acted as mediators.[205] These Pythagoreans died fighting the Thurians and the chastened citizens sacrificed to them at the temple of the Muses — a temple the philosophers had built.[206]

The Pythagoreans attempted comebacks in other cities as well. In Zancle and Rhegium *stasis* broke out some time before the middle of the fifth century, enabling Pythagorean influence to grow and continue growing in these cities, even after the break-up of the society in Croton. There is no agreement as to whether Zancle and Rhegium ever came under Pythagorean rule.[207] Iamblichus names two Pythagorean constitutions at Rhegium and his catalogue of Pythagorean worthies include ten Rhegians.[208] Rhegium became a gathering place for expatriate Pythagoreans. However, the political situation in Rhegium also became unstable and a second exodus from the west ensued as 'all except Archytas of Tarentum' left Italy.[209]

Archytas and Empedocles

Under Dionysius the Elder, Syracuse again became a dominating, growing power in 405. By this time Crotoniate domination had crumbled and the Italian cities had banded together in a league which met at Heraclea.[210] The leader of these cities was Tarentum, with its modified, more democratic Pythagorean rule. In Tarentum, as in Rhegium, the development of Pythagoreanism was a relatively late phenomenon. Of the Tarentines Iamblichus lists, none date from the early history of the movement.[211] There is a strong temptation to compare Tarentum with Locri, for both were Spartan colonies and aristocratically governed. Neither city was of any great help to the wandering Pythagoras in his hour of need, albeit Tarentum apparently let him in.[212] Tarentum's history was dominated by fierce fighting with the Italian tribes of the interior. In 471 the Iapygians slaughtered a great mass of Tarentine aristocrats.[213] The nobles made some sort of comeback and a compromise between democracy and aristocracy was effected.[214] Another compromise centred around the redivision of land; as Archytas put it, 'when found correct calculation puts an end to evil strife and increases concord'.[215]

Such compromises had not been characteristic of earlier Pythagorean politics and an important difference seems to have been the personality of Archytas. True to their founder's doctrines, most Pythagoreans had been wary of ambitious individuals. The fact that Archytas had some sympathy with democratic forms of government and was not chary of being known as a thinker in his own right reminds one of Hippasus. Unlike the latter, Archytas managed to establish himself in power by the time of Plato's second journey to Syracuse in the 370s. His diplomatic and military skills gave him authority not only in Tarentum but over a confederacy of Greeks in Magna Graecia. The philosopher-general had two tasks: one was to deal with the Italian tribes; the other was to keep the Syracusans at bay. His military abilities accomplished the first; as for Syracuse, Archytas kept his own counsel. He had a valuable ace in Dion and a useful trump in Plato.

George Grote has commented on the synthesising nature of Pythagoras' life and works, his ability to bring together men of different temperaments and abilities.[216] The force of the philosopher's personality played this role, but so did the laws and the society he founded. The success of one initiate, whether it be of a political or of a religious nature, reverberated equally on all the other members of the society. We tend to think of the Greeks as pre-eminently individualists, each engaged in his own Odyssey. Herodotus' story of the aftermath of the battle of Salamis, when all the Greek commanders voted for themselves as foremost in bravery, testifies to this, as do the lives of any number of Greek leaders.[217] The two groups who strove most successfully to counter such individualism (at least in the eyes of others) were the Spartans and the Pythagoreans. Envious Greek aristocrats attributed this success to the 'good laws' of Lycurgus and Pythagoras, but it takes no great psychological or sociological insight to notice that both groups, besides successfully arresting change, provided their members with a controlled form of individuality that also served as a safety valve. When marching to war, Xenophon tells us, the Spartan wore scarlet and allowed his hair to grow long.[218] Of course, there were practical reasons for the red cloak; symbolically, however, it was the analogue of the Pythagoreans' pure white clothing. One society dressed for war, the other for salvation. The *syssitia* and the *synedria* set saints and warriors apart from the rest of the Hellenic world, even as the inflexible regimens crushed the individuality of their respective members.[219] To what extent territorial empire and political rule were by-products or primary objectives of these two societies can never be known. The fact remains that the 'new men' who consciously followed the old ways as they perceived them were remarkably successful.

However, these isolated Greek experiments broke down and mercenaries and philosophers unleashed themselves on to the Hellenic world after the break-up of the Pythagorean societies. Many of the Pythagoreans drifted back to their Orphic roots. The failure of humility, the demise of the strict Pythagorean ways, can best be seen in Empedocles. He describes himself in Nietzschean terms:

> I go about among you an immortal god, no mortal now, honoured among all as is meet, crowned with fillets and flowery garlands. Straightway, whenever I enter with these in my train, both men and women, into the flourishing towns, is reverence done me; they go after me in countless throngs, asking of me what is the way to gain; some desiring oracles, while some, who for many a weary day have been pierced by the grievous pangs of all manner of sickness, beg to hear from me the word of healing.[220]

Empedocles was not without influence in his native city of Acragas. He came from a politically important family and played a significant role in the transformation of his native city from a tyranny to a democracy.[221] He dissolved an oligarchic organisation known as the Thousand, but, when offered the kingship by the grateful citizenry, he refused. The stories about him suggest an extremely egomaniacal individual who at some point had to leave Acragas and died in exile.

The discrepancy in Empedocles' character was noted by Timaeus: 'He seems to have held opposite views when in public life and when writing poetry.'[222] How such a man could be a democrat puzzled the ancients, but haughty individuals often take up popular or even radical causes to emphasise their uniqueness, and Empedocles came from a family which had opposed tyrants in the past.[223] An equally glaring discrepancy surfaced between the wonder worker and the politician. He was a politician only in his native city and there only because he was born into the position. The fact of the matter seems to be that Empedocles was not interested in any social organisation with hereditary or legally binding functions. This is to be interpreted in a religious as well as a political sense. Although Empedocles' high opinion of Pythagoras is known, he refused to join the latter's cult. Rather, as Max Weber notes of magicians, Empedocles preferred to be self-employed.[224]

There is no doubt about Empedocles' debts to the Pythagoreans. He taught reincarnation: 'For I have been ere now a boy and a girl, a bush and a bird and a dumb fish in the sea.'[225] He promised to teach his pupils to journey to the underworld to bring back the strength of a man who has died.[226] However, he was not known primarily for his dogma or his students, but for his charismatic magic.[227] Timaeus reports some of his tricks and his pupil, Gorgias, testifies to his magical abilities as well.[228] Empedocles was as little concerned with setting up a cult or subsuming his personality under the rigid Pythagorean rule as he was in remaining a lifelong partisan of democracy. Leaving out his philosophical achievements, Empedocles most closely resembles Epimenides, the charismatic wonder-worker.

Pythagoras had successfully united two important Hellenic streams of thinking in his person and philosophy. These two tendencies can be personified by the names of Solon and Epimenides. For a while, the Pythagoreans managed to combine these opposites within their system, but systems break down and Solon and Epimenides, the pious rationalist and the wonder-worker, emerged once more in the personalities and achievements of Archytas and Empedocles.

3 PLATO AND THE ACADEMY

Plato

> I lived among great houses,
> Riches drove out rank,
> Base drove out the better blood,
> And mind and body shrank.[1]

So wrote Yeats in *Last Poems* describing the depressing era in which he lived. Events in Ireland had disappointed him. As a member of the Irish Senate from 1922 to 1928, he had hoped to influence his country's affairs, but came instead to the conclusion that 'the greatest weakness of a democratic state was the inability of the electorate to tell a true philosopher king from a windy political opportunist'.[2] Equally discouraged by the state of European culture and flattered that his biases were shared by Spengler and Gentile, Yeats flirted with Fascism, but finally drew back, his sense of aestheticism bruised.[3] (Lady Gregory would have felt ill at ease among the Irish Blue Shirts.)

Yeats's experience with the twentieth century can be utilised to pinpoint the mental and spiritual outlook of a number of important Greek aristocrats of the fourth century. To none does this apply with greater apposition than those Athenians who grew up in the aftermath of Periclean Athens and who witnessed the defeat of Athens by Sparta. The aristocrats considered taxation by democrats to be onerous and unjust and viewed with even greater repugnance the ascendancy and power of the renewed democracy. Feeling out of kilter with the times, individuals such as Plato and Isocrates retreated to the Persian Wars to find examples of correct conduct and polity. While assessing the plans and behaviour of Greek intellectuals, their emotional vertigo should be kept in view. What went through Yeats's mind can be used as clues to the attitudes of Plato and Isocrates as they sought to make sense of the world of the fourth century and the role in it of the elite with which they identified. Although Athens remained a major power, both thinkers came to see that it could no longer be pre-eminent in Greek affairs, ruled by those who deserve to rule, the heirs of Solon, the peers of Pericles. Yeats laments,

64 *Plato and the Academy*

> Things fall apart; the centre cannot hold;
> Mere anarchy is loosed upon the world,
> The blood dimmed tide is loosed, and everywhere
> The ceremony of innocence is drowned;
> The best lack all conviction, while the worst
> Are full of passionate intensity.[4]

Arguably, the most famous example of a philosopher who was also a political activist is Plato. William James posits an interesting duality which serves to throw light on Plato's political involvement:

> The deepest difference, practically, in the moral life of man is the difference between the easy-going and the strenuous mood. When in the easy-going mood the shrinking from present ill is our ruling consideration. The strenuous mood, on the contrary, makes us quite indifferent to present ill, if only the greater ideal be attained. The capacity for the strenuous mood probably lies slumbering in every man, but it has more difficulty in some than in others in waking up.[5]

Thoughts along these lines must have occurred to Plato's illustrious relations when they considered the political participation, or, rather, the lack of political involvement of their young relative. Plato's reluctance to engage in Athenian politics could not be explained as due to a fragile constitution. He was a healthy, robust individual who participated in gymnastics and wrestling as a youth and at an advanced age undertook overseas excursions.[6]

Nor could Plato's lack of political involvement be due to a rejection of his family's political past and what they had stood for. Plato shows every sign of pride in his noteworthy relatives. In the *Charmides*, Critias boasts about the qualities of his cousin, Charmides, saying there is more to him that meets the eye, for he is a philosopher and a poet 'not in his opinion only, but in that of others'. Socrates replies 'that, my dear Critias ... is a distinction which has long been in your family, and is inherited by you from Solon.'[7] Perictione, Plato's mother, was a descendant of Solon and such a lineage carried weight in democratic Athens. Relatives on his mother's side included the oligarchs, Critias, Charmides and Antiphon. His father's family was also aristocratic, claiming descent from the last king of Athens, the mythical Codrus, scion of lawgivers and kings. Plato was forever conscious of his upper-class roots. Further, the family did not rest on its laurels, but maintained a high visibility throughout the latter part of the fifth century. Pyrilampes went on embassies to the Persian king and other monarchs of Asia.[8] A true *kalos kagathos*, he combined beauty and stature with temperance and position. Plato never abandoned his admiration for these aristocratic qualities.

Probably, Charmides and Critias stood for more in the philosopher's life than either his parents or his brothers.[9] His references to Critias consistently show respect and even affection. Plato's Critias is the unsullied follower of Socrates and engages with the Master in mutual admiration and *eros*: the younger man fascinated with the mentor's dialectical skills and *daimon*; the older man impressed with the youth's mental and physical characteristics, not to mention good name.[10] The Critias who speaks in the *Charmides* and the *Protagoras* in no way corresponds to the villain portrayed by Xenophon in the *Hellenica*.[11] In 404 Plato had every reason to be interested and expectant when men who 'happened to be relatives and acquaintances of mine . . . invited me to join them at once in what seemed to be a proper undertaking'.[12] The relatives, of course, were Critias and Charmides; the acquaintances consisted of the social circle that Plato's family moved in. Plato was invited to play a role in the rule of the many by the few. On both sides this was regarded as a proper undertaking, and the oligarchs required his services at once. At this point, however, Plato balked.

It would not be far off the mark to assume that Socrates influenced Plato in his decision. In a different context, he restrained Plato's brother Glaucon when he wished to speak in the Assembly before the legally acceptable age of 20. As Xenophon tells the story, Glaucon patently had nothing to say in any event.[13] But Socrates had also locked horns with Critias and the gentle Socratic irony was missing when 'Socrates, it is said, exclaimed in the presence of Euthydemus and many others, "Critias seems to have the feelings of a pig: he can no more keep away from Euthydemus than pigs can help rubbing themselves against stones." '[14] This remark caused Critias to take a dislike to Socrates, adds Xenophon laconically. Since Critias had just been shamed before a gathering of his peers, the wound penetrated deeply. Anxious or not to take his place among his relatives and acquaintances, Plato was aware of the hatred that Critias now bore towards Socrates and wished to see what the immediate future held in store for his teacher.

For Plato, Socrates was more than a beloved mentor. Plato's father, Ariston, died while he was still a boy and, whatever one may think of Georges Devereux's model of displaced fathering as applied to classical Greek society, the fact remains that at some point Plato's father ceased to counsel him and the youth was forced to turn to one or more father surrogates upon whom to model himself.[15] His portrayal of Pyrilampes was quite flattering, as was the depiction of Critias and Charmides in the dialogue, *Charmides*. In his writings, Plato created not only a series of ideal states, but also an ideal family for himself. Behind his two maternal relatives stood Socrates, the father surrogate *extraordinaire*. Although there is no way of knowing just how close Plato and Socrates were, the young man was probably admitted to Socrates' inner circle.[16] There can be little doubt that Socrates saw admirable qualities in Plato, just as Plato in his turn appreciated the acumen of Aristotle. The older man exercised on Plato both a direct and, through his relatives, an indirect influence. Commenting on Socrates, Plato says through Alcibades in the *Symposium*: 'Personally I think the most amazing thing about him is the fact that he is absolutely unique: there is no one like him, and I don't believe there ever was.'[17]

It was this unique individual who was ordered by the Thirty to fetch Leon of Salamis from his home for execution. According to Plato, Socrates saw the purpose quite clearly. 'This was a specimen of the sort of commands which they were always giving with the view of implicating as many as possible in their crimes.'[18] Socrates would have none of it and only the rapid fall of the government spared the philosopher's life. 'When I saw all this and other like things of no little consequence,' laments Plato, 'I was appalled and drew back from that reign of injustice.'[19] Previously Socrates had tangled with the democracy and Plato found that constitution to be 'generally detested', but the brutalities of the Thirty 'showed in a short time that the preceding constitution had been a precious thing'.[20]

No longer as keen as before, Plato still desired to take part in public and political affairs upon the return to power of the democrats under Thrasybulus, but again he was content to look on.[21] Like most intellectuals, Plato was less interested in playing the game or even scoring the goals than in refereeing the match or, at the least, calling the plays. Denied this role throughout most of his life, he seemed content to stand on the sidelines criticising, moralising, editorialising. The restored democracy at Athens gave the philosopher cause for complaint, for, although 'in general those who returned from exile acted with great restraint', they tried, condemned and executed Plato's friend and associate, Socrates.[22] In his defence, Plato has Socrates say,

> No man who goes to war with you or any other multitude, honestly striving against the many lawless and unrighteous deeds which are

done in a state, will save his life; he who will fight for the right, if he would live even for a brief space, must have a private station and not a public one.[23]

Plato took these words to heart. His reluctance to throw himself into a revolutionary situation had been strengthened by Socrates' unwillingness to take part in the rule of the Thirty. Any further adventurism on Plato's part had to compete with the spectre of Socrates drinking the hemlock 'he, of all men, least deserved'. Throughout his long life, Plato had cause to elaborate on this theme and the fact that someone of his background did not take an active role in governing required explanation.

In the *Republic* Plato repeats the argument:

Such a one may be compared to a man who has fallen among wild beasts — he will not join in the wickedness of his fellows, but neither is he able singly to resist all their fierce natures, and therefore seeing that he would be of no use to the State or to his friends, and reflecting that he would have to throw away his life without doing any good either to himself or others, he holds his peace and goes his own way.[24]

Again, in the *Seventh Epistle*, the aristocrat Plato likens himself to a physician who has to deal with a recalcitrant patient; 'anyone who would put up with him is without spirit or skill'.[25] Likewise, someone who would advise the city in the face of threats and intimidations and preconceived notions of right and wrong is a man 'without spirit, and he who refuses is the true man'.[26]

Another track that Plato took and one which was used as an argument in his defence as early as Speusippus is found in the *Fifth Epistle*.

If anyone hears this and says, 'Plato apparently claims to know what is good for a democracy, but though he is at liberty to speak in the assembly and give it his best advice, he has never yet stood up and said a word,' you can answer by saying, 'Plato was born late in the life of his native city, and he found the demos advanced in years and habituated by former advisors to many practices incompatible with the advice he would give.'[27]

He goes on to say that he would give advice to the *demos* 'as to a father' if there was no unnecessary danger involved.[28] But personal risk was never far away in Greek politics. Plato's ancestor, Solon, had written about fusing

> justice and power into an iron weapon,
> I forced through every measure I had pledged,
> I wrote the laws for good and bad alike,
> and gave an upright posture to the courts, . . .
> I put myself on guard at every side,
> spinning like a wolf among a pack of dogs.[29]

Such heroics never appealed to Plato, but neither could he escape the guilt that came from a lifetime of inaction towards his own city. His strategy to cope with such feelings was to reverse the traditional moral order: 'The true champion of justice' confines himself to private life and leaves politics alone. In point of fact, the man who enters an unstable arena of politics 'spinning like a wolf among a pack of dogs' is the man without spirit and he who refuses is the true man. It was not the young, physically robust Plato acting with the timidity and caution associated with old age, but rather the *demos* itself which had become senile and servile.[30] Giving advice to such an institution would be a futile exercise and accomplish nothing besides personal risks.

In the *Gorgias* this technique is applied to politicians and statesmen as well. Only Kierkegaard's contempt of journalists can match Plato's dislike of democratic statesmen.[31] Far from being an ideal statesman, Pericles was a demagogue of the highest order, 'for I hear that he was the first who gave the people pay, and made them idle and cowardly, and encouraged them in the love of talk and money'.[32] Socrates concludes that the democratic leaders 'have fitted the city full of harbours and docks and walls and revenues and all that kind of rubbish, and have left no room for justice and temperance'.[33] Who then is the true statesman? Socrates has the answer in hand: 'I think that I am the only or almost the only Athenian living who sees the true art of politics: and the only practising politician.'[34] He backs up these words with the oft-repeated physician analogy and, anticipating his impending trial by the democratic jury, he asks, 'what do you suppose that the physician would be able to reply when he found himself in such a predicament?'[35] The desperate situation is the obtuseness of the *demos* who would sentence him to death.

Where does all this leave Plato? It should come as no surprise that the answer is the position of the philosopher-king. Guthrie, relying on the *Republic*, aptly assesses Plato's dilemma and his solution:

There is one curious point about the philosopher's fitness to rule. It may sound logical (even if we remain skeptical) that because his mind is fixed on the immutable realities of the divine order, he alone can order human affairs according to the highest standards. But it is freely admitted that for the same reason he will despise the world of men and be most unwilling to take an active part in it. Plato frequently says that he will only govern under compulsion (500d, 519c *et al*.), and it even becomes an advantage that he would prefer a different life (520d-521b). Stranger still, he has no time to look down on the affairs of men and *therefore* will be good at inplanting in society the divine pattern of justice and civic virtue as a whole (500b). This is one of the points at which philosophy becomes autobiography (if indeed it is not that all the time), for surely this mirrors the conflict in Plato's own *psyche*. Unwilling himself to enter politics, he yet felt ashamed of his reluctance ... and so evolved the remarkable idea that a philosopher could not take part in the politics of any existing society, but only in an ideal one (cf. esp. 9.592a), and at the same time that the ideal one would never be realized until the philosopher agreed to take part in politics.[36]

Soon after his master's death, Plato, along with Socrates' other disciples, withdrew to Megara — a move that Athenian democrats had ardently hoped Socrates would make. There, the disciples associated with the philosopher Eucleides, an intimate member of the Socratic circle, who along with another Megarian, Terpsion, had witnessed Socrates' death.[37] It is generally agreed that Plato was back at Athens in 395, summoned to active service in the Corinthian War. This detail is related by Aristoxenus, who also mentions campaigns fought at Delium and Tanagra.[38] While these last two episodes seem unlikely, Plato did see fighting in the last years of the Peloponnesian War and in the early part of the Corinthian War. G.C. Field reminds us that 'what is important to remember is that an Athenian philosopher in Plato's time could not be a mere cloistered scholar, but had to know what it was like to be a man of action too'.[39] He then goes on to note that scholars of his own generation who had fought in the First World War 'will be able to estimate the differences that this must have made to their understanding of many problems'.[40] Whether this understanding included in every case a heightened appreciation of practical political problems may be doubted. To know what it is like to be a man of action is one thing; to want to have anything to do with such a life is quite another. A goodly number of any war generation make successful attempts to forget their annoying 'man of action' years and to re-enter the cloister. However, it is clear that no Greek *polis* ever resembled a cloister. There was too much change and uncertainty. Though Plato hated social, political and economic change and however much he sought to flee into a realm of pure forms and ideas, the truth is as Field states it: an Athenian philosopher of that time was likely to be or, better, could not avoid being a man of action too.[41] Certainly Plato's life was adventurous enough, in spite of his best efforts to the contrary.

After 391 no more large-scale expeditions of citizen forces were sent out by Athens against Corinth and Plato undertook a new cycle of trips.[42] The purpose of these travels was to acquaint himself with the leading logicians and mathematicians of his day. Eucleides was a follower of Parmenides and Zeno and even further removed than Plato from the empirical world, preferring dialectical abstractions and 'either-or' dilemmas.[43] In Cyrene, Plato visited the mathematician Theodorus. Finally, he went to Italy and met with Pythagoreans.

The presence of this sect had already made itself felt in Greece. In an otherwise silly book, A.D. Winspear and T. Silverberg highlight an intriguing episode during the last days of Socrates. After solemnly asserting on the basis of the flimsiest of proof that 'Socrates at the end of his life was a more or less orthodox Pythagorean', they continue: 'Members of the sect visited him in prison and offered to pay his ransom. It is to Thebes and Megara, strongholds politically and philosophically of the Pythagorean brotherhood, that he would have escaped, had he made the decision to escape and not faced death with resignation.'[44] Thebes and Megara could by no stretch of the imagination be considered Pythagorean strongholds in any political sense. It is true that Lysis, after fleeing the mob at Croton, wound up in Thebes after a sojourn in Achaea; and that Lysis was the teacher of Epaminondas, who was devoted to the old man and 'preferred that grave and rigid old gentleman to those of the same age as himself'.[45] In the *Rhetoric* Aristotle says, 'At Thebes no sooner did the leading men become philosophers than the country began to prosper.'[46] But to imply that Epaminondas was a Pythagorean is an exaggeration and the brief primacy of Thebes was due less to philosophy being put into practice than to military innovations and skills.

A Pythagorean colony was present in Thebes and a number of Pythagoreans found their way into Plato's dialogues. In the *Crito* Simmias and Cebes of Thebes were willing to buy Socrates' way out of prison and they encouraged him to escape to Megara or Thebes.[47] Pythagoreans were willing to bail one another out through financial and other means. Although it is far-fetched to claim on this evidence that Socrates was a Pythagorean, it can be assumed that Socrates and the Pythagorean community were acquainted with and respected each other and that this admiration passed from Socrates to Plato.

According to the *Seventh Epistle*, between the time that Socrates died and Plato's first trip to Sicily in 389-388, the author came to a few crucial conclusions. He saw that 'it was impossible to do anything without friends and loyal followers'.[48] In Athens, given 'the corruption of our written laws and customs', to find such a group would amount to a piece of extraordinary good luck amounting to a miracle.[49] During this period Plato formulated his famous dictum 'that the ills of the human race would never end until either those who are sincerely and truly lovers of wisdom come into political power, or the rulers of our cities, by the grace of God, learn true philosophy'.[50]

Such was the frame of mind with which Plato sailed to Italy and Sicily for the first time. The Epistle goes on to record the philosopher's repugnance with what he saw in the west: Italian and Syracusan banquets, men gorging themselves twice a day and never sleeping alone at night and so on. 'I was profoundly displeased,' writes the old moralist.[51] Plato may be trying to impress upon the reader the inevitability of Dion's failure in Syracuse. However that may be, Philodemus claims that Plato's motive for the visit was a desire to see the Pythagoreans.[52] In his *Republic* Cicero enlarges on this theme:

> After Socrates' death Plato went on journeys ... to Italy and Sicily in order to become acquainted with the discoveries of Pythagoras ... He spent a great deal of time in the company of Archytas of Tarentum and Timaeus of Locri, and also got possession of Philolaus' notes. And, as Pythagoras' reputation was then great in that country, he devoted himself entirely to that teacher's disciples and doctrines.[53]

Syracusan banquets there may have been, but most of his time in Italy was spent in the subdued atmosphere of Pythagorean *synedria*.

Part of the reason Plato went to visit the Pythagoreans was to continue his discussions with mathematicians. Timaeus was a scientist who had 'scaled the height of philosophy' and Archytas was a noted mathematician. Equally important, Plato wanted direct observation of 'friends and loyal followers'. From the adherents of Pythagoreanism in Greece, Plato had gathered some idea of the nature of Pythagorean groups, their closeness and loyalty and their political activism. As Plato reflected on the cause of the death of Socrates, the only true politician, the trial and condemnation of the man must have depressed him. Alienated himself from the mainstream of Athenian society, Plato found consolation and direction from the followers of Pythagoras. Morrison rightly emphasises that

> the drawback to the Socratic *politike* had been its ineffectiveness, the fatal isolation and vulnerability of the *politikos*. It is true that the Pythagorean *synedria* had run into trouble in the end, but they achieved much and enjoyed a long period of ascendancy, and Archytas remained as a surviving example of a successful Pythagorean statesman. Plato's contact with the surviving Pythagoreans seems to have convinced him that something like the Crotonian *synedrion* would provide 'the trustworthy friends and supporters' necessary for successful political reform.[54]

At Tarentum, Plato may have met Philolaus. Among these three Pythagoreans, Plato would have broadened considerably his knowledge of the sect.

According to Nepos, when the report made its way to Sicily that Plato had come to Tarentum, Dionysius II 'could not refuse Dion's request to invite him to his court'.[55] If this tradition is true, Archytas and Dion were most likely in contact with each other even at that early date. This would not be surprising if Dion had expressed interest in philosophy prior to his meeting with Plato.[56] We do not know how long Plato stayed in Sicily, but it was long enough for him to make two widely disparate impressions on two important individuals.

Plato's effect on Dion was great and permanent. One should not unduly exaggerate, as Plutarch does, any personality changes on Dion's part resulting from his meeting with Plato.[57] He had served tyrants for most of his life; and, however hedonistic the mood of the court, Dion had never been a worldly *élégant*. Whatever changes may have occurred were due to the differences in temperament and ruthlessness between the Elder and the Younger Dionysius. Still, there can be no doubt that Plato and Dion were attracted to each other.[58] As with so many intellectuals, with Plato the key word is receptivity: 'For Dion was in all things quick to learn, especially in the matters upon which I talked with him; and he listened with a zeal and attentiveness I had never encountered in any young man.'[59] One can almost sense in Plato the renewed interest in life that Dion occasioned. The younger man listened with enthusiasm as Plato 'imparted to him my ideas of what was best for men and urged him to put them into practice'.[60] The fact that Dion resolved to spend his life differently from other Italians and Sicilians meant that Plato had found a fellow traveller and a highly placed one at that. For his part, Dion was greatly flattered by the interest and approval of the older man. No doubt, there were those in Syracuse who found even the young Dion a cold and boring individual. True, tyrants might come to appreciate Dion's calculating ways and try to utilise them for their own ends, but nobody was fond of him except for a few philosophers. Plato's later lament for the murdered Dion 'who didst madden my soul with love', is both touching and sincere.[61]

No such vibrations floated in the air between the philosopher and the tyrant. Dionysius had sought out poets and philosophers in the past, trying thereby to achieve respectability in the eyes of the Greek world. Obviously wishing to be known as a cultured ruler, he engaged in artistic patronage and wrote poems and tragedies. There may have been other reasons as well. As J.K. Davies points out, the Herodotean stereotype of the king as a tyrant was being revised in Dionysius' day by various political thinkers who attempted to create a new theory of monarchy.[62] With Plato, Dionysius was to be disappointed in his search for legitimacy. The conversation between the two resembled Herodotus' narrative of Solon and Croesus as the philosopher distanced himself from the tyrant.[63] In exasperation, Dionysius asked Plato why he had come to Sicily and Plato replied, 'to seek a virtuous man'. Dionysius retorted angrily: 'Well, by the gods, it appears that you have not yet found such a one.'[64] Before the tyrant had much more time to ponder Plato's statement and perhaps link Dion's name to it, the latter sent Plato away on a trirene. 'Plato was eager for it,' notes Plutarch.[65]

The majority of the sources relate that on Plato's return from Sicily he was made a prisoner on Dionysius' orders by the Spartan captain Pollis and sold at Aegina.[66] Plato himself has nothing to say on the matter. His failure with the ruler was complete and the incident was shameful to an Athenian aristocrat. If the Aeginean story is true, then his redemptor, Anniceris, refused to accept the money remitted him by Dion or by Plato's friends in Athens. Instead, he purchased land on which the Academy came to be located.[67]

In the *Fifth Epistle*, Plato had said that towards Athens, he would always be like a faithful son to his father, senile though the old man might be. He reiterates this sentiment in the *Seventh Epistle*: 'To use compulsion upon a father or mother is to me an impious act, unless their judgement has been impaired by disease.'[68] Such an attitude towards the home base of the Academy was necessary for the school to function there. Ancient democracies did not knowingly foster within their premises institutions which worked for the open overthrow of their form of government. For Plato, an aloof attitude towards Athenian politics in return for the city's toleration of his school was a fair trade-off. In the course of time other cities, influenced by Plato's reputation and thoughts, would ask for his assistance in setting up laws, not always successfully. Plato rejected Cyrene because he thought the city too addicted to luxury to make the implementation of his regimen practicable.[69] When Megalopolis was founded, the Arcadians and Thebans asked Plato to be *nomothetes* to the new colony. On finding out that all things were not to be held in common, Plato refused.[70]

Syracuse, however, was a different matter. To begin with, there was Dion's personal plea. If the philosopher expected to keep the admiration of his most valued pupil, he had to respond positively, especially as some of Dion's unstated arguments appeared to imply that, if his faction was not shored up, his influence and life were ultimately in danger.[71] Dion felt confident of the present state of his influence over the tyrant and wished to press home his advantage. Plato figured prominently in his plans, 'so that now, if ever, might we confidently hope to accomplish that union, in the same persons, of philosophers and rulers of great cities'.[72] In the *Republic* Plato had argued how the divorce between the world and philosophy, so detrimental to both, might be brought to an end, for it is not impossible that a ruler may arise who ordains laws and institutions of a Platonic nature and, if this be the case, 'it is surely not impossible that the citizens should be content to carry them out'.[73] The possibilities of such events happening were not overwhelming and Plato had expected to spend the remainder of his life, as he had spent the last 20 years, among his students and groves on the outskirts of Athens. Yet, Dion had written that exactly such a constellation had appeared in the west and Plato had to face the challenge.

In a revealing statement Plato says, 'I was ashamed lest I appear to myself as a pure theorist, unwilling to touch any practical task.'[74] Here the self-image of the aristocrat came to the fore, the person to whom as a youth political ascendancy had seemed 'a proper undertaking'. Whatever one may think of Karl Popper's Plato (and in particular his description of Socrates, the social democrat), it is worthwhile to engage with Popper in speculating about Plato's ambitions, the secret dreams that fuelled the philosopher's enthusiasm and caused him to see himself an object of shame among those whose opinions he valued:

Plato and the Academy 75

Even where he argues against ambition, we cannot feel but what he is inspired by it ... He who has had communion with the divine may descend from his heights to the mortals below, sacrificing himself for the sake of the interest of the state. He is not eager; but as a natural ruler and saviour, he is ready to come. The poor mortals need him. Without him the state must perish, for he alone knows the secret of how to preserve it — the secret of arresting degeneration ... I think that behind the sovereignty of the philosopher king stands the quest for power.[75]

More than self-image was at stake. Plato had made himself the leader of a group of aristocratic youths to whom he was in the habit of discoursing on subjects such as political leadership and the theory of the state. We know that the members of the Academy took an active interest in the world around them and in Sicily in particular. For Plato to maintain a moral hegemony over these students, he had to demonstrate to them that it was possible, given the appropriate circumstances, to put theory into practice. His lack of political activity had earlier alienated him from members of his family and class. The desire not to repeat this incident with members of the Academy played its role.

Charges of the other-worldliness of the Academy had been levelled by Isocrates and his rival school. The competition between them for worldly influence was and remained great. Isocrates had addressed a letter to one of the Dionysii wishing to set himself up as an adviser to the tyrant and warning him about 'one who is neither statesman nor general [who] presumes to speak in the cause of Hellas and to you'.[76] The letter leaves off on a competitive note. 'But you shall at once judge for yourself whether my advice is worth anything.'[77] When Dion wrote to Plato and entreated him to come to Syracuse 'before certain others came in contact with Dionysius and diverted him to a less worthy ideal of life', he may well have had in mind some agents of Isocrates' in addition to Philistus, Aristippus and Aeschines.[78]

Another group Plato listened to with respect were the Pythagoreans, who had also written letters to him urging him to come and exert an influence over the young ruler.[79] Their own positions in power in Italy and especially Tarentum depended to a large extent on maintaining proper relations with the powerful Syracusan city and they did not hesitate to enlist Plato in their cause. Plato obliged them and the two forces worked closely together.

Plato arrived in Sicily with trepidations, but he must have had some hope of success. The Younger Dionysius accorded the philosopher a hero's welcome upon his arrival at Syracuse in 376.[80] At first all went according to plan. Like most weak and indolent men, Dionysius was genuinely fascinated by strength and self-control. He threw himself unquestioningly into the new regimen. Geometry became his new passion and his court, attuned to following the tyrant's whims, emulated their master's zeal.[81] The palace was filled with dust, says Plutarch, owing to the number of geometricians there. Plato had brought with him assistants who concentrated on training the court. Parallels for such behaviour may be found in the rage for pastoral settings at the court of Marie Antoinette. Shepherds or geometricians: the commitment was shallow in both cases. What Dionysius lacked was staying power and the geometricians of the tyrant's court quickly longed for the less abstract pleasures of yesterday.

The acme of Plato and Dion's success with the tyrant came after a post-sacrificial prayer by a herald pleading to the gods that the tyranny abide unshaken for many generations. On hearing this Dionysius cried, 'Stop cursing us!'[82] Statements such as this finally galvanised Philistus and his group to take counter-measures. For the historian Philistus it was the dynasty that counted. As M.I. Finley points out, Dionysius the Elder had anticipated the practices of the Hellenistic monarchs: 'If one were to ask the name of the empire which Dionysius acquired and ruled, there could be no answer ... This kind of ruler was monarch wherever his writ ran, so long as he would enforce it.'[83] The empire which Dionysius had bequested his son was a formidable one. At a heavy price, he had wrested almost total control of the island from the Carthaginians.[84] The empire was large but fragile and, now, it seemed to Philistus and his faction, Plato and Dion wished to destroy the institution that had made the empire possible.

The philosopher had written 'do not subject Sicily nor any other State to the despotism of men, but to the rule of laws; this at least is my doctrine'.[85] From the *Eighth Epistle* it would appear that Plato and Dion had worked out a division of authority that cut back drastically the powers of the tyrant.[86] Plato would also have restored the Greek cities of Sicily that Dionysius had destroyed.[87] That such destruction had been accomplished only through much bloodshed and suffering is obvious; however, Davies' point must be kept in mind: 'by 389 ... it had largely run its course, and had created an empire which was to be stable for over twenty years'.[88] To Philistus, it was the empire and the dynasty which fashioned and could alone preserve it that mattered. The historian could console himself that he was not alone in his sympathies.

Plato and the Academy 77

Writing to his pupil, Nicocles, Isocrates had neatly extolled absolute rule and the advantages of mercenaries:

> And not only in matters of ordinary routine and of daily occurrence do monarchies excell, but in war they have compassed every advantage; for in raising troops, and handling them so as to mislead and forestall the enemy, and in winning people over, now by persuasion, now by force, now by bribery, now by other means of conciliation, one man rule is more efficient than the other forms of government.[89]

Mercenaries were an important fixture of the Greek world of the fourth century. They were not new to the fourth century — Greeks had been serving for pay since the eighth century — but it was in the period following the Peloponnesian War that they came to be a serious political and social problem. Nowhere were they more effectively embraced and utilised than by Dionysius the Elder, who had no illusions about the real foundation for his rule; and nowhere were they more rigorously resisted as the basis of a land force than in Athens, where the Periclean ideal precluded any but citizen soldiers.[90]

Although terrified by them, Plato never understood the importance of mercenaries, but they and not law were the glue that held empires together. In the *Laws* Plato had sketched a lengthy blueprint for a military force composed exclusively of citizens between the ages of 20 and 60. He was very much a product of his native city in such matters and viewed the mercenaries as a force alien to the spirit of a Greek *polis*.[91] For their part, the mercenaries felt that Plato posed a threat to their continuing existence and their survival depended on Plato's removal from Sicily. Additionally, they may have thought that Plato was profoundly ungrateful to them and undervalued their role as the effective protector of the Younger Dionysius from a hostile citizenry: because they were there so was Dionysius; and it was the presence of the tyrant that had drawn the Athenian philosopher to court.[92]

Before examining Plato's two failures in Sicily, it will be worthwhile to dwell for a moment on Plato and his still willing student, Dionysius. Although it can be presumed that Plato did not wish to establish the utopian *Republic* in Syracuse, even for those reforms which he and Dion wished to set in place it was necessary to make Dionysius into a philosopher, to make philosophy the alpha and the omega for the young man. Only complete dedication to philosophy and its teacher would give him the strength of character and conviction to push through a series of reforms in the face of the opposition of Philistus and his faction.[93] What this meant in practical terms is expressed by Grote:

> He and Dion began to deal with Dionysius as a confessor treats his penitent; to probe the interior man; to expose him to his own unworthiness: to show that his life, his training, his companions, had all been vicious; to insist upon repentance and amendment upon these points before he could receive absolution, and be permitted to enter upon active political life.[94]

When Dionysius expressed an interest in resettling the Greek cities of Sicily and modifying his tyranny, Plato rejected such remarks replying, 'first go through your schooling, and then do all these things; otherwise leave them undone.'[95] The master wanted more than surface enthusiasm; he had not yet finished probing the interior man. Like so many intellectuals in politics, Plato was not interested in ruling *per se*; others could do that. What interested the philosopher was in establishing himself as the conscience behind the throne.[96] The Athenian *demos* had Socrates: Dionysius was to have Plato. This indirect approach allowed Plato (as was probably the case with Pythagoras) to create a distance between himself and the everyday world of events. Unsullied by the world, the philosopher was left free to moralise at will. Other things may go wrong, the intellectual remains pure. Even so, Plato was clearly on the defensive in answering Dionysius' later charges that Plato had deterred him from putting the philosopher's own reforms into place.[97] The line between a saint and a fool is a thin one and Plato was clearly feeling the razor's edge.

The situation Plato imagined for himself — had things not gone wrong — may be illustrated by the example of Euphraeus of Oreus, who managed to gain an ascendancy over Perdiccas, the monarch of Macedonia. This Academician 'lorded it as regally as the king himself, though he was of low origin and given to slander; he was so pedantic in his selection of the king's associates that nobody could share in the common mess if he did not know how to practice geometry or philosophy'.[98] This charge probably comes from Theopompus' *Attack on Plato's School*, which explains the personal slander against Euphraeus. But the programme Euphraeus and Plato followed with varying degrees of success was common to members of the Academy. Erastus and Corsicus demanded it of the pliant Hermias and so did Aristotle of Themison of Cyprus.[99]

Philistus was shrewd enough to realise that the weak link in the chain of Dion-Dionysius-Plato was between Dion and Dionysius. Dion had made a play for power just before the elder tyrant's death. This had failed, but Dion had skilfully managed to impress upon Dionysius his indispensability.[100] Philistus had two cards to play. The young tyrant had formed a genuine attachment to the philosopher. Plato reciprocated in part, but he could never be as close to Dionysius as he was to Dion. Plato was always diplomatic in his relations with people, but he could not hide his great love of Dion from Dionysius. The way to the philosopher's heart was by being a model student, but Dionysius lacked the perseverance for this — or possibly he realised that Plato's methods were not relevant to the situation in Sicily.[101] People may give up on a human relationship when they have signally failed to satisfy the other individual's criteria of values; a young tyrant, on the other hand, may have some reason to expect that he can have relationships entirely on his own terms. Even when he placed Plato under house arrest, the tyrant continued to crave Plato's respect. Dionysius also used another ploy and became increasingly open to accusations concerning Dion. If Dion were to disappear, then surely he, Dionysius, would be raised in Plato's estimation. In his truly formative years, the tyrant had grown up making wagons and lampstands and wooden chairs and tables.[102] Throughout his life, Dionysius remained childlike, trying to manipulate men and affairs as once he had fashioned chairs and tables of wood.

This childlike feeling of omnipotence, diametrically opposed to the views of Plato and Dion, was fostered by cliques at the court. The battle for Dionysius' mind was not waged between a philosopher and a historian alone, but between philosopher and philosopher. Between Plato and Aristippus, competition was fierce: competition as to who was the true Socratic and competition for the tyrant's favour.[103] During Plato's third visit to Sicily, Plutarch records an example of such rivalry. Helicon of Cyzicus, a Platonist, successfully predicted an eclipse of the moon. The delighted tyrant presented him with a talent of silver. 'Thereupon Aristippus, jesting with the rest of the philosophers, said that he himself could also predict something strange. And when they besought him to tell what it was, "Well then", said he, "I predict that ere long Plato and Dionysius will become enemies".'[104] Since Plutarch had just previously informed us of Plato and Dionysius' attempt to conceal their private bickerings over Dion from the public, Aristippus obviously had reliable sources upon whom he could draw. Quite possibly the tyrant himself had become exasperated with Plato. Knowing once he had sold Dion's estate there would be no turning back, Dionysius had confided in Aristippus, thus emboldening him to declare publicly the spat.[105]

There is also the allusion to 'the rest of the philosophers', some of whom had come with Plato, while others were Pythagorean agents of Archytas. Those Aristippus jested with probably felt more in sympathy with him. He had assumed the role of the court jester and, in return for playing the fool, Aristippus was allowed to express himself with a certain frankness which may have extended to politics. According to a passage in Athenaeus, those who sided with Aristippus and against Plato were given political duties. Aristoxenus names a certain Polyarchus (nicknamed the High Liver), whom Dionysius sent as an envoy to Tarentum.[106] Polyarchus extols the life of the Persian king who experiences the most pleasures in the widest variety of forms. The empire is scoured to pander to the great man's sensual needs; novelty is important, otherwise jadedness sets in. To combat feelings of *déjà vu*, rewards are offered to all who could invent a new pleasure. He is truly the happiest man on earth, and 'next to him ... one might set down our own ruler, though far behind. For in the case of the king, all Asia supplies [his pleasure] as well as [Egypt and Europe], whereas the service rendered to Dionysius must appear as something utterly trifling when compared with the other'.[107] Trifling perhaps, but none the less the minor empire in the west is an accurate image of the great Persian empire and Dionysius a lesser king of kings. This is legitimacy through association, for no one questioned the credentials of the Persian monarch. Also bestowing legitimacy was the fact that such an empire corresponds to man's *phusis*.[108] Opposed to this are 'lawgivers [who] in their desire to reduce the human race to one level and to bar every citizen from luxury, have caused a class of things called virtues to bob up'.[109] Going further, they deified Justice and then Sobriety and Self-control. Pleasure perversely was assigned the name 'greed', and 'thus it came about that the man who obeyed the laws and the voice of the common herd was moderate in his bodily pleasures'.[110] Dionysius, as he really was and not as he ought to be, possessed a regal nature. In so far as he submitted himself to a dour lawgiver's regimens and conventions, the ruler reduced himself to the common herd.[111] This may not be a very profound theory of monarchy and empire, but it had the inestimable advantage of corresponding to the facts of Dionysius' personality.

Philistus' trump card, however, was a tangible piece of evidence damning Dion. Dionysius had come into possession of a letter Dion had written to Carthaginian officials urging them to include him in any dealings or interviews with the tyrant 'since he would help them to arrange everything securely'.[112] As Gilbert Ryle puts it, Dion was and remained, apparently, a *persona grata* in Carthage.[113] Armed with this letter as well as his own fears and misgivings, Dionysius exiled Dion.

His political patron gone, Plato sought means to follow him to Athens. Dionysius, however, did not wish to let Plato go. No doubt, he knew the stories circulating about Plato and the Elder Dionysius. The Younger Dionysius no less than his father wished to be known as a patron of culture. Although Plato was placed under house arrest, the tyrant intensified his efforts to win the philosopher's respect, but to no avail.[114] Plato may also have been placed in protective custody to keep him away from the tyrant's mercenaries. It has been pointed out that Plato did not comprehend this new variable, the role of the mercenaries in the political life of Greece. With Dion exiled, Plato knew that his status had slipped from being the prospective conscience of the philosopher-king to that of a voice of merely another philosopher at the court of the tyrant. The Athenian aristocrat in Plato was repelled by the thought of being considered a sycophant such as Aristippus. Before he was finally given permission to leave Sicily Plato achieved a solitary success: 'Before my departure I had established relations of friendship and hospitality between Archytas and his Tarentine friends and Dionysius.'[115] With Dion gone, Plato turned for protection to these Tarentines who no doubt did their best; in return, Plato exercised his waning influence on the tyrant to forge this new bond. Unlike the Athenian philosopher, Archytas was a realist who could utilise either the hedonist Polyarchus or the idealist Plato in establishing a *modus vivendi* with the powerful Syracusan state.

Only the most persistent of pressures could induce Plato to return a third time to Syracuse in 362, but the pressures came from the same sources as had pushed the philosopher westward 14 years before and this time they were intensified. Dionysius wrote to Plato asking him to return, reminding him that he had promised to do so once hostilities with Carthage had ceased and the empire had become more consolidated. Dion's return would have to wait another year, he added.[116] In the same or another missive, the tyrant resorted to threats, saying in effect that if Plato did not sail Dion's possessions would be seized. This prospect galvanised Dion who 'consented and even entreated me to set sail'.[117] Plato vacillated: he knew that his ambitious plans for Dionysius and Sicily were at an end and, although half-felt obligations towards Dion and Dionysius continued to pull at him, he resisted, claiming he was too old 'and that what they were doing now did not at all accord with the agreement we had made'.[118] To satisfy a tyrant's vanity and a grandee's desire to maintain his vast wealth: where was philosophy in all this, the burning desire to reformulate the state according to the

Good? Plato had reason to feel old.

The Pythagoreans also pushed for Plato's return; and towards Archytas and his friends Plato was less inclined to offer excuses. Plato's one success in the west had been the treaty between Syracuse and Tarentum. Archytas and other Tarentines now wrote him that, should he not return, the treaty between the cities would be abrogated. Do not betray your Pythagorean friends, they wrote in a well-coordinated epistolary campaign.[119] There was also collusion between the western philosophers and Dionysius – not for the first time. Dionysius had sent a trireme to Athens 'to ease the journey for me' and on it were a number of Sicilian acquaintances of Plato, men of whom he thought highly. Included in this group was an associate of Archytas, Archedemus, whom Plato valued above all other men in Sicily.[120] 'These all brought me the same story of the marvelous progress Dionysius was making in philosophy.'[121] Apparently, Plato's earlier trips had not been in vain; the tyrant was making genuine progress. However, they insisted, such tentative steps as the tyrant had taken were in jeopardy unless the philosopher came once more to finish the job. Plato's venture into practical politics could still be crowned with success.

The philosopher probably believed little or none of this. However, he set sail for the west a third time in order to forestall future criticism that the real cause of failure in Sicily was his philosophy and not the tyrant's character.[122] This was the beginning of a rearguard action on Plato's part to salvage his reputation, which was to culminate in the *Seventh* and *Eighth Epistles*, *apologiae pro vita sua*, from there to blend into the favourable tradition of Plato's life and personality, waging war down to the present against the unfavourable accounts of Plato the tyrannophile and Plato the political idiot.[123]

The philosopher decided that at the next meeting with Dionysius he would cast caution aside and talk to him about the deepest and most important parts of his philosophy. Perhaps the inductive approach was not the correct one to take with the tyrant. Revealing the central problems of philosophy would set the tyrant's soul on fire, causing him to desire more enlightenment from his master, Plato. All would follow if Dionysius were a true lover of wisdom. But there was only the initial conversation. The tyrant was either content with what he knew or uninterested in pursuing matters further and thus stood self-condemned.[124] Plato's own position could be described in similar terms. Feeling betrayed by Dionysius and no doubt by the Pythagoreans, he tried to make himself useful to Dion by safeguarding the latter's interests. Dionysius had after all given his word, but J. Harward reminds us that in a matter of this sort Plato was a child in the hands of Dionysius, who tricked him at every turn, and, after cajoling him by promises into staying the winter in Syracuse, sold Dion's estates, and kept the money for his own purposes. Plato was very sore about it, and treats the robbery of Dion as an affront to himself and as evidence that Dionysius felt no gratitude for his teaching.[125]

Plato's other tactic was to ally himself with Dion's faction in Syracuse. He attached himself to Dion's uncle, Theodotes, who attempted to use Plato's influence with the tyrant to extract lenient treatment for Heraclides. A former ally of Dion, Heraclides had escaped Dionysius' wrath by fleeing to the Carthaginians. The strategem failed and the tyrant, as jealous as ever, accused Plato of preferring Dion's friends to himself.[126]

In the intrigues at court, Philistus and his faction had prevailed. If Dionysius wanted a philosophy congenial to his tastes, Aristippus and others were glad to oblige. The tyrant had confiscated Dion's property and was soon to hand over Dion's wife to a loyal follower, Timocrates.[127] Plato's life was again in danger both from the tyrant's whims and the mercenaries' dislike of him. Placed under arrest, he ultimately wound up at the house of Archedemus, from where he addressed letters to Archytas and his other friends in Tarentum beseeching their aid. Archytas, who felt responsible for having placed Plato in such dire straits, dispatched a ship to Syracuse and asked Dionysius, as an ally, to let Plato go. The tyrant complied and even supplied the philosopher with travelling expenses. What last words Dionysius and Plato had to say to each other is not known: but Plato does write that he did not bring up the subject of Dion's property.[128]

Dion and the Academy

Before discussing Dion's misadventures in Sicily, it will be useful at this point to attempt an analysis of Plato's Academy.[129] There is a passage in Plato's *Laches* where Lysimachus, son of Aristides 'The Just' and Melesias, son of Pericles' rival Thucydides, address two elderly, distinguished military figures, Nicias and Laches:

> Both of us often talk to the lads about the many noble deeds which our own fathers did in war and peace — in managing the affairs of the allies and those of the city — but neither of us has any deeds of

his own which he can show. The truth is that we are ashamed of this contrast being seen by them, and we blame our fathers for letting us be spoiled in the days of our youth, while they were occupied with the concerns of others. And we urge all this upon the lads . . . but if they take pains they may perhaps become worthy of the names which they bear. They, on their part, promise to comply with our wishes, and our care is to discover what studies or pursuits are likely to be most improving to them.[130]

Lysimachus and Melesias have military training in mind, a fertile enough field of endeavour in Plato's time. Socrates enters the discussion and the conversation slowly shifts over to the nature of courage. No firm definition can be fixed, but in the end a decision has been made and agreed on by all that Socrates should see to the education of the two aristocratic youths.[131]

It was from the scions of Aristides and Thucydides that Plato wished to enlist his pupils. Basing his assessment on the *Pinakes* of Callimachus, Grote noted that Plato had originally received the philosopher Eudoxus coldly: he was in fact passed over, in spite of the fact that Eudoxus was considered a brilliant youth who did not lack sponsors for his programme of studies.[132] Later on, after he had made his reputation as a mathematician and had pupils of his own, the two men were reconciled. It is obvious that Plato received his students from the aristocratic segment of society much as had Pythagoras before him. One of Plato's criticisms of the Sophists had been that they accepted anybody and dealt 'wholesale or retail in the food of the soul'.[133]

There are interesting glimpses of life in the Academy afforded us by the comic poets. There may be some exaggeration in their sneers and jibes, but there is truth as well. Ephippos comments on a member of the Academy, a disciple of the Master, who rose to speak in the assembly before his 'peers':

> He wore his hair trimmed by the knife — so fine
> And did not tamper with the fullness of his beard — so fine
> His foot enclosed by shoes whose laces — so fine
> He'd tied most evenly around his legs,
> And by the richness of his cloak well-fortified,
> His stately figure leaning on a cane,
> Not in the home town's manner, but in foreign style
> He began to speak: Oh men of the Athenian land.[134]

In general, an Academician could be known by 'a cloak of white, the grace of line, gray garments elegant and fine,/ Soft cap and shapely cane.'[135] No wonder Eudoxus was not allowed to join the Academy — he could not afford the school tie.

Some of these affectations of dress harken back to the Pythagoreans. The wearing of white, the symbol of purity and the external manifestation of a soul unsullied by contact with the world, has Pythagorean parallels. The Italiote Greeks, however, never acquired the reputation for effeteness that the members of the Academy had. The parodied Academician in the assembly has an 'Alcibiades in Croton' air to him, but the Academic dandies never submerged their personalities in the doctrines of their master as had the Pythagoreans. If silence was the key to inspiration for the latter, the former searched for truth through dialectics. For the Pythagoreans it is always an *ipse dixit* that decides every question, for the godlike Pythagoras had already in his various incarnations confronted the great problems of life and the student could only follow in the great man's footsteps.[136] With Plato it was different. For him, knowledge comes 'after long-continued intercourse between teacher and pupil, in joint pursuit of the subject, suddenly, like light flashing forth when a fire is kindled, it is born in the soul and straightway nourishes itself'.[137] In theory, the pupil was given an equal share of the credit for the kindling of such ecstatic illumination. In effect, the egos of the Academians were less repressed. Although contact with Plato was considered important and memorable, truth could be arrived at independently of him, with other teachers, such as Helikon or Theaetetus. What had originally been a monolithic relationship between a master or his golden verses and a student now became more complex as various human and intellectual relationships began to take place.[138] The unity of the Academy was more fragile than the brotherhoods of the Pythagoreans and, as early as Speusippus, we can see Plato's successor trying, by deifying Plato as Apollo's son, to create a 'catholic' doctrine against the assorted protesting individuals and groups.[139] Politically, as well, Plato's students enlisted in a variety of political causes, from democracy to tyranny, that reveal the lack of central planning such as had been found in Croton.

Plato had founded the Academy in 388 after his first visit to the west. The influence of the Pythagoreans is obvious. Plato had been impressed by the way philosophy had become a way of life for them and he tried to emulate this model in Athens. Socrates had been an urban dweller, but Plato rejected this mode of life with its passionate interest in the politics of the *polis* in favour of the Pythagorean idea that elite associations should hold themselves apart from the *polis*. The site of the Academy was at Colonus, a secluded and unhealthy spot, away from the bustle of Athens.[140] The woods there were sacred, dedicated to the hero Academos. All around were sanctuaries of Poseidon, Adrastus and Dionysus. In this holy atmosphere, the members of the Academy formed a religious organisation, a *Thiasos*, dedicated to the Muses.[141] The cult took the form of festivals and the students arranged with the utmost care the series of sacrifices and banquets: in fact, the same care that they showed about clothes and general manners.[142]

Life at the Academy would seem to corroborate Max Weber's views about the upper classes in political decline: 'In such a case, the ruling strata came to consider their intellectual training in its ultimate intellectual and psychological consequences far more important for them than their practical participation in the external affairs of the mundane world.'[143] The author of the novel, *Chion of Heraclea*, seems to corroborate this view. He has his Academic hero write:

> As a young man, I did not set my heart on magistracies or official honours, but from the beginning I was seized with a passionate desire to become one who contemplates the nature of things. And this brought me to Athens and made me the friend of Plato, and I have still not had enough of him.[144]

But the protagonist, Chion, is being disingenuous here, for he wants to lull the tyrant of Heraclea, Clearchus, into a false sense of security. His real wish is to assassinate the tyrant. Although a philosopher, Chion is also a man of action and had learned to be both by observing Xenophon: 'I saw a man wearing long hair, a person of beautiful and mild aspect, striding in their midst and stilling their passions.'[145] Chion engaged the student of Socrates in conversation and learned that 'even when it comes to bravery, philosophers are better off'.[146] The natural decision for the young nobleman was to go to Athens and study with Plato who 'endeavors to make philosophy appear to his disciples as not incompatible with an active life, in fact as something with its face turned towards practical life as well as towards contemplation'.[147] Chion spent five years in Athens and was intending to remain another five, when he learned of the tyranny of Clearchus in his home town. He realised that he was needed back home because (i) the tyranny must not turn into a perpetual despotism; and (ii) he could not live in freedom as long as his own city was under a tyrant.[148] Having a premonition of his heroic death, Chion nevertheless wrote a final letter to his revered teacher at Athens: 'Singing the Paean to Apollo and winning the prize of victory, I shall depart this life, if I die after having liberated mankind from this tyranny.'[149] Chion is the perfect Platonic revolutionary, the noble counterpart of the young man leaning on his cane in the *Ecclesia*.

The truth is far more prosaic. Heraclea was suffering from class warfare and the people had demanded remission of debts and redistribution of the lands of the rich.[150] The Council looked in vain for outside help from Timotheus and Epaminondas. Finally, in desperation, they called in Clearchus, whom they had previously exiled. Once in power, Clearchus turned against the aristocratic body:

> He summoned the people to Assembly ... Roused by his speech, the people conferred full powers on him and in anger against the power of the Council put themselves and their wives and children under the yoke of a tyrant's domination ... The people were delighted to see the Council destroyed by the Council's general.[151]

One Heraclean not delighted by this turn of events was Chion who spoke of 'a strong group of fellow conspirators, stronger still through loyalty than through number'.[152]

These aristocrats naturally were few as opposed to the many and their loyalty was that of a family that had much to lose should the reign of Clearchus continue. In 353-352 Chion and his co-conspirator, Leonidas, managed to assassinate Clearchus before being killed in turn. Protecting their privileges from a popular tyrant, an important noble family had hoped to return the government to its old, aristocratic basis. Clearchus had ruled for ten years prior to his assassination and Chion had spent part of his time in the Academy, waiting for the right moment to strike. He was not alone in Athens: two other prominent Academicians were exiles from Heraclea, Heracleides Ponticus and the mathematician Amyclas.[153]

Although Memnon depicts Clearchus as a cruel and vain tyrant who rouged his face and dressed outlandishly, the aims of the tyrant in such behaviour were sensible enough.[154] Clearchus called himself the son of Zeus and appeared in public with a golden eagle as a token of his parentage. He wore purple robes, 'buskins like kings in tragedies, and a crown of gold'.[155] Like the Dionysii before him, Clearchus tried to legitimise his rule, and Dionysius the Elder may well have served Clearchus as a role model. Like the Syracusan tyrant, Clearchus attempted to make his court a showplace of culture. He founded a library and, according to Justin, a small group of Platonists met at his court.[156] The leader of this group was Chion. The resident philosopher may initially have flattered himself that he could transform the tyrant into a Platonic ruler; if so, he met with no success. Clearchus may have had prolonged exposure to philosophy at Athens, but his views as to the role of philosophers at court matched those of the Dionysii.

Both Plato and Isocrates courted Dionysius the Younger and, later, Philip; why Clearchus should become an object of scorn to the Academy requires explanation. In fact, Clearchus was the student of both Plato and Isocrates and he was the latter's student for four years. Isocrates claimed that Clearchus was the kindest, the most humane and the most liberal pupil in his school.[157] The future tyrant was sponsored for Athenian citizenship by Timotheus in 375 and the friendship may still have been in force in 362 when Clearchus named his son after the Athenian general.[158] After gaining power, however, he changed greatly and Plato would not have approved of his treatment of the aristocrats in Heraclea. Like Callippus with Dion, Chion felt that Clearchus had gone too far.[159] Having less invested in Clearchus than in Dion, the Academy felt that Chion could and should be treated as a noble tyrannicide whose sole motives were idealism and liberty. And so the legend grew, enshrined finally in the first-century AD novel, *Chion of Heraclea*.

In attempting to legitimise his rule, Clearchus was probably following the views of Isocrates, who had given similar advice to Nicocles, a ruler as vicious as Clearchus.[160] An interesting letter from Isocrates to Timotheus, Clearchus' son and ruler of Heraclea, is a good example of his technique. The orator begins by pointing out the friendly relations that exist between Timotheus' family and himself.[161] Like a good management consultant, Isocrates points out how Timotheus can profit from his family's past misfortunes and how he can make the worse appear the better: 'For most men are wont to praise and honour, not so much the sons of fathers who are of good repute, as those born of harsh and cruel fathers, provided that they show themselves to be similar in no respect to their parents.'[162] With Clearchus in mind, Isocrates warns the king not to pillage the best, wealthiest and most sagacious citizens through taxation.[163] Having dispensed these invaluable guidelines ('blessings greater than these it would be difficult to discover'), Isocrates holds out the example of Cleomnis of Methymna, a noble and wise ruler, who 'restores the exiles, returning to those who come back their lost possessions, and in each case recompenses the purchasers the price they had paid'.[164] It may well be that Isocrates was playing a double game and was in the employ of Heracleote aristocrats who were in exile at Athens.[165] Having made peace with his father's enemies and with his father's money in hand, Timotheus can look forward to a noble and wise rule. Should there by any need of counsel, Isocrates strongly encourages Timotheus to look to Autocrator, the bearer of his letter. The Isocratean agent is interested in the same pursuits, 'and I have often profited by his skill, and finally, I have advised him about his visit to you ... Use him well and in a manner profitable to us both.'[166] After a few concluding flatteries, the old rhetor bows out, awaiting the verdict of his latest sally into the political arena. Plato had similar views in the *Laws*:

> Clinias: What is the theory, once more? There is to be an autocrat, you say, and he must be young, temperate, quick to learn, retentive, bold, and high souled?
> Athenian: And you must add, fortunate, – fortunate, that is, in the single point that there is a contemporary legislator of distinction with whom chance brought him in contact. With that one coincidence, God has done his utmost toward his purpose of heaping blessings on a community.[167]

It was indeed difficult to keep intellectuals away from autocrats.

Given the social makeup of the Academy, it is not surprising that some 'legislators of distinction' attempted to become autocrats themselves. Timolaus of Cyzicus emulated aspects of Clearchus' career by shifting his personality structure upon assuming power. From being a 'good man' who distributed free grain and money to fellow citizens, he suddenly tried to overthrow the constitution of Cyzicus.[168] Euaeon of Lampsacus' ploy was to lend money to his native city, 'taking as security the acropolis which he retained with the design of becoming tyrant, until the people of Lampsacus combined to resist him; and after paying back his money they threw him out'.[169] Chaeron of Pellene proved even more extreme than Clearchus. The tyrant drove out the male nobility, redistributed their land to their slaves and forced aristocratic women to marry the slaves – 'these were the beneficial results he derived from the noble *Republic* and from the lawless *Laws*!', sneers Athenaeus.[170] All three men were used by Sophocles of Sunium's lawyer, Demochares, as exhibits to justify the ban on philosophers at Athens in 307-306.

The most famous case of Academic misrule, however, was Dion.

Between 365 and 361, he was the toast of the Academy and visited a number of cities on goodwill trips.[171] Dion's task was made easier by the fact that his wealth had been shipped out to him from Syracuse.[172] Besides being able to defray Plato's civic expenses, Dion used the money to create a high public profile for himself, but he had more than just money working for him. Even before Plato's third Sicilian voyage, most shrewd observers had expected Dion to extend diplomatic feelers for possible support for a Syracusan *coup d'état*. His acceptance of Spartan citizenship was especially provoking to Dionysius.[173] There could be no doubt that Dion was waiting in the wings for his time to come.

Plato's failure in Sicily coupled with the seizure of Dion's property made Dion take action. Even had Dion been disinclined towards warfare — which he was not — Dionysius' decision to remarry Dion's wife, Arete, to one of the tyrant's supporters would have led him to that decision. Moreover, the tyrant's determination to educate Dion's son in the manner of an anti-Plato — 'the boy was supplied with courtesans, gorged with food and wine, and kept in a constant state of drunkenness' — must have been the final straw.[174] He was a man provoked.

Additionally, his friend Speusippus gave him encouraging news. Speusippus had been among the coterie of Academicians who had sailed with Plato to Syracuse. There he engaged in intelligence activity, sounding out the Syracusans as to their political sentiments.[175] He concluded that even a small force could defeat Dionysius. Although noncommittal at the time, Plato did nothing to discourage members of the Academy from joining Dion's entourage. From Speusippus' point of view, this was an enterprise in which the Academy was actively involved. The leader, Dion, was a member of the Academy; Speusippus had done some groundwork in Syracuse and back in Athens he could be expected to publicise the event to the Greek world. To this end, Timonides was dispatched with Dion. His role would be to supply an eye-witness narrative for the momentous events and Chapters 22-53 of Plutarch's *Dion* are taken from his report.[176] Speusippus' goal can be gleaned from a few quotations; Dion's mercenaries are praised; 'What joy must we suppose those men themselves felt, and how great a pride, who, with the fewest resources, overthrew the greatest tyranny that ever was!'[177] That the Academy was instrumental in this can be seen symbolically from Dion's initial triumphal entry into Syracuse, where on the one side of him was his brother, Megacles, on the other side the Academician, Callippus, 'both crowned with garlands'.[178] The grand partnership between the leading aristocratic family and the Academy had temporarily succeeded. Dion came in for his share of praise: 'But as for himself, he lived with simplicity and moderation on what he had, and men wondered at him ... He was nevertheless so modest ... just as though he were messing with Plato in the Academy, and not living among captains of mercenaries and paid soldiers.'[179] In the world and yet firmly apart from it; an Academic Achilles blessed with birth, wealth, power and the respect of the masses: none of these things does he consider important and, yet, somehow, he has them all. The recurrent fantasy at its height.

Plato at some point also came around and wrote to Dion urging him to promote and rely on the philosophers 'so that the rest of mankind will be as children in comparison. We must make it manifest that we are really the sort of men we say we are.'[180] Dion is exhorted to surpass Lycurgus and Cyrus in character and statesmanship.[181] Plato ends his epistle to Dion with a warning: 'Don't forget that one must please men if one would do anything with them, whereas self-will is fit only for solitude.'[182] However, the more Dion consolidated his power, the more he took pride in showing that he despised everything which looked like courting popularity.[183] Besides his dour disposition, there was his determination not to give in to the Syracusan *demos*.[184] The people had voted for a redistribution of land and houses, but Dion summarily repealed this measure.[185] In effect, the Syracusans were divided into two factions: the wealthy supporting Dion and the *demos* supporting Heracleides 'because it was believed that he would never aim at tyrannical power'.[186] The contest between these two men has been distorted by the Academic biases of the sources, especially Timonides: Heracleides' victory over Philistus was a piece of luck, his democratic proclivities proof that he wished merely to pander to the mob.[187] The demagogue had even dared to complain when Dion had sent to Corinth for counsellors and, probably, troops. A thoroughly worthless individual, 'turbulent, fickle, and seditious', Heracleides should be killed and the state freed of the hunt for mob favour; so argued the philosopher friends of Dion.[188] Dion at first refused to go along, saying his Academic experience had taught him to master such impulses, yet in the end he gave in and ordered the murder.[189]

Increasingly isolated from the people, Dion turned to his mercenaries. A redistribution of property of sorts was effected when Dion divided first his rivals' and later even his friends' lands among his soldiers.[190] Platonic principles had given way to the demands of the mercenaries and when Dion refused to demolish the fortifications in Ortygia the people's suspicions were further provoked. Dion had turned into a tyrant. Additionally, he had lost the support of the aristocracy by his shabby treatment of them in favour of his mercenaries. At some point, certain members of his Academic following began to demur. Suspicion joined with isolation and Dion began to make use of spies. One in particular was a fellow Academic, Callippus, who cleverly insinuated himself into the tyrant's good graces and ultimately had him slain.[191]

Dion's last days show a man who was less than philosophical about his fate. He developed a Macbeth-like sense of guilt for the murder of Heracleides. If in fact he did not initially kill his popular opponent because of Platonic principles, the subsequent murder must have left him with a moral void. Intensifying the matter, the two had once been good friends. Dion's much vaunted self-control had broken down before. In Leontini, after Dion had been forced to retreat from Syracuse, messengers had brought him news that he was requested back by the Syracusans who had suffered a reversal of fortune. To rally his troops 'he rose and began to speak, but copious tears checked his utterance'.[192] Dion had similarly broken down when reunited with his wife, although this is understandable.[193] Dion's self-mastery was punctuated by bouts of hysteria. One day, alone, lost in thought and racked with guilt, he saw a vision of 'a tragic Fury, sweeping the house with a sort of broom'.[194] It was a vision of his own failure to change the situation in Syracuse and his impending punishment. The man who had manipulated portents just a few months ago was now 'terribly shocked, and, becoming apprehensive, summoned his friends, told them what he had seen, and begged them to remain and spend the night with him, being altogether beside himself, and fearing that if he were left alone the portent would appear to him again'.[195] His son's death then occurred. The young man fell from the roof of his house; he may or may not have been drunk.[196] Dion's own death, when it came a few days later, was hardly less pathetic; Timaeus is more than willing to give us the graphic details.[197]

From his point of view, Callippus regarded himself as a tyrannicide, worthy of praise from his old school, and he detailed his exploits in a letter sent to Athens.[198] However, the Academy found it easier to disown Callippus than Dion and Callippus' subsequent actions showed him to be no better than the man he had replaced.[199] Callippus brought dishonour upon his city, writes Plato, never mentioning him by name; holding two men responsible for Dion's death, he adds that they were never of any consequence.[200] In spite of this, the fact that one member of the Academy had slain another who had become a tyrant and then in turn became a tyrant himself could not be so easily swept under the rug. It was brought up regularly by Plato's numerous detractors.[201] Plato writes with hindsight that 'what seems to be the end of an old difficulty always involves the beginning of a new one'.[202] Dion's posthumous legacy was an increasingly bitter factional dispute between the tyrannical and the democratic party and the philosopher feared for the very existence of the Greek language in Sicily.[203]

Not all of Plato's students met with such misadventures, but as Meyer notes, 'aller Augen waren auf Syrakus gerichtet'.[204] The Academy made a name for itself in the fourth century by the lawgivers it sent to assorted Hellenic cities. As opposed to the anti-Platonica of Athenaeus, Plutarch gives us a favourable picture of Academic activists. Of course, he has his own axes to grind and uses the Platonists as a whip with which to lash out at Epicureans who 'if they write on such matters at all, write on government to deter us from taking part in it'.[205] Among Academicians in power, Plutarch mentioned Aristonymus who reformed the constitution in Arcadia, Phormio who modified the severely oligarchic rule of the Eleans and Menedemus who was sent to the Pyrrhaeans. Further, Eudoxus legislated for his fellow Cnidians and Aristotle gave laws to the Stagirites.[206] Leaving aside Aristotle for the moment, it can be safely assumed that the philosophers in question were successful because they had influential backing from aristocratic friends back home as well as the prestige of being Plato's students. The exception is Eudoxus who became famous as a scientist and could rest on his reputation without having a clique behind him.

The Academy's greatest success occurred in Atarneus with the tyrant Hermias. Most details of Hermias' early life come from a hostile source, Theopompus, who called Hermias a barbarian and a eunuch.[207] Hermias was not an aristocrat and may have started his career as a money lender. Shrewd and intelligent, he began to rise in the world politically, even buying a princely title from the Persian administration.[208] The purchased status shows a man who may have been unscrupulous in his early years, but who sought legitimacy for reasons other than those of security. Such an individual would have been ideal for the attentions of the Academy. Hermias, however, was an aggressive dynast, and it is a safe assumption that his close friendship with two of Plato's students, Erastus and Corsicus, involved more than theoretical enthusiasm for Plato's philosophy. The pair must have been locally important.[209] As young men who had spent a good deal of time at the Academy, Erastus and Corsicus lacked worldly experience. Plato accordingly asks Hermias to protect them in order that their hothouse morality not wilt through contacts with wicked and unjust men.[210] In return, Plato promises Hermias trustworthy and loyal friends in these young nobles. Of course, in protecting two leading citizens of Scepsis, Hermias was committing himself to protecting Scepsis from wicked and unjust designs, such as he himself may have had. His support would have enabled the two philosophers to carry out whatever reforms they had in mind with considerably less external threat. The tone of the letter suggests that the three are to consider each other as equals as much as possible. Each side had what the other wanted. Hermias had power and the philosophers had status and were versed in noble doctrines. That some sort of equality was kept can be seen from an inscription in which an alliance is made with the city of Erythrae by 'Hermias and his companions'.[211] Such a situation is what Plato must have had in mind in Sicily.

The letter written by Plato to Erastus, Corsicus and Hermias also shows the philosopher's mystical side. D.E.W. Wormell has correctly pointed out the epistle's 'religious atmosphere reminiscent of an oracular utterance ... His letter is to be to them a "covenant and binding law", binding because of his immense prestige'.[212] Plato alludes to the respect in which he is held, his words are 'the prophecies I have just uttered'.[213] Like many other examples of sacred writ, the value of the letter is enhanced by repeated readings and Plato urges the three of them to do this whenever they are gathered together.[214] If problems arise, Plato, like Isocrates, says they should not hesitate to write to Athens. It may be noted that there is much in common between the *Sixth Epistle* and Isocrates' letter to Timotheus. In both cases, advisers are gingerly offered to a despot whose power, although real, lacks a firm foundation. These advisers are filled with the spirit of the great man who sent them and are to be trusted in every way. As the writer of the *Fifth Epistle* points out to Perdiccas of Macedon, 'constitutions, like species of animals, have each their own language ... I believe that ... [Euphraeus] can search out the words appropriate to monarchy as well as any man in your service.'[215] Any problems that cannot be solved on location are to be referred to the home base. Success in all cases depended on indispensability. Politically, if not personally, Plato had become dispensable to Dionysius. There is reason to believe that the effect of the Academy on Hermias was more pronounced. Hermias, like Dionysius II, Perdiccas and Themison, took up the Platonic regimen of geometry and dialectics.[216] He had more staying power than the rest, however, and may actually have continued to take it seriously once the novelty had worn off. As to the political role of the Academy, there is the text from Didymus:

And into the surrounding country, he made expeditions; and he made friends of Corsicus and Erastus and Aristotle and Xenocrates; hence all these men lived with Hermias ... afterwards ... he listened to them ... he gave them gifts ... he actually changed the tyranny into a milder rule; therefore he also came to rule over the neighbouring country as far as Assos, and then, being exceedingly pleased with the said philosophers, he allotted them the city of Assos. He accepted Aristotle most of all of them, and was very intimate with him.[217]

Upon the death of Plato in 348 Aristotle had left Athens because the leadership of the Academy had been retained by Plato's family. When Speusippus, Plato's nephew, was made the new head Aristotle must have been miffed and the fact that Xenocrates, a more orthodox Platonist than either Aristotle or Speusippus, accompanied Aristotle into a voluntary exile also indicates that the departure was a secession.[218] Another reason for Aristotle's exit was his unpopularity with the Athenians. Being a member of the Academy was difficult enough in Athens; but coming from the semi-barbaric north where Aristotle's father had been associated with King Amyntas II would have guaranteed Aristotle a cold reception in that city. Indeed, he writes that 'in Athens things which are considered proper for a citizen are not permitted to an alien, and it is dangerous to live in Athens'.[219] The fact that these sentiments were written to Antipater goes a long way towards explaining the Athenians' hostility, but, even earlier, friends of Macedon were looked on with suspicion by Athenians.

Aristotle returned to the north and soon established himself as Hermias' favourite. Aristotle's sister was a friend of the family and Hermias no doubt also heard good reports about him from Erastus and Corsicus. Since the philosopher married Hermias' niece, it became obvious that Aristotle was not just a philosopher at court, advising his patron when requested. He was a member of the ruling family. At some point, Hermias offered the philosophers, for services rendered, the city of Assos. Joining Erastus, Corsicus, Aristotle and Xenocrates, at the dynast's court was Aristotle's grand-nephew, Callisthenes. Neleus, son of Corsicus, took part in philosophical discussions and Theophrastus who came from the neighbouring town of Eresus was also there.[220] As Werner Jaeger notes, 'nothing less than a colony of the Athenian Academy was taking shape in Assos at this time'.[221] Yet, after three years at Atarneus and Assos, Aristotle, rather than pressing home the Academy's advantage, distanced himself from the court by moving to Mytilene. By 343-342, he was in Macedonia. Jaeger's view, which has won widespread acceptance, is that this physical movement parallels an intellectual transition on the philosopher's part from the ethical radicalism of the Academy towards *Realpolitik*. The change in attitude was accomplished under the influence of the experienced statesman, Hermias.[222] Between the tyrant and his son-in-law, no rupture occurred. A treaty between Philip and Hermias was made sometime shortly before the latter's death in 341 and Aristotle, who was in Pella, would have been instrumental in forging it.

There is another aspect to Aristotle which surfaces as well, his activity in the area of political intelligence. Peter Green puts forward the plausible suggestion that 'quite apart from his scientific and philosophical activities, he was also acting as a confidential political agent, a link-man between Hermias and Philip'.[223] Speusippus and Callippus had spied for Dion; Aristotle now did the same for his own patron. Although Philip had destroyed Aristotle's home town, the king shared the openly hostile attitude of Aristotle and his companions towards Persia. Hermias had carved out an impressive position for himself in the Troad between the empire of Persia and the rising power of Macedon. Though supposedly under Persian control, the dynast was trying to achieve independence and offered Philip the use of his territories as a bridgehead for any future invasion.[224] It would have been in these secret and dangerous moves that Hermias employed Aristotle as a 'link-man'.[225]

How far Aristotle's revised political thinking went can be gauged by noting that, according to Themistius, Aristotle taught that, far from being a prerequisite to correct rule, a king would do better to avoid philosophy in the strict sense and content himself with advisers who are genuine philosophers. The ruler or rulers should, however, practise philosophy in the broader sense of that term which Aristotle has described as *philomuthos*, a lover of culture. Carnes Lord accurately describes such a man as one who 'shares with the philosopher ... a sense of awe or admiration for the noble and beautiful rather than the sense of his own ignorance and the desire to remedy it ... the lover of culture remains within the horizon of habit and convention'.[226] Such a concept was far more congenial to rulers than the more radical idealism of Plato and the Academy. Gentlemen, not philosophers, would rule Aristotle's ideal state. Aristotle criticised Plato's philosophical ruling elite for being too harsh and called for the rule of magnanimous men, not those of a stern disposition.[227] Such was the case with Hermias, who, flattered by his philosophical advisers, honoured them in turn by giving the sages the city of Assos. Such was the case with Philip who rewarded Aristotle by rebuilding his home *polis*, Stagira, and bringing back the citizens who had been enslaved or driven into exile.[228]

In the *Laws*, Plato had advocated a community less utopian than in his *Republic*. Aristotle, in his discussion of marriage and the family, takes the retreat a step further and points out that 'what is common to the greatest number gets the least amount of care. Men pay most attention to what is their own.'[229] What became Aristotle's 'own' was a share in the ruling family of Atarneus through his marriage to Pythias. The marriage was by all accounts a happy one and Aristotle served the tyrant's family well and with sincerity as can be judged by his hymn to the fallen tyrant.[230]

Zealous members of the Academy were probably shocked that Aristotle left the tyrant's court for the obscurity of Lesbos. However, Aristotle obviously felt that those Academics who remained could exercise sufficient influence with Hermias. Aristotle was close enough to continue contact with him; as a member of the family he would remain appraised of his plans. Nor can Green's speculations be ignored that Aristotle sensed that Artaxerxes' vigorous new policy meant physical danger to Hermias and his followers and so moved across the straits to Mitylene to join his friend Theophrastus.[231]

Aristotle writes:

For while a philosopher as well as a just man or one possessing any other virtue, needs the necessaries of life, when they are sufficiently equipped with things of that sort the just man needs people towards whom and with whom he shall act justly, and the temperate man, the brave man, and each of the others is in the same case but the philosopher even when by himself, can contemplate truth, and the better the wiser he is; he can perhaps do so better if he has fellow-workers, but still, he is the most self-sufficient.[232]

Buoyed by the revenues of Assos, protected by his father-in-law, Hermias, and a subject of interest to the powerful Philip, Aristotle could indeed feel that temporarily at least his boundless curiosity could be indulged. With Theophrastus, he pondered the inner meaning of marine biology for two years before being called to Pella by Philip. Since Philip was a friend of the family and it was important for Hermias to be represented at the court by his son-in-law, Aristotle gave up his self-sufficiency. Besides, there was the matter of Stagira. For his services, Aristotle did not demand the transformation of a city into a utopian model, but rather the rebuilding of his own *polis*, replete with the old *status quo*. In a similar manner, no attempts were made to change Assos into either a Callipolis or a Magnesia.

Not being an Athenian, Aristotle lacked the home base of Plato and Socrates. His departure from Athens deprived him of his intellectual home and the important circle of the Academy. His parents died while he was quite young and his native city, Stagira, was destroyed by Philip. Aristotle was not a cosmopolite. His ventures into Troad and Macedonian politics were attempts to remedy this aloneness and to seize something solid in increasingly turbulent times. Therefore the marriage to Pythias, the connection with the wily dynast, Hermias, the companions at Assos and in particular his life-long friend, Theophrastus. When Hermias was executed, Aristotle turned to Macedon. His relationship with Philip was good and, although his relationship with Alexander was ambivalent, he maintained close ties to Antipater throughout his life. Naturally, such security was purchased at the price of great unpopularity, particularly in Athens, but it was a price the philosopher was willing to pay. There was one other attempt on Aristotle's part to come to terms with his shaky condition, through political theory. T.A. Sinclair underscores the difference between Plato and Aristotle. The latter

> saw in his good citizen primarily a reflection of himself, or of himself as he would wish to be seen, dignified, intelligent and moderate, full of good sense, knowledge and manly virtues. Plato, if he could have pictured himself in the city of the *Laws* at all, which is doubtful, would certainly be sitting on the Nocturnal Council. But Plato was devising a city for another people, for ordinary people, not for himself. Aristotle was planning one where he and his friends could have lived happily; he pictured the Ideal State as one which would both produce such men and provide them with the right kind of life.[233]

Aristotle's family connections, both past and present, were instrumental in Philip's decision to ask the philosopher to come to his court and tutor the heir apparent, Alexander. It was a bitter disappointment to Isocrates who was the loser of an intense *agon* between his school and the Academy for Philip's patronage. The old rhetor wrote a letter to Alexander warning him against the sophists from the Academy with their pseudo-problems and fine sounding answers which, however, fly in the face of common sense and cannot benefit a monarch in his kingly duties.[234] That the eventual victor was the sarcastic Aristotle made the setback all the more difficult for Isocrates to bear.

4 FROM POLIS TO MONARCHY

Isocrates and Panhellenism

In his autobiography, *Antidosis*, Isocrates writes:

> It occurs to me as I am speaking, what a change has come over Athens ... for, when I was a boy, wealth was regarded as a thing so secure as well as admirable that almost everyone affected to own more property than he actually possessed, because he wanted to enjoy the standing which it gave ... Now, on the other hand ... it has become far more dangerous to be suspected of being well off than to be detected in crime.[1]

The statement admits of rhetorical hyperbole, for Isocrates grew up during the Peloponnesian War when wealth could hardly be regarded as a secure possession, as the fortunes of Isocrates' father show. Before losing his fortune, Theodorus was a prosperous flute manufacturer who was able to provide Isocrates with a superior education.[2] In practice, this meant that the young man was acquainted with the leading sophists of his day.[3] His most important contacts were with Gorgias and Socrates. From the former, he learned to refine his powers of rhetoric and to exalt the Panhellenic ideal; from the latter, he learned moral philosophy. Like so many of his age, Isocrates was deeply impressed by Socrates' defence of his activities and his execution moved Isocrates deeply. In a passage from the *Phaedrus*, Plato has the master prophesy a distinguished future for his young companion.[4] For his part, Isocrates remained true to many of Socrates' teachings.[5] Although a cautious man throughout his life, there are two anecdotes which show courage on Isocrates' part. When Socrates was executed, Isocrates made his feeling known by donning clothes of mourning; and when Theramenes was being led to execution, Isocrates alone dared to defend him.[6] If these stories are true, they reveal a man loyal to his teachers. Later in life he was especially proud of students whose loyalty he had retained.

Two things came in the way of Isocrates playing a direct, active role in the affairs of his city. During the Peloponnesian War, Theodorus lost his wealth, leaving his son without patrimony. This discouraged the young man from entering politics, for Isocrates was not one to go into penniless exile. Taking advantage of his education, he set himself up as a teacher. He was financially successful as, for that matter, were Plato and Aristotle, but while they downplayed their financial gains, Isocrates did not hesitate to boast about how he had reversed Fortune's reversals.[7] Also, the rhetor liked to see himself as the spokesman for the Athenian rich. The second factor that came in the way of an active political career was Isocrates himself. Like Plato he had a weak voice; additionally, he lacked the self-assurance necessary for success when speaking in front of others.[8] According to Pseudo-Plutarch's *Life of Isocrates*, when Theramenes had fled for safety to the altar of *Hestia Boulaia*, Isocrates rose to speak in his defence, but words eluded the young man until finally Theramenes told him to stop his well-directed efforts. Such a traumatic experience would have reinforced his initial lack of confidence. Also leading to inertia were his rhetorical standards, which were too high. Vain and thin-skinned, Isocrates did not trust himself to handle the give-and-take of democratic repartee. He was the man with the perfect retort, but it took him years to think of it.[9] As he wrote to Philip, 'I was not given a strong enough voice nor sufficient assurance to enable me to deal with the mob, to take abuse, and bandy words with the men who haunt the rostrum.'[10]

Demosthenes overcame handicaps as great, but Isocrates came to prefer the quiet life. Men who live as I do, he says, are looked up to both in Athens and elsewhere.[11] On a pleasure-pain scale, Isocrates sought dignity and avoided indignity. Temporarily setting aside what they had learned from him, Aristotle and others mocked Isocrates because as a young man he had written forensic speeches. Isocrates came to regard that episode in his life with some embarrassment; but at the time he had needed the money, for the greatest indignity is poverty, 'a thing that breaks up friendships, perverts the affections of kindred into emnity, and plunges the whole world into war and strife'.[12] Avoiding poverty, Isocrates became rich; having become independently wealthy, he turned to culture — in particular the Panhellenic ideal.

Isocrates taught over a hundred pupils in his career, engaging them in a course of studies which lasted from three to four years. He surrounded himself annually with five or six pupils and with these he maintained a prolonged and intense contact.[13] These 'associates' paid high fees and came from all over the Greek world to study with the master. Some became teachers in their own right or expert debaters, but those who interested Isocrates the most were the future politicians. In fact, says Cicero, his school was like a Trojan horse from which came forth nothing but princes.[14] Like Plato and Pythagoras, Isocrates chose to exercise power through his students. Studies with Isocrates took less time than a course in the Academy and the subject matter was more practical than what the mystical Plato could offer. A person could have difficulty being both a politician and a Platonist, but no such dilemma faced Isocrates' students. For example, Timotheus was a member in good standing of Isocrates' school, but could the same thing be said of Phocion or Chabrias with regard to the Academy? Plato had created such a gap between theory and practice that a practical politician could do no more than admire this Hellenic 'Castellia' from outside. It was exactly such a gap that Isocrates tried to breach through his school and his writings.

While discussing his letter to Timotheus, the son of Clearchus, some of Isocrates' techniques in dealing with political rulers have been noted. More realistic than Plato, Isocrates stressed team-work.

> And I believe that if the rest of the Greek world also should be called upon to choose from all mankind both the man who by his eloquence would best be able to summon the Greeks to the expedition against the barbarians, and also the leader who would be likely most quickly to bring to fulfillment the measures recognized as expedient, they would choose no others but you and me.[15]

The 'you' varied, but the rhetor always included himself in these ventures, although 'my part, it is true, is the smaller'.[16] What was sought was the union of the sage and the hero. If Plato desired to be the conscience of Dionysius, Isocrates was more concerned with supplying the brains to his future world conqueror, 'for the master must painstakingly direct his pupil, and the latter must rigidly follow the master's instruction'.[17] We can see Isocrates trying to manoeuvre himself into an influential position with Philip. They share in common the fact that they are misunderstood and disliked by the masses, the king on account of his power and prestige, the sage because of his superior wisdom.[18] The union of power and prestige directed by superior wisdom was Isocrates' lifelong goal.

This goal eluded him, but his best chances for success came with his pupils. His relationship with Nicocles throws light on the manner in which Isocrates hoped to create for himself a role in the political world of the fourth century. For Greeks, Cyprus was to the east what Sicily had been to the west, the furthest outpost of Hellenism against a formidable barbarian foe.[19] There were even similarities between Evagoras and Dionysius the Elder. Evagoras had worked his way to the top from private estate and relied heavily on mercenaries. At one point he controlled practically all the cities of Cyprus, as well as cities in Phoenicia.[20] Unlike Dionysius, he was unable to hold his empire together and, after a ten-year war with the Persians, he agreed to limit his kingdom to Salamis, pay an annual fixed tribute to the Persians 'and obey as a king the orders of the King'.[21] Though wily and ruthless, from Isocrates' point of view Evagoras had some redeeming characteristics. Most importantly, he had his son educated by Isocrates. Taking aim at the Academics, Isocrates writes: 'For it has not escaped the notice of me or anyone else that you, Nicocles, are the first and the only one of those who possesses royal power, wealth, and luxury, who has undertaken to pursue the study of philosophy.'[22] A friend of the family, Isocrates saw as his duty the elevation of Evagoras and his descendants to a status of legitimacy in the eyes of the Greek world.[23] This meant glossing over or ignoring a number of unsavoury facts concerning their political and personal lives, but Isocrates was prepared to do this.[24] In turn, he expected his students to pay close attention to what he had to say about governing, how to dress, the nature of a king's bodyguard and so on. It was particularly important that the king associate with the wisest men possible and, lacking such individuals, to import them from abroad.[25] Poetry should be read, but comedy ignored.[26] In general, people such as Isocrates are indispensable in order that the tyrant equip his mind 'to judge those who are inferior and to emulate those who are superior to himself'.[27]

Evagoras had made another important move. He had befriended Conon, the Athenian admiral, giving the Evagorids an important Athenian connection.[28] Evagoras' son, Nicocles, associated with Timotheus, the son of Conon, at the school of Isocrates. Relying on his pivotal position, Isocrates desired to bring Athens and Salamis into closer accord with one another and Timotheus as *strategos* had often concluded alliances with monarchs.[29] Isocrates' letters to Nicocles can be seen to have a dual purpose: they offered his pupil advice on how best to shore up his rule in Salamis by modifying what must have been a harsh personal rule; a 'milder government' in Salamis in turn would make an alliance between Athens and Salamis more palatable to the Athenian *demos*.[30] Such an alliance would rebound to the credit of Timotheus, the Athenian general and star pupil of Isocrates. Isocrates was very ambitious for Timotheus in this and other ways.

Success for one of the philosophical schools provided no cause for rejoicing to its rivals. Isocrates had warned Dionysius of Plato and the rhetor's student, Theopompus, had sneered at Aristotle's efforts in

Macedonia. Both schools vigorously contested access to Philip's patronage. Isocrates' success in Salamis went unheralded by the Academy, but, when in the 350s the Evagorids made an alliance with Persia, the Platonists saw an opportunity to discredit Isocrates. Their spokesman was Aristotle, who by teaching rhetoric at the Academy had already indicated that the rival school was to be challenged head on on its home ground.[31] Cicero observes that, 'stimulated by the fame of the rhetorician Isocrates ... [Aristotle] began to teach young men to speak and to combine philosophy with eloquence'.[32] By appropriating Isocrates' specialty and modifying it to suit their own ends, the Academics hoped to steal some of Isocrates' students as well and supplant the rival school in reputation. This new spirit is made clear in an early work of Aristotle, the *Protrepticus*, which takes the form of a letter to Themison and is hortatory in content. But the challenge is not merely literary and philosophical.[33] Of Themison, we know only that he was a wealthy prince of Cyprus; but 'he was probably the most prominent Cypriot the Academy could muster for its designs'.[34] A.H. Chroust also notes that in the *Protrepticus* 'the Platonists serve notice that they are determined to extend their political and intellectual influence to Cyprus, where hitherto Isocrates had held an uncontested monopoly in speaking on the political, intellectual, and cultural ideals of Greece'.[35] We do not know what happened with Themison, but it is very unlikely that Aristotle achieved a greater success with the prince than Isocrates had with Nicocles. On the other hand, the fact that Isocrates' monopoly was broken in Cyprus meant to the Platonists that their poaching had not been in vain.[36]

Isocrates is best known as the leading publicist of a Panhellenic crusade against the Persians. He was not the first to advance such an idea, nor was he the last:

> The kingdom of the Greeks is now dismembered by them and deprived of territory so vast in extent that it cannot be traversed in a march of two months. On whom therefore is the labor of avenging these wrongs and of recovering this territory incumbent, if not upon you? You, upon whom above other nations God has conferred remarkable glory in arms, great courage, bodily activity, and strength to humble the hairy scalp of those who resist you ... This land which you inhabit, shut in on all sides by the seas and surrounded by the mountain peaks, is too narrow for your large population; nor does it abound in wealth; and it furnishes scarcely food enough for its cultivators. Hence it is that you murder one another, that you

wage war, and that frequently you perish by mutual wounds. Let therefore hatred depart from among you, let your quarrels end, let wars cease, and let all dissensions and controversies slumber.[37]

The speaker is Pope Urban II at the Council of Clermony, 27 November 1095. His themes are familiar to readers of Isocrates. The answer to the problems that afflict Christendom lies in destroying 'a race from the kingdom of the Persians' and wresting 'that land from the wicked race, and subject[ing] it to yourselves. That land which, as the Scripture says, "floweth with milk and honey".'[38]

Like Urban and Gregory VII, Isocrates was a leading publicist for a great crusade against the infidel. Isocrates was a man possessed of a great idea — to save Greece. Unlike Academics who laid down laws for individual cities — an anachronistic enterprise at best — Isocrates took in the big picture: 'Men of wisdom ought to concern themselves both for the interest of our city and for the interest of Hellas, but should give preference to the broader and worthier cause.'[39] Isocrates was the victim of witticisms directed at him by both sophists and the followers of Plato: the former thought him incapable of thinking on his feet; the latter of thinking deeply about things at all. But Isocrates felt that he had outflanked his critics. Intellectually, his notion of *philosophia* was much broader than that of the Platonists. He was aiming at a universal culture, whereas his opponents had in mind a particular method. Politically, as well, Isocrates emphasised Panhellenism and contrasted it with the more particularistic views of his opponents.

'In an age when the old beliefs were losing their binding force and the long established structure of the city-state was breaking up ... the new dream of national achievement appeared to be a mighty inspiration. It gave life a new meaning.'[40] So Werner Jaeger assessed the mood of the fourth century. Isocrates certainly saw his life enhanced by becoming the foremost publicist for this new dream. What he had in mind is succinctly stated in the *Panegyricus*:

> It is not possible for us to cement an enduring peace unless we join together in a war against the barbarians, nor for the Hellenes to attain to concord until we wrest our material advantage from one and the same source and wage our wars against one and the same enemy. When these conditions have been realized, and when we have been freed from the poverty which afflicts our lives ... then surely we shall enjoy a spirit of concord, and the good will which we shall feel towards each other will be genuine.[41]

Internal rather than external pressures were principally responsible for bringing the Christian Crusade into being. Similarly, in his writings Isocrates dwells at length on the socio-economic situation in Greece.[42] He notes that internecine war and factional fighting have created instability and poverty in Hellas and that this poverty forces Greeks to enlist as mercenaries. When Greek fights Greek, the Persians are the only victors.[43] As a wealthy man, he was naturally worried about the political and economic dislocations. Writing to Philip, Isocrates points out that, unless some sort of solution is offered to the problem of the indigent poor, 'they will grow before we know it into so great a multitude as to be a terror no less to the Hellenes than to the barbarians'.[44] The solution lies in collecting this large, floating population, enlisting them as mercenaries, overthrowing the Persian empire (or at least vast areas of it) and settling the Greeks in Asia from Cilicia to Sinope.[45] Isocrates invites his audience 'to picture to yourselves what vast prosperity we should attain if we should turn the war which now involved ourselves against the people of the continent, and bring the prosperity of Asia across to Europe'.[46]

Isocrates does not trust arguments premised on economics to do all the work for him. The war against Persia is a war of revenge, for 'eternal is the wrath which [the Athenians] cherish against the barbarians ... and ingrained in our nature is our hostility to them'.[47] After giving an emotional and tendentious account of Persian-Hellenic history, he concludes: 'These things may well rouse our indignation and make us look to the means by which we shall take vengeance for the past and set the future right.'[48] Like his papal counterpart, Isocrates assures his audience that the struggle will be an easy one, for 'in every quarter the Persians exposed their degeneracy ... and none of these things has happened by accident, but all of them have been due to natural causes'.[49] The Persian commons lack discipline and the taste for war and the aristocracy's 'whole existence consists of insolence toward some, and servility towards others'.[50] Effeminate and utterly degenerate from luxurious living, the Persian aristocracy manifests its perversity by honouring men more than gods.[51] Relying on the account of his friend, Xenophon, Isocrates recounts the story of the *Anabasis* as proof of the lack of martial spirit on the part of the Persians.[52]

Isocrates lacked the religious fervour of Pythagoras and the mysticism of Plato; however, as the deliverer of Greece from its present ills, he felt it incumbent to call upon the gods as allies in the holy war. He labours to find a divine cause for the contemporary troubles and finally locates one by linking the proposed endeavour with the Trojan

War, of which he says, 'some god out of admiration for their valor brought about this war in order that men endowed by nature with such a spirit should not be lost in obscurity'.[53] The present crusade is a sacred mission:

> For this war is the only war which is better than peace; it will be more like a sacred mission than a military expedition; and it will profit equally both those who crave the quiet life and those who are eager for war, for it will enable the former and the latter to win great wealth from the possessions of our foes.[54]

Harking back to the Trojan War once more, Isocrates asks: 'If those who made war against an Alexander [Paris] and took a single city were accounted worthy of such praise, what encomiums should we expect these men to win who have conquered the whole of Asia?'[55] Immortality through the memory of valour is what Isocrates offers for Greeks who march against the barbarian; and who better to compose the deathless encomiums than the inheritor of the tradition of Hesiod, Theognis and Phocylides?[56] Isocrates has made himself indispensable, as he reminds Philip: 'It may be that even now the gods have assigned to me the task of speech while to you they allot the task of action.'[57]

Isocrates may be seen as the high priest of the church of the Deified Logos, the members of which are educated Hellenes who share a common culture. *Logos* serves a mytho-poetic function.[58] In *Nicocles*, Isocrates composes what Glen Marrow has rightly called a hymn to *logos*:

> For the power to speak well is taken as the surest index of a sound understanding, and discourse which is true and lawful and just is the outward image of a good and faithful soul . . . None of the things which are done with intelligence take place without the help of speech, but that in all our actions as well as all our thoughts, speech is our guide . . . Therefore, those who dare to speak with disrespect of educators and teachers of philosophy deserve our approbrium no less than those who profane the sanctuaries of the gods.[59]

Even Isocrates admits that rhetoric cannot directly teach morality and he has no system of salvation besides the emotionally weak concept of immortality through the recording of noble deeds.[60] Being entirely this-worldly in orientation, he must place himself at the service of a secular power and hope that the value of his counsel would increase his influence in the running of the state. As Jaeger notes, 'Such an association could hope to influence society at second hand — by moulding the characters of great leaders who could either be, or seem to be, capable of transforming it.'[61]

Isocrates spent his long life looking for such a leader. He had pinned great hopes on his Athenian pupil, Timotheus. If Dion was beloved of Plato, and Hermias' passing 'left the sun's beams desolate' for Aristotle, Timotheus was Isocrates' favourite. In the *Antidosis*, the normally cautious rhetor boldly defends his discredited pupil: 'Timotheus was superior to all the rest in that he did not hold the same views as you with regard to the affairs of the Hellenes and of your allies and the manner in which they should be directed.'[62] Isocrates had accompanied Timotheus during his tenure as *strategos* and written glowing accounts of his military and political actions.[63] Timotheus was an imperialist, one of a group of men who briefly constructed the Second Athenian Confederacy after 378. *To Nicocles* was partly pro-Timotheus propaganda and the *Plataica* was also written in the service of Timotheus and Callistratus.

Isocrates' most important work of the period was the *Panegyricus*. It is interesting to note the similarities between this speech and a document of the Second Athenian Confederacy, the *Decree of Aristoteles*. The rhetor was working very closely with the new imperialists and the correspondence between theory and action was also close. The decree is anti-Spartan in tone, as is the work of Isocrates, and the aim of the *Panegyricus* is to make a second Athenian empire palatable to the rest of the Greeks.[64] The economic motivations of empire are said in reality to benefit all Hellas. The Piraeus, after all, was established in the centre of the country, equidistant to all.[65] Artistic and intellectual arguments are put forth, reminiscent of Pericles' famous funeral speech. Made the most gentle of people by philosophy, the Athenians are eager to share their culture with anyone who is willing to join their empire.[66] The first Athenian empire is portrayed in the best possible light, partly by describing the plight of Greece under Spartan and Theban rule: 'On the contrary, we regarded harmony among our allies as the common boon of all, and therefore we governed all the cities under the same laws ... but leaving each member of it free to direct its own affairs.'[67] The Decree of Aristoteles makes the same point: Greeks and barbarians are to have the form of government they desire free from any Athenian garrison, governor or tribute.[68] In the early days of the empire, the Athenians, as Callistratus noted, seemed to have learned from their mistakes.

However, by the years 362-358, Athens had again overextended itself. At first Isocrates viewed the problem of the Athenian empire as largely an outgrowth of unresolved internal politics and wrote the *Areopagiticus* in support of Timotheus.[69] By the time of Timotheus' third downfall and the disastrous Social War of 357-355/4, Isocrates knew that Athens was not capable of being the leading power in Greece, much less the leader of an anti-Persian crusade.[70] He reversed himself completely and wrote that the war had impoverished Athens; he complained of the perils faced in a war which did nothing but give the Athenians a bad name among the Greeks.[71] What was good and to be actively pursued had become imbecilic and to be given up forever. A typical member of 'the best and the brightest', Isocrates swung between extremes with the greatest of ease.

Timotheus had been relieved of his command once and tried twice by the *demos*. The second trial in 358 resulted in a fine of one hundred talents and the son of Conon had to leave Athens in disgrace. Wealthy, arrogant, impulsive and aristocratic, Timotheus resembles Dion in many ways. Isocrates emphasises the aloofness of his pupil in order to deflect attention away from Timotheus' conduct in battle, but Timotheus' arrogance at the trial played a role in his downfall. Like Plato, Isocrates warned his student of the consequences of such behaviour, but Timotheus 'could not change his nature. He was a good man and true, a credit to Athens and to Hellas, but he could not lower himself to the level of people who are intolerant of their natural superiors.'[72] Once again an elitist politician and an elitist thinker found much to admire in each other. Due in part to a natural affinity, the philosophers tolerated their difficult pupils and saw virtues where others were repelled by faults. Dion and Timotheus flattered their teachers by bringing them in close to political action and were rewarded by a loyalty they knew could never be found among other men. As opposed to Hermias, there is no evidence that their teachers effected any transformation of their personal behaviour or outlook on life. However, Hermias did not start life with all the advantages of Dion or Timotheus and so used philosophy as a social and cultural crutch. Aristotle could not repeat his success with Alexander. Even with Hermias, he learned more about politics from his student than he could expect to teach the worldly ruler.

When Timotheus was tried in 373, he brought in as witnesses for his defence Alcetas, king of Epirus, and Jason, the despot of Pherae. Their testimonials were enough to get Timotheus acquitted. It was to the dynamic Jason that Isocrates next turned his attention, 'for he kept talking as if he intended to cross over to the continent and make war upon the King'.[73] Unfortunately for Isocrates, Jason was soon assassinated. Although Isocrates' letter to Dionysius the Elder breaks off just when the rhetor is beginning to give the tyrant a lecture on Greece, the fact that this letter is alluded to in *To Philip* would indicate that a Panhellenic theme was again being assayed.[74] Dionysius' death in 367 brought this episode to a close. Undaunted, the octogenarian wrote a speech for a young prince of Sparta, Archidamus. However seriously Archidamus may have taken Isocrates' advice, affairs at home took up all the king's interests.[75]

In Philip, Isocrates finally thought that he had found the strong man he was seeking. In the fourth century, however, a monarch of an expanding empire could be assured of a number of intellectuals competing among themselves for his attention. The battle for Philip was waged between Plato's successor, Speusippus, and Isocrates. Isocrates' address to Philip in 346 marks the beginning of an important volley from that corner. As well, the *Philippus* and the *Second Letter* provide programmatic statements similar to the policies Androtion, a pupil of Isocrates, carried through the Assembly in 344.[76] Isocrates saw himself linking the two men. Another of his students, Python of Byzantium, represented Philip on an embassy to Athens in 343. His mission was unsuccessful and Hegesippus claimed that Isocrates prompted the diplomat's thinking.[77] Finally, Theopompus was in Macedonia doing double duty for his teacher. On the negative side, he was writing scurrilous attacks on Hermias, trying to undermine Aristotle's influence on the politics and patronage of that area. While at the royal court Theopompus was also engaged in writing his *Philippica*, a work supportive of Philip's aims.[78]

Speusippus' counter-attack came in the form of a letter addressed to Philip and written after the failure of Python and the exile of Androtion. The letter was ideally timed and Speusippus pulled no punches: 'Ancient history would have been fitting for Isocrates to relate, ancient as he himself is.'[79] Employing sophistries, empty rhetoric and cheap tricks, the rhetor's worst sin was in omitting the many benefits the Macedonian king has bestowed on the Greeks.[80] Relying on a research assistant, Antipater of Magnesia, Speusippus sought to outflank his rival, both temporally and spatially. Historically, Isocrates' genealogy did not do Philip justice, claimed Speusippus. In particular, not enough stress was placed on the royal family's contribution to Greece — a sensitive point to the Macedonians. Isocrates' examples were 'grotesque, irrelevant, and contradictory'. Buttressed by the Academy's manipulations of the past, Philip could now in good conscience lay claims to the lands of the Olynthians and the region of Amphipolis, 'all Heraklid property'. He was also the prior claimant to the cities of Potidaea and Torone, displacing Athenian control in that area. Finally, the epistle took a swipe at Theopompus (who might by now have been getting on Philip's nerves) and accused him of slandering Plato.[81] Speusippus also reminded Philip of past Academic favours done during the reign of Perdiccas, though Euphraeus of Oreus, the Academic at court, had a chequered career in Macedonia.[82] Euphraeus may have been instrumental in obtaining for Philip the beginnings of his kingdom, but he later became an enemy of the king and committed suicide when the latter moved to seize Oreus. As this occurred at about the same time as Speusippus' letter, the subject was a delicate one and Speusippus prudently drew upon the name of Plato alone. In any event, Antipater of Magnesia was a known quantity and Philip was advised to replace the caustic Theopompus with Speusippus' agent.

Philip was content to play the rivals off against each other, just as he manipulated politicians and political events. The Macedonian king often travelled with actors and musicians, and continued the royal pattern of stocking the court with well-known Greek intellectuals and artists. Although Athens remained the centre of dramatic production, plays were now taken on the road and Philip arranged dramatic festivals himself.[83] Those philosophers who were the invited guests of Philip, had the dubious privilege of seeing their revered teachers parodied on stage, for in the Middle Comedy philosophers were frequently objects of attention.[84] In more serious moments, Philip might turn to intellectuals for edification, or listen to their own peculiar intellectual *agones* among themselves.

Besides adornment and amusement, Philip had a better use for intellectuals. In general, intellectuals can be usefully employed at two distinct points: before a given event, they serve as propagandists; and after a given event, when consequences need the same treatment as the motives, they again provide symbolic or mythological justification for what has just taken place. During the event itself, intellectuals merely get in the way of history and, if some of them get knocked about because they consider themselves indispensable to the action, any politician will be quick to point out that the blame lies not with him.[85]

The Panhellenic propaganda promoted by Isocrates and other intellectuals served the interests of Philip, who used it as a justification 'to champion the cause of concord among the Hellenes and of a campaign against the barbarian'.[86] However, when the old Athenian actually began telling Philip how such concord should be achieved, the king simply ignored him. In point of fact, Philip did build his power 'not in behalf of Hellas, but against her ... plotting against us all' and, if Isocrates was not willing to give the *ex-post-facto* justification for what happened, Philip knew he could find someone who would.[87]

A specific example of Philip's use of intellectuals involved the Sacred War against the Phocians. There was more symbolic import to this campaign than in Philip's other wars, for Delphi and the Amphictyony were involved. In his capacity as *archon* of Thessaly, Philip was easily persuaded to lead the members of the Holy League against the sacrilegious Phocians. As befitted the sacred task, Philip's soldiers were garlanded with crowns of laurel and the king proceeded to battle under the stated leadership of the god.[88] The unnerved Phocians fled and Philip assumed the title of 'the avenger of the god, and the defender of religion'.[89] He had manipulated the scene effectively: his artistic friends advised him how to dress his soldiers for maximum effect and from the intellectuals in his entourage he could expect arguments from mythology justifying his leadership of the Amphictyonic league and his assumption of the guardianship of Delphi.[90] As for deification, there again philosophers were handy with 'sound arguments which can help your power'.[91]

The one case where Philip had to choose between the Academy and the followers of Isocrates involved the education of his son, Alexander. To Isocrates' consternation, the king chose Aristotle. If Isocrates had no one better to put forth as a candidate for royal tutor than Theopompus, he was at a disadvantage to begin with.[92] Markle believes the appointment of Aristotle was an award given to the Academy by Philip because of Speusippus' letter, an epistle which outdistanced its rival in courting the king's favour.[93] But given the opportunity, Isocrates would not have hesitated to find new arguments which promised the king more than Speusippus could muster and Philip knew that. Equally unpopular with the majority of Athenians, the two schools offered the king no opportunity to improve his own standing among the citizenry, so there was no meaningful choice in that direction. Philip picked Aristotle because of his 'proven qualities'. The two families were close and Aristotle had committed himself to Philip's cause. Aristotle was also close to Antipater who was to prove a useful ally on a number of occasions.

Aristotle and Alexander

Philip was a shrewd judge of men and he wanted Alexander educated away from the court and Olympias in remote Mieza. The king reckoned that the not overly gregarious Aristotle would be the right man to have in that spot. The philosopher had by now given up Plato's mathematical notions of education and concentrated on the natural sciences, rhetoric, literary criticism and political theory. Alexander was least interested in political theory, although Aristotle tried hard to exert his influence in that area. He wrote:

> If there is one person ... so pre-eminently superior in goodness that there can be no comparison between the goodness and political capacity which he shows ... and what is shown by the rest, such a person ... can no longer be treated as part of a state ... for a person of this order may very well be like a god among men.[94]

Young Alexander had already announced that he would only enter the races at the Olympic Games if all his competitors were kings.[95] At best, Aristotle was verbalising the prince's thoughts and, like Plato and Isocrates before him, he now had to deal with a self-assured and headstrong ruler. Aristotle hectoring Alexander to be a hegemon to the Greeks and a despot to the barbarians, to look to the former as friends and relatives and to deal with the latter as with 'beasts or plants', made little impression on the prince.[96] Nor did Aristotle's proofs of the inferiority of barbarians have much effect on his pupil. Isocrates in his *Fifth Epistle* had written to Alexander warning him of Aristotle's eristics; such studies were not meant for a prince whose role in life was not to persuade, but to command.[97] In time, Alexander came to associate Aristotle closely with eristic learning and he would also recognise the philosopher as an ally of Antipater and Cassander. Once, arguing with Cassander, the king angrily retorted that 'these are the famous quibblings of the Aristotelian school, arguing for both sides of a point'.[98]

Another example of Aristotle's limited impact on Alexander was the manner in which the king treated Callisthenes. When Alexander left for Asia in 334, he took with him a retinue of intellectuals: philosophers such as Anaxarchus and his student Pyrrho, historians like Callisthenes and others. In part, the inspiration came from his teacher. However much he may have wanted to introduce Greek culture to the east, Alexander was serious in revealing to the Greeks, or at least to Aristotle and his students, the nature and culture of Asia.[99] Alexander had been strongly influenced by reading Homer whose heroes would have felt more at home in fourth-century Macedon than in Isocrates' Greece. The young ruler identified himself with Achilles and regarded Aristotle's annotated *Iliad* as his most valuable possession. Callisthenes was a student of geography, history and Homer and Alexander made use of him to correct the text of the *Iliad* on the basis of local information and lore collected in Asia Minor.[100] More than this, Alexander hoped for another Homer to record his deeds in a suitably heroic mode and Callisthenes was agreeable to the task.

Alexander's visit to Siwah gave Callisthenes an early opportunity. He dramatically narrates how Alexander followed the tracks of Perseus and Heracles to the oracle, guided by two crows and aided by a providential rain. Once at the shrine, Alexander was assured that he was descended from Zeus.[101] As his incredibly successful campaign progressed, Alexander became increasingly megalomaniacal, but his historian also began to draw inflated conclusions as to his own independent worth. Arrian reports that Callisthenes stated that 'without the history he was writing, Alexander and his work would be forgotten ... If Alexander was destined to have a share of divinity, it would not be owing to Olympias' absurd stories about his birth, but to the account of him which he should himself publish in his history.'[102] Aristotle's verdict on his grand-nephew was that he was an unsurpassed speaker who lacked common sense. According to a late source, the philosopher repeatedly warned Callisthenes 'to speak as seldom and as pleasantly as possible in the presence of a man who had at the tip of his tongue the power over life and death'.[103]

Since the sources indicate that Callisthenes had been with Aristotle at Mieza, Alexander was aware of his pedantic manner. Presumably, the king hoped that his merit as a chronicler would overcome any personal boorishness. He had two additional uses for Callisthenes and the other philosophers in his entourage. One was entertainment. An inveterate competitor, the king enjoyed pitting members of his court against each other and, on occasion, matched wits with the likes of Callisthenes himself. It amused the conqueror to play the more sullen, 'old-fashioned' Macedonians off against his clever Greek retainers, externalising conflicts within his own psyche.[104] In the case of Clitus, this tension led to murder. When the depressed emperor needed consolation, Callisthenes and another philosopher, Anaxarchus of Abdera, were brought in as alienists.[105] Even here, the two competed as to who could better succeed in lightening the sufferings of the king. Anaxarchus employed a rather risky form of shock therapy — laughter followed by stock sophistic arguments about the Great Man being above human law — and came out ahead. As Anaxarchus' stock rose, that of his Peripatetic rival dropped.[106] Later, the sophist would encourage Alexander in his delusions of divinity. Ironically, Anaxarchus would die a hero's death refusing a Cypriot king the flattery he had so freely bestowed on Alexander.[107]

The *proskynesis* affair finally ruptured irreparably relations between the king and his chronicler.[108] Paralleling the historian's inflated opinion of himself was a lessening of respect for the king. The student of Aristotle bristled at Alexander's policy toward Asiatics. To the Peripatetic, 'barbarians' were slaves by nature and should be treated as such. Further, Callisthenes' refusal to participate in *proskynesis*, a form of obeisance the Greeks reserved for divinity, drew the admiration of the Macedonians. Although Alexander might enjoy a *riposte* as much as another Greek, sarcastic remarks about his *pothos* and his political ideas would not be tolerated indefinitely. Truesdale Brown correctly measured Callisthenes when he wrote: 'Happy and pleased with himself, he brought out stinging little quotations from the poets, particularly Euripides; and apparently Alexander replied in kind ... To Callisthenes, this would have seemed simply learned amusement to which the Greeks had long been accustomed.'[109] Alexander had had enough of his Homer and let the vain writer work his own downfall. On request, Callisthenes made an impromptu speech in praise of the Macedonians and was awarded with a standing ovation.[110] Baiting him with a line from Euripides, Alexander challenged Callisthenes to argue the reverse as a real proof of his eloquence. Filled with *hubris*, the orator did so with great vigour and naturally infuriated the Macedonian audience. He must have been doubly confused when Alexander declared his palinode a proof not of eloquence but of hatred of the Macedonians. By the time of his death in the Hermolaus affair in 328, Callisthenes must have had time to reflect on Aristotle's caution: 'Speak as seldom and as pleasantly as possible.'

Plutarch cites a letter from Alexander to Antipater in which the king ominously notes: 'The Pages were stoned by the Macedonians, but I personally will punish the sophist, as well as those who sent him out, and those who are harboring in the Greek cities men who plot against me.'[111] This outburst was a thinly veiled threat against Aristotle and Antipater, both of whom had maintained a correspondence with Callisthenes and no doubt found Alexander's orientalising repugnant. Under the protection of his good friend, the viceroy, Aristotle had established the Lyceum at Athens. Alexander now decided to patronise the rival Academy and Aniximenes of Lampascus was honoured by the king, who also sent presents to Xenocrates.[112] In spite of Alexander's threats, Aristotle allowed Theophrastus to eulogise Callisthenes. As much as anything else, the essay on Callisthenes' 'martyrdom' was an apology for Aristotle, who is not to be held responsible for Alexander's barbarous actions. While under Aristotle's tutelage, the young prince showed great promise; however, the vicissitudes of fortune and his great success corrupted him. Like Socrates and Plato before him, Aristotle refused to take responsibility for a student's subsequent behaviour.[113]

Aristotle's return to Athens in 335-334 had coincided with the city's surrender to the Macedonians. It has been conjectured that Aristotle had a moderating influence on Alexander, who was lenient to the Athenians. The citizens of Athens duly noted their thanks in an inscription. 'Hence, the people of Athens wished to make it quite clear ... that they bestowed upon you [Aristotle] ... distinction, honor, and praise; and that they would forever keep him in faithful and honored memory.'[114] As long as Macedonian troops were garrisoned in Athens, Aristotle was safe, if not loved. At some point his honorific *stele* was destroyed by the anti-Macedonian, Himeraeus, and it is reasonable to assume that this occurred in 323, the year Alexander died. During the Lamian War, Aristotle became the focus of anti-Macedonian feeling at Athens and was indicted for impiety.[115] This same charge had been levelled against Socrates and, as in the past, the philosopher was given the chance to escape. Not a citizen like Socrates, Aristotle left the city, contenting himself with a verbal Parthian shot that he did not want Athens to sin twice against philosophy.[116]

Impiety may have been the formal charge, but the Athenians threw Aristotle out for political reasons. In his famous speech against the philosophers, Demochares claims that Aristotle passed intelligence reports to Antipater, that some of these were intercepted and that they contained information detrimental to the city's interests.[117] It is known that Aristotle wrote nine books of letters to Antipater and, though the old general may have been interested in Aristotle's researches, the philosopher's primary value to him was as an incisive reporter of what was taking place in Athens.[118] From the rapidly increasing enrolment of students at the Lyceum, Aristotle could have obtained additional information about other parts of Greece. Probably, he analysed the mood of the volatile city, where orators such as Demosthenes, Lycurgus and Hyperides stirred up anti-Macedonian feeling whenever possible.

In a letter written from Chalcis in 323, the philosopher informs Antipater that the city was crowded with informers, that it was becoming increasingly dangerous for a Macedonian to live in Athens and that aliens in general were victims of discrimination.[119] The death of Hermias had left a vacuum in Aristotle's life that may have been filled by Antipater and the viceroy utilised his brilliant friend as an agent. The psychological links between an agent and his control are extremely close. It is no surprise that Aristotle named Antipater the executor of his will.[120]

The Hellenistic World

Assuming a populist stance, Demosthenes had stated in his famous defence *On the Crown*:

> It is not a speaker's words nor the modulations of his voice in which the value lies, but in his political agreement with the people, the accord of his likes and his dislikes with those of his country. A mind of this sort will give words based on goodwill. But to cultivate persons from whom the state anticipates some danger is to anchor one's boat away from popular feeling and to abandon the expectations of the same secure harbour.[121]

Demosthenes was never specific about the menace of resident philosophers in Athens, but his nephew Demochares in a speech by 307 lacked no such compunctions. The suicide of Demosthenes and the regime of the Peripatetic Demetrius of Phaleron separated the two speeches. Demosthenes had had a major effect on Athenian public opinion: to be an Athenian patriot meant to be anti-Macedonian. To Athenian nationalists the alien intellectuals, with Aristotle and his school in the foreground, were 'a clear and present danger'. The Academy did not attract the same ire as the Peripatetics, but the orators surely pointed out that except for Plato and Speusippus all the prominent members were aliens, often from far-off countries.[122] As for the two Athenians, their relations with Macedon were well known. Speusippus' successor, Xenocrates, might accompany an Athenian delegation to Antipater to plead Athens' case, but by then the defeated city had turned its back on the patriots and was more interested in coming to terms with Antipater. It was hoped that the head of the Academy could do what Aristotle had accomplished in earlier years and deflect a conqueror's wrath.[123]

During the Wars of the Successors, Antipater died and in 319 Polyperchon became the new regent. Antipater's son, Cassander, refused to accept the situation and quickly outmanoeuvred Polyperchon, who turned for support to Athens. The regent promised to remove Antipater's oligarchic constitution and grant a general amnesty, in effect returning the *polis* to the situation prior to the Lamian War.[124] The Athenians greeted the news with joy and in their brief freedom condemned two men to death: Phocion who had strong Academic ties and a Peripatetic philosopher, Demetrius of Phalerum.[125] Before the decree was passed, Demetrius had left Athens and made his way to his friend, Cassander.

The new government was dominated by the democratic orator, Hagmonides of Pergase, who tried to eradicate philosophical influence in Athens. Though primarily revenge on a political foe, the execution of Phocion was an indirect stab at the Academy, for the old man was known to have been a student of the Academy, a close collaborator of another Academic sympathiser, the general Chabrias, and a good friend of his teacher, Xenocrates.[126] Indeed, anticipating Demetrius of Phalerum's later treatment of Theophrastus, Phocion had tried to enrol Xenocrates as a citizen in order that the Chalcedonian could avoid paying tax as a resident alien. In Athenian politics, Phocion had advocated that men of education and culture — that is, men educated at the philosophical schools — should monopolise offices while those not of the elite should stay at home and tend to their produce.[127]

Hagmonides also struck at the Peripatetics by indicting Theophrastus on a charge of impiety:

> He, doubtless, cared little for the religious views of the Peripatetic, but for his political opinions and affiliations, as a good democrat, he could entertain nothing but hatred. Was not Nicanor, who had done Athens so much harm, the adopted son and son-in-law of the teacher of Theophrastus?[128]

William Ferguson goes on to remind us that the Lyceum was a hotbed of aristocratic influence both in the ideas it disseminated and in its membership. Hagmonides' political influence was soon in eclipse, however, and he could barely muster one-fifth of the votes in the *Areopagus*.[129] No doubt, the occupation of the Piraeus by Nicanor by 318 convinced many Athenians of the need to look at the trial with a good deal of foresight.

Like his father, Cassander favoured Peripatetic philosophers.

Although not known as an intellectual, he knew most of Homer by heart and was not averse to patronising utopian projects.[130] Euhemerus was his trusted friend and was employed on numerous missions.[131] To his brother, Alexarchus, Cassander gave land at Mount Athos and allowed him to build and settle a new city, Uranopolis. With some exaggeration John Ferguson notes that this city 'is our only example of a practical attempt to produce a foundation of a new kind to incorporate the values of a new age'.[132] On Euhemerus' fabulous Sacred Isle 'all the accepted deities were generals, admirals, and kings who lived a long time ago'.[133] In an age when kings were assuming divinity, Euhemerus provided welcome propaganda. Alexarchus, who may have used Euhemerus as a guidebook, identified himself with the sun and the citizens of his city were called Children of Heaven. Either a philologist or a schizophrenic, Alexarchus invented a private language with which he addressed his brother.[134] A borderline intellectual at best, he was reacting to the opening up of the world by Alexander. Cassander put up with his bizarre experiment because Alexarchus was his brother, but the Macedonian ruler was also comfortable enough with intellectuals to be able to countenance such behaviour.

Demetrius of Phaleron was a different sort of individual. He ruled Athens competently for ten years and was able to put many of Aristotle's and Theophrastus' political ideas into practice. Although less severe than Antipater, Demetrius reduced the electorate to half that of 322. Magistrates were to be elected rather than selected by lot. As the superintendent of the state, the *epimeletes*, Demetrius went about changing laws with great vigour, closely advised by his teacher, Theophrastus.[135] His concern for the propertied classes resulted in the revision of the law of real property and the reform of the national festivals so as to relieve the wealthy of the burden of outfitting them.[136] Closely connected with such economic measures was legislation on morals. Imitating Solon, a number of sumptuary laws were enacted. To protect such laws, Demetrius drew on Aristotle and set up two new bodies. The *nomophylakes*, who guarded against public violations of the laws, were given the insignia of priests and prominent positions at religious events.[137] Equally intrusive were the *gynaeconomi* who enforced female morality.[138] Essentially an expanded vice squad, the Boards 'looked in at banquets, counted guests, examined sepulchral monuments, checked debauchery, and made general inquisition into the private lives of citizens'.[139]

Part of Demetrius' motivation was economic, the need to put Athens on a firm financial footing. However, like most intellectuals in power or desirous of power, the Peripatetic spent much of his time telling other men (and especially women) how to behave. He now had to be taken seriously. Demetrius skirted the line between theory and action better than most: the major tension in his life seems to have been the contradiction between how he expected others to behave and how he behaved himself. Vain to the point of dyeing his hair blond, he dressed with great affectation, 'was fond of social pleasures, and his dinners, drinking parties, and *liaisons* with beautiful courtesans were matters of common knowledge and conversation'.[140] Apparently, Demetrius distinguished between his own instincts and the hedonism of others. If the contradiction bothered him, we do not hear of it. The *demos* hated him because he had restricted the franchise and was a thorough-going hypocrite; nor could Demetrius ever make the Athenians forget that he was an agent of Cassander. The philosopher's policies were a financial success and kept the city at peace for ten years, but, when Demetrius Poliorcetes sailed into the Piraeus in 307 with 20 ships and rhetoric about a free Athens, the issue was never in doubt. The restored democracy erected sumptuous statues of Demetrius and Antigonus and crowned each with diadems worth two hundred talents.[141] The deposed philosopher fled to Cassander.

During Demetrius' regime, two philosophers had been brought to trial for impiety, Stilpo and Theodorus the atheist.[142] As a result of the Phalerian's influence, Theodorus was acquitted. With the removal of the powerful Demetrius from Athens, no one of importance remained to protect philosophers from harassment. Generally, the restored democracy under Demetrius Poliorcetes was lenient in its treatment of the Peripatetics. However, in 306 a certain Sophocles of Sunium proposed a law banning any philosopher from setting up a school in Athens without the express permission of the *demos*.[143] The real force behind this measure was Demochares, the nephew of Demosthenes and the heir of the orator's politics. Demochares, as were so many opponents of philosophers, was also a historian. Polybius provides a sample of Demochares' style:

> Demetrius of Phalerum plumed himself on the increased prosperity of the city, but what praise did he deserve that was not due to any *banausic* tax-jobber? And at what a price the riches had been purchased! The state had been dragged across the stage of great and noble actions, like a donkey in a play. It had abandoned the leadership to others. And a fine set of laws this blondined Solon had drawn up. Let them be revised at once.[144]

The sarcasm is heavy but not without point. Philosophers had looked back to Solon as the ideal legislator, not least because his enforcement of morals struck a responsive chord with their own solemn assessment of the ills of the day. What Lewis Feuer has called the Mosaic dream of giving the weak and the wicked commandments engraved in stone in order to restrain and form their characters has been a persistent dream of intellectuals down through the ages. Egged on by Theophrastus, Demetrius of Phalerum freely indulged this fantasy, going so far as to give priestly functions to the *nomophylakes* and *gynaeconomi*. The ruler's own private life accentuated the absurdity of such legislation. Demochares did not disapprove of Demetrius' economic stringencies as such, but, rather, as a good democrat and imperialist, he felt that the money should be put in the service of a restored Athenian democracy.

Sophocles' proposal was carried and the philosophers fled. The law was in effect only a few months when it was challenged by a disciple of Aristotle, Philo, on a technicality. It was impious and illegal, claimed Philo, to attack a religious club dedicated to the muses. 'The old law of Solon was thus in substance cancelled by the new law of Sophocles.'[145] In defence of Sophocles' law, Demochares launched his famous calumny against philosophers. In spite of his efforts the law was overturned and Sophocles was fined five talents.[146]

The reasons for this change of heart are open to speculation. The *demos* no doubt had second thoughts on the matter and concluded their original assessment was too hasty. It was known that Demochares and Poliorcetes did not get along and the Macedonian was the more powerful of the two. Poliorcetes may not have loved the philosophers, but he knew that they served as a useful counterweight to the Athenian nationalists. Also, while he controlled Athens, the philosophic schools added to his prestige. Athenians too realised that their cultural supremacy — which had softened the heart of more than one conqueror — was intimately linked with the names of Plato, Aristotle and their *epigoni*. Finally, there were material advantages to being a university city.

Since Anaxagoras, the Athenians had been putting philosophers on trial for impiety. As Derenne has carefully shown, 'En effet, dans la plupart des cas, se sont des rivalités politiques et personelles qui ont déterminé les accusateurs à agir ... dans la plupart des cas, la religion n'était qu'une arme au service de la politique.'[147] While not denying the religious import of the trials, Derenne has shrewdly noted that other thinkers, who were equally hazy or eccentric in their religious convictions but of no account politically, were not brought to trial.[148]

Intellectuals came to be identified not just with eccentric thinking, but as partisans of Macedonian rule. Further, to be anti-intellectual meant more than just adhering to 'common sense' and customs tried and true; since Demosthenes, opposition to the philosophical schools meant that one identified oneself as an Athenian patriot. The anti-intellectual mood in Athens had gradually hardened in the course of the fourth century and the trials of intellectuals accelerated accordingly. The action of Sophocles marked not only the culmination but also the end of an era in Greek politics.

Ingemar Düring writes that after 300 'politics had practically ceased to exist at Athens', and the philosophical schools of Plato and Aristotle mirrored this reality by concentrating their attention on theoretical problems, away from active political life.[149] On the whole, this generalisation is accurate. As compensation, polemics among the intellectuals themselves grew 'more and more vulgar and scurrilous'.[150] W.W. Tarn provides eulogies for the two schools — the moribund Academy 'had nothing new to say to the world, nothing to meet men's present needs. It had become merely orthodox; it was on its way to becoming orthodoxy in decay, and, like other decaying matter, to breed strange forms of life alien to its own substance.'[151] The Peripatetics never recovered their pre-eminent position of the Phalerian's days. Theophrastus had been recalled and his successor was the eminent Straton, but 'the Macedonia of ... [the Peripatatics'] sympathies had been the Macedonia of Antipatros and Kassandros. It had no part or lot in the Macedonia of Demetrios, and its heart went to Alexandria with his namesake; Straton was the tutor of Ptolemy II, and corresponded with Arsinoe.'[152]

Of course, Tarn's statements admit of exceptions. The Peripatetic Olympiodorus was a devoted democrat who opposed Cassander, supported Demetrius and was subsidised by Lysimachus.[153] The head of the Peripatetics, Lycon, 'often gave the Athenians advice on various subjects and thus conferred on them the greatest benefits'.[154] The Pergamine dynasts, Eumenes and Attalus, gave Lycon gifts, and the Seleucid ruler, Antiochus II, would have as well, were his offers not refused. Lycon's successor, Ariston of Ceos, may have been employed by Antigonus Doson in various state affairs.[155] The Macedonian king was also a friend and pupil of the philosopher Euphantus of Olynthus who dedicated to him his work *On Kingship*.[156] Finally, Doson employed a well-known member of the Peripatetic school, Prytanis, to draw up a code of laws for Megalopolis.[157] Nor was the Academy politically autistic. Although he went out of his way to shun political involvement, Arcesilaus was a friend of the Macedonian commander at Athens,

Hierocles, and dedicated books to Eumenes, from whom he accepted large sums of money.[158] Towards Athens, the philosopher probably maintained what Tarn likes to call 'a quiet but well understood patriotism'.[159] In the classroom he may have been bolder, for Ecdemos and Demophames were his students.[160] In Plutarch's words, these two philosophic adventurers

> were natives of Megalopolis, but had escaped from the oppression of the tyrants, and after being with Arcesilaus the philosopher during their exile liberated their country by organizing a plot against the tyrant Aristodemus, and also took part in the overthrow of Nicocles, the tyrant of Sicyon, joining Aratus in that enterprise. In addition to this, when the people of Cyrene sent for them, they had championed their cause in a brilliant manner and preserved their liberty.[161]

There was an anachronistic quality in such careers, an activism which was alien to an era where intellectuals preferred to write about history rather than make it, or compose tracts on kingship rather than overthrow tyrants. Significantly, Ecdemos and Demophames were the teachers of the so-called 'last of the Greeks'; and 'among their best actions, they themselves counted the education of Philopoemen, thinking they had done a general good to Greece by giving him the nurture of philosophy'.[162] Regrettably, Philopoemen was a military man who was more interested in war and hunting than in philosophy and his political vision was narrowly Achaean. From Dion to Philopoemen, the Academy failed signally to find a philosopher-king who could rescue the Hellenes from widespread misery and political annihilation.

In the third century, the Academy and the Lyceum had to compete with other schools for the allegiance of educated and influential Greeks. One important reason for the increase in philosophers and philosophical schools was that more wealthy and educated Greeks had time on their hands. Polybius explains: 'But in our own times . . . owing to Alexander's empire in Asia . . . our men of action in Greece are relieved from the ambitions of a military and political career and have therefore ample means for inquiry and study.'[163] Schools rose to meet this demand; though the Stoa and the Garden were primarily responses to the problems of the Hellenistic age. It was an era that called for a new message. In Tarn's words, the want was met. Plato and Aristotle had desired above all things to *know*; and when they turned to politics and ethics, they had dealt — they could not otherwise — with the city state, and with man as a member thereof and in relation thereto. But man had now become a citizen of the world; philosophy had to deal with him as such; and the question he asked of his teachers was, how was he to act in relation to himself. Inevitably the philosophy of *knowledge* was to be replaced by the philosophy of comfort.[164]

Politically, the framework of the world of the *polis* had been broken up and replaced by a new world of Hellenistic territorial monarchies under absolute rule.[165]

On the whole, the conduct that Hellenistic monarchs approved was non-political. For Epicurus and his school, political life was inconsequential for the wise man. Since happiness was not to be found in the political arena, a sage should concentrate on his studies, his friends and his garden, as did the venerable Epicurus.[166] Aalders has correctly diagnosed the Epicurean position as one of political quietism, an acceptance of the *status quo*, 'a conventional and conformistic attitude in political and social respects, with a kind of indifferent conservatism'.[167]

Still, political life was not closed off completely. There are people for whom politics provides a certain pleasure, says Epicurus, and these ambitious individuals should not be hindered from pursuing what is for them an attractive business.[168] Epicureans in politics included Philonides, who pleaded for the restoration of his city's freedom at the court of Demetrius Soter, and Pyrrhus' adviser, Cineas, who attempted the impossible task of bridling Pyrrhus' ambitions.[169] While Cineas was primarily a courtier and a diplomat, Philonides was first and foremost a mathematician for whom politics was of secondary interest. Most Epicureans heeded their founder's advice and stayed out of politics.

The founder of Stoicism, Zeno, also felt that the way to avoid the uncertainties of living in an unsettled period was by becoming a sage. Political activity was not to be engaged in at the expense of virtue. Should a clash occur between moral law and the law of the state, a Stoic's obligation is clear. Products of their time, the Stoics regarded citizenship as less important than had either Plato or Aristotle.[170] On the one hand, the state was expanded into a cosmopolis incorporating the entire human race; on the other hand, the individual's role in it was to find self-sufficiency. Both these extremes are found in Cynic thought as well and early in his life Zeno had come under the influence of Crates. Zeno's utopia, written during this period, has strong Cynic overtones and was a direct attack on Plato's *Republic*.[171] M.I. Finley's verdict on the *Politeia* of Zeno is harsh but essentially correct:

> Zeno proposed to cure the ills of society by ignoring all but the good men and by abolishing social institutions, not by changing them, just as later Stoics preached the equality and universal brotherhood of all men as an ideological justification for the preservation in real life of the grossest inequalities, ending with absolute monarchy.[172]

The Stoics differed from the Epicureans in that they did not discourage their followers from entering the world of affairs. Chrysippus, the third head of the school, wrote rather grandly — if Plutarch is to be believed — that 'the sage will voluntarily assume kingship and make a profit from it and, if he cannot reign himself, will dwell with a king and go campaigning'.[173] The Stoics divided humanity between the wise few and the multitudes, and 'since not only are the wise free, they are also kings', Chrysippus' assertion is not surprising.[174] Nevertheless, no Stoic assumed a royal mantle and probably only one king in our period, Antigonus Gonatas, took Stoicism seriously. Not even Antigonus attempted to put Zeno's *Politeia* into practice. Few Stoics became politicians, though more of them 'dwelt with a king' and some even went campaigning.

On the attractions of patronage for Stoics, T.W. Africa notes that

> Stoics were found in the courts of kings and the tents of Roman commanders, enlightening the minds and enjoying the bounty of the great of the earth. Of the two Stoics associated with radical popular movements, Blossius escaped the Gracchan debacle to perish with Aristonicus, but Sphaerus ended as the courtier of the voluptuary Ptolemy IV. More typical was the Stoic Persaeus, who was Antigonus' governor of occupied Corinth. Chrysippus, Hecaton, and Diogenes the Renegade defended private property, and Panaetius was the confident of Scipio Aemilianus, as Posidonius was the familiar of Pompey the Great.[175]

The Stoa's greatest success came with Antigonus Gonatas, who, like Marcus Aurelius, was drawn early to philosophy. Part of the explanation for such an interest lies in his long rivalry with Pyrrhus, who had been given an honoured place at Demetrius' court. Always popular with the soldiers, the colourful Pyrrhus may have supplanted Antigonus somewhat in the eyes of his father and the more serious, introverted prince found solace in the company of philosophers. Antigonus' first teacher was the Megarian philosopher, Euphantus of Olynthus, who wrote a treatise on the art of governing a kingdom for his pupil.[176] The prince next befriended the Eretrian philosopher, Menedemus, who had gathered around him a circle of artisans and thinkers and was only too happy to offer Antigonus the pleasure of his company.[177] Menedemus was a practical man and an Eretrian patriot, who hoped to parlay his friendship with the king into concrete political favours for his city. He was later to be bitterly disappointed when Antigonus refused to restore Eretrea to its former freedom.[178] By this time, Menedemus had been supplanted in influence by Zeno's pupil, Persaeus, who helped doom Eretrea.

'The history of philosophy is to a great extent that of a certain clash of human temperaments,' says William James, and the truth of this statement has been demonstrated in our narrative numerous times.[179] James emphasised that a philosopher's 'temperament' exerted a primary claim on an individual's choice of a line of thinking; a philosopher's 'temperament ... loads the evidence for him one way or the other, making for a more sentimental or a more hard-hearted view of the universe'.[180] The peculiar relationship that exists between a man and his principles can be extended to interpersonal relationships as well, which is the case with exteriorisations or projections. Analytical psychiatrists point out that a projection is not a deliberate defence manoeuvre but a choiceless original state and is the avenue by which the unconscious complex attempts to reach our consciousness. 'In this condition, one finds his friends and his enemies, his hopes and his fears, his sources of support and his threats of failure, concretised in outer persons, objects, and events.'[181] Hence, the complicated and sometimes difficult, emotionally laden relationships between Plato and Dion, Isocrates and Timotheus, Aristotle and Hermias, Alexander and Diogenes, and Antigonus Gonatas and Zeno.

From all accounts Zeno was an exceedingly cautious individual, all the more so after his early treatise on government with its strongly Cynic overtones. According to Diogenes Laertius, 'King Antigonus often broke in on him with a noisy party, and once took him along with other revelers to Aristocles, the musician; Zeno, however, in a little while gave them the slip.'[182] This anecdote suggests the relationship that came to develop between the Younger Dionysius and Plato. The reluctant philosopher is cast in the role of the royal super-ego, for the moral of Diogenes' tale is that Zeno 'readily adapted to circumstances'.[183] Such self-sufficiency, the ability to present the smallest possible target to fortune's darts, impressed and engaged the Macedonian king, who likened his reign to that of a 'noble servitude'.[184] It had long been customary for Macedonian kings to adorn their courts with imported Greek intellectuals and Antigonus wished to set up a circle of intellectuals in Macedonia, similar to Menedemus' group in Eretrea. Since Antigonus alternated between philosophy and wine and occasionally tried to combine the two, Zeno declined the Macedonian king's offer to join him at his court.[185] Pleading old age, Zeno did agree to send two of his pupils, Persaeus of Citium and Philonides of Thebes, to Macedonia.[186]

Of Philonides we know nothing, but Persaeus was a laconophile like Sphaerus and wrote a treatise on the *Laconian Constitution*.[187] Paradoxically for a Stoic, he was also interested in the hedonistic aspects of life and wrote such works as *Convival Reminiscences* and *Dialogues of the Boon Companions*.[188] No doubt, these essays were written to please Antigonus, as was the treatise *On Kingship*.[189] A many faceted individual — philosopher, jester and soldier — Persaeus found no difficulty in bridging the king's interests. Characteristically, the philosopher died at his post as commandant of Corinth in 243.[190]

Of our remaining two Stoics, Sphaerus, a student of Zeno, served Cleomenes III, while Blossius was the adviser of Tiberius Sempronius Gracchus. Plutarch's pairing of the Spartan kings Agis IV and Cleomenes III with the Roman brothers, Tiberius and Caius Gracchus, was an obvious choice and the comparison already had been in Cicero's mind when he criticised the Gracchi's agrarian reforms, alluding darkly to that 'contagious evil' which emanated from Sparta.[191] As the comparison between the Spartans and the Romans became more embellished, so did the role of Sphaerus, who had to be to Cleomenes what Blossius had been to Tiberius Gracchus.

Sphaerus has been labelled a revolutionary by J. Bidez, F. Ollier and Tarn, but Africa and others have argued that Sphaerus' role in the Spartan Revolution was slight.[192] As can be judged from such titles as *The Laconian State* and *On Lycurgus and Socrates*, Sphaerus' interests were pedagogical and antiquarian. Another of Sphaerus' works was entitled *On Monarchy* and he spent time as a courtier at the Spartan and Egyptian courts. Cleomenes III made use of Sphaerus' talents to overhaul the Spartan educational system, but whether Sphaerus was the instigator of this 'reform' is doubtful; rather 'as the mouthpiece of Cleomenes ... he attempted to justify the royal revolution by historical arguments'.[193]

Blossius of Cumae was the student of Antipater of Tarsus, the sixth head of the Stoa. Although Cumae was a Greek city, it has been conjectured by D.R. Dudley that Blossius came from a Capuan family that had a tradition of anti-Roman and pro-democratic behaviour.[194] Blossius found his way to Rome where he was a *hospes* of the family of P. Mucius Scaevola.[195] Both Scaevola and his brother, P. Licinius Crassus Mucianus, were to become supporters of Gracchan legislation and Blossius' introduction to the Gracchi may have come from either of them. As opposed to another philosopher, Diophanes of Mytilene, the sources do not say that Blossius was a tutor to Tiberius, nor do we know when the two became acquainted. In his work *De Amicitia*, Cicero has this to say about Blossius: 'For he did not follow, but he directed the infatuation of Tiberius Gracchus, and he did not offer himself as the comrade in the latter's fury, but as the leader.'[196] Cicero had no use for the Gracchi and gloats over Blossius' 'heavy and righteous' penalty for his crimes against the Republic.[197] In his emphasis on Blossius' role as the *éminence grise* behind the elder Gracchus, he is followed by Valerius Maximus and Plutarch.[198] It is impossible to assess the extent of Blossius' influence. He may have been influential in suggesting to Tiberius that the allotments of land parcelled to the people from the *ager publicus* be inalienable, backing this claim with Greek political theory.[199] However, as is true of Cleomenes III, everything that either the Spartan king or Tiberius ventured can be explained as a pragmatic and traditional approach to the problems of the day. It had also become a tradition that a king or a grandee have an intellectual at his elbow providing ideological and historical support.

After the debacle of 133, Blossius escaped the purge of Tiberius' followers. The Tribunes' more illustrious supporters were left alone by the wary Senate, but Blossius' release is a question mark. According to Cicero and Valerius he was interrogated privately by C. Laelius.[200] Blossius' line of defence was that his esteem for Tiberius was so great that it was his duty to carry out any and all of the Tribunes' requests. Laelius next asked Blossius the famous question: 'Even if he requested you to set fire to the Capitol?'[201] The Stoic responded in the affirmative. Plutarch's account of the incident is more dramatic.[202] Blossius is hauled before a Commission of Inquiry. As in the earlier accounts he is asked the pregnant question concerning arson, this time by Scipio Nasica. There is a dramatic pause before Plutarch allows Blossius reluctantly to reply that if Tiberius had ordered him to do so, he would have done so. According to Plutarch, Blossius was acquitted, but Cicero's claim that Blossius fled Rome rather than face the Commissioners is to be preferred.[203]

The philosopher left for Asia Minor and joined the retinue of the rebel king, Aristonicus.[204] The last king of Pergamum, Attalus III, had been a staunch ally of Rome, currying Roman favour whenever possible. In his will he bequeathed the Pergamene kingdom to Rome, an act either of great realism in sensing the coming times or of great spite to those who had the most to gain from the continued independence of the kingdom.[205] Aristonicus, the bastard son of Eumenes III, clearly felt himself among the latter and led a brief rebellion against the Romans. Aristonicus motives and actions were not atypical of the times. John Ferguson writes:

> He was not the first or last pretender of the period, but he was perhaps the ablest and certainly the most interesting. Hostility to and suspicion of Rome was an easy and sincere emotion. The eradication of Carthage and Corinth was not long past, and men had only to use their eyes to see how Rome emptied the coffers of her provinces and filled the slave market. Alongside this, whether from idealism or expediency, or a mixture of both, Aristonicus appealed to the spirit of social justice which was always latent in the Hellenistic Age.[206]

Scipio Nasica, who was sent out to organise the new province, died before he could complete his mission. In 131 a military command was given to the highly esteemed but militarily inept P. Licinius Crassus, who was killed while invading Leucae. But despite initial successes and despite making some headway in Leuca and other Hellenised *poleis*, Aristonicus was never able to take Pergamum and at Cyme Ephesus defeated the Pergamene fleet. The next two Roman commanders, M. Peperna and M. Aquilius, were experienced and skilled campaigners. Together with Rome's client kingdoms in the area, Pontus, Cappadocia, Bithynia and Paphlagonia, they defeated the pretender's forces. Aristonicus was strangled in a Roman dungeon.[207]

Throughout his career Aristonicus managed to juggle a number of perceptions about himself. As a patriot, he attempted to unite the subjects of his kingdom against the Roman occupiers. When this failed, he became a radical social reformer and encouraged the poor to rebel against the rich, slaves against the masters.[208] Finally, as a mystic and a nationalist he appealed to the rural proletariat to rise up against the cities and the Asians of the interior were stirred up against the coastal Greeks. This last phase occurred after the battle of Cyme and it was during this period that Blossius joined Aristonicus. We are told by

Strabo that Aristonicus went 'up into the interior and quickly collected a vast number of propertyless men and slaves bewitched by liberty whom he called citizens of the sun'.[209] The role of Blossius in all this is unclear. Undoubtedly, he wished to make himself at least as useful to Aristonicus as he had to Tiberius Gracchus. However, against his enemies, the pretender was no more successful than the tribune. Having nowhere further to run, Blossius, like Hannibal, committed suicide in the east.[210] After Blossius, intellectuals, both Greek and Roman, would support the dominant power and, indeed, even had they wished, they could do little else. The world was soon to become Rome's.

The above accounts of Sphaerus and Blossius show them occupying an interesting, ambiguous, but, on the whole, unimportant role in the events of the time. They were ideologues to ambitious rulers who knew their own minds and required no intellectuals to fire their visions. To some historians, this role of the intellectual as essentially a Homer or a Boswell to a prince intent upon taking his place in his people's history is not enough. The intellectuals, be they Pythagoreans, Platonists or Stoics, take centre stage. A.J. Toynbee identifies Blossius as Marx's 'Hellenic prototype':

> The Stoic prophet of revolution ... was not only Zeno's disciple but was also the master of Tiberius Gracchus and Aristonicus. And if it had pleased the Goddess fortune to crown Aristonicus' proletarian insurrection with success, then no doubt the names of the Italiot Greek prophet and his Pergamene khalifah would be resounding down to this day as loudly as the names of Marx and Lenin.[211]

Firm believers in the power of books, Toynbee and others maintain that the Stoics armed themselves with the wisdom and ideology found in two Hellenistic utopias written by Euhemerus and Iambulus.[212] Thus, like Moses on Mount Sinai, they did not descend to the land of the wicked empty-handed. If Blossius has been christened as Marx's Hellenic prototype, Joseph Bidez calls Iambulus 'le Jules Verne du Marxisme'.[213] To be sure, the Jules Vernes and the Iambuluses of the world are widely read, but escapism rarely leads to political activism. Significantly, Zeno's *Politeia* is not mentioned in connection with either Sphaerus or Blossius. In fact, there is no great Stoic International, no movements of intense Stoic missionaries out to convert the world to a new order of Heliopolis. Stoics never achieved the cohesiveness of the Pythagoreans, nor did they attain the discipline that in the case of the western Greeks had elicited the admiration of Plato.

5 EPILOGUE

A story in Diogenes Laertius sums up the role of the intellectual as a political activist in the classical and Hellenistic periods:

> One day Dionysius over the wine commanded everybody to put on purple and dance. Plato declined, quoting the line: 'I could not stoop to put on women's robes.' Aristippus, however, put on the dress and as he was about to dance, was ready with the repartee: 'Even amid the Bacchic revelry/True modesty will not be put to shame.' He made a request to Dionysius, on behalf of a friend and, failing to obtain it, fell down at his feet. And when some one jeered at him, he made reply, 'It is not I who am to blame, but Dionysius who has his ears in his feet.'[1]

Some of the themes are familiar; an autocrat with 'philosophical proclivities' and a fondness for wine has gathered around him the court philosophers. Under the influence of alcohol, the tyrant makes the philosophers literally dance attendance on him. Such were the hazards of dealing with tyrants. Philosophers flattered themselves that they were indispensable to the tyrant's self-image as a cultured individual and a legitimate ruler and to a certain extent legitimisation was one of the most important services performed by intellectuals. For their services, they were tolerated and even courted and paid. However, the court *consiglieri* had to put up with the whims of capricious hosts. The deflation of philosophers provided amusement for those rulers who had had their own inconsistencies pointed out to them by these same individuals. Accustomed to study and take advantage of human behaviour in concrete situations, shrewd rulers were aware that the philosophers themselves were all too human: differences of personality and temperament existed and the failure of one sage or school occasioned glee to others. The contest between Aristippus and Plato for the favour of Dionysius did not take place through tracts, but on the floor of a drunken dinner party. Alexander enjoyed setting similar 'comedies', where philosophers were the butt of jokes.

This underside of the intellectuals' dealings with men of power helps explain why the incursions of intellectuals into politics were ultimately failures.[2] They were willing to offer counsel and utilise their expertise to help a grateful patron find a higher truth; they were unwilling to be dragged off to a dinner party by a drunken king like an exotic pet, as was Zeno by Antigonus. The attachment of intellectuals to symbols which transcend everyday life must be kept in mind.[3] When empathy with the sacred was combined with an aristocratic background, as was the case with Plato, intellectuals were unable to serve for maximum effect as confidants of the mighty. Most members of the philosophical schools came from the leisured classes and never forgot it. No wonder that, at the first opportunity, intellectuals left the political arena and retreated into established and patronised schools or became apolitical altogether. Mannheim's vision of a free floating intelligentsia, loosed from control of the past and free of regional and class biases, proved an illusion then and has been no more successful since.[4]

Those philosophers who became politicians themselves proved in most cases to be no better than the men they replaced. For every tyrannicide, there was a tyrant; for every Phormio a Timalaos, for every Menedemus a Chaeron. The heirs of Plato, Aristotle and Isocrates were equally ready to become yogis or commissars, in Arthur Koestler's terms, and all could find in their respective philosophies adequate reasons for their choices. As Raymond Aron observes, the attitude of intellectuals towards politics is very similar to that of non-intellectuals: 'In the opinions of teachers or writers, there is the same mixture of half-baked knowledge, or traditional prejudices, of preferences which are more aesthetic than rational, as in those of shopkeepers or industrialists.'[5]

Finally, the episode at Dionysius' court helps to define the perimeters of the intellectuals' place in politics. In Plato and Aristippus, two very different responses were given to the tyrant's order to don purple robes and dance. The aristocratic Plato refused and sulked in wounded dignity, but the less complex Aristippus joined in. The role of most intellectuals in politics in this period lies somewhere between Plato and Aristippus, the hedgehog and the fox. Kolakowski has formulated similar differences between the priest and the jester:

> The priest is the guardian of the absolute; he sustains the cult of the final and the obvious as acknowledged by and contained in tradition. The jester is he who ... doubts all that appears self-evident ... Priests and jesters cannot be reconciled unless one of them is transformed into the other, as sometimes happens. (Most often, the jester becomes a priest — as Socrates became Plato — and not vice-versa.) In every era, the jester's philosophy exposes as doubtful what seems

> most unshakable, reveals the contradictions in what appears obvious and incontrovertible, derides common sense and reads sense into the absurd ... Depending on time and place, the jester's thinking can range through all the extremes of thought, for what is sacred today was paradoxical yesterday, and absolutes on the equator are often blasphemies at the poles. The jester's constant effort is to consider all the possible reasons for contradictory ideas. It is thus dialectical by nature.[6]

It follows that jesters are more interested in the multiplicity of things, 'often unrelated and even contradictory', while priests have a propensity to relate everything to a single, related, coherent system which endows everything with meaning.[7]

Most intellectuals, especially those who regard themselves in a romantic manner as an aristocratic elite at war with the demands of a new age, opt for the vision of the hedgehog, the posture of the priest. And yet, Greek history suggests that it is the jester, Aristippus, who makes the request of the tyrant, has the better chance of influencing events and cuts the better figure. His request was not granted, which should surprise neither the historian nor the student of human nature.

NOTES

1. Introduction

1. The terms intellectual and intelligentsia both came into common usage in the nineteenth century. For *les intellectuels*, see Louis Bodin, *Les Intellectuels*, 6-9; Victor Brombert, *The Intellectual Hero: Studies in the French Novel, 1880-1955*, 21-31. *Intelligently* is discussed briefly in James Billington, *Fire in the Minds of Men*, 400-2, and more fully in his article 'The Intelligentsia and the Religion of Humanity', *American Historical Review*, 65 (1960), 807-21. See also Hugh Seton-Watson, 'The Russian Intellectuals', in George B. de Huszar (ed.), *The Intellectuals*, 41-50. For the word's American introduction and its linguistic and other connections with the Russian original, see Lewis S. Feuer, 'The Political Linguistics of "Intellectual": 1898-1918', *Survey*, 16 (1971), 156-83.

2. The literature on intellectuals is immense. An anthology of the classic studies and statements is edited by George B. de Huszar, ibid. Philip Reiff (ed.), *On Intellectuals*, contains a number of important articles by leading thinkers. More recent methodology and results are found in Aleksander Gella (ed.), *The Intelligentsia and the Intellectuals: Theory, Method and Case Study*. Ray Nichols, *Treason, Tradition and the Intellectual: Julien Benda and Political Discourse*, has a good selection of the most recent literature in the notes to Chapter 1, 'Politics and the Intellectual', 1-19. Of the historical surveys, three may be mentioned, Lewis A. Coser, *Men of Ideas*, and Lewis S. Feuer, *Ideology and the Ideologists*. Seymor Martin Lipset and Asoke Basu, 'Intellectual Types and Political Roles', in Lewis A. Coser (ed.), *The Idea of Social Structure: Papers in Honor of Robert K. Merton*, 433-70, attempt to analyse the political activism of intellectuals. Bernard Frischer, *The Sculpted Word: Epicureanism and Philosophical Recruitment in Ancient Greece* (University of California Press, Berkeley and Los Angeles, 1982), 1-66 surveys the Greek scene. Unfortunately, it appeared too late for me to utilise in this book. The ideal place to begin an examination of the issue is Max Beloff, 'The Intellectual in Politics', in his book of the same title (Weidenfeld & Nicolson, London, 1970), 3-18. Typically, Beloff's brief and cogent remarks are right on the mark.

3. Nichols, *Treason, Tradition, and the Intellectuals*, 10.

4. Max Weber, *Economy and Society*, II, 925.

5. Shils, *The Intellectuals and the Powers*, 3.

6. Florian Znaniecki, *The Social Role of the Man of Knowledge*, 21.

7. This is true of the Pythagoreans and the Academics. By the third century family standing had become less important. See John Patrick Lynch, *Aristotle's School*, 79-80.

8. *Ap.* Stob., 4.29C 52. Trans. M.T.W. Arnheim.

9. M.T.W. Arnheim, *Aristocracy in Greek Society*, 181.

10. Karl Mannheim, *Ideology and Utopia*, 159.

11. Ibid., 155.

12. Thomas W. Africa, *Science and the State in Greece and Rome*, 35, 36. Demetrius of Phalerum, though of low birth, put on aristocratic airs, D.L.7.6. Aristotle was the son of a physician, but married the niece of Hermias of Atarneus. Throughout his life he maintained close ties with Macedonian nobles. Pythagoras was the son of a merchant, but discounted this in favour of a genealogy that made clear his aristocratic intent. Even Zeno and his successors were acquaintances of

the Hellenistic kings. By this time being the head of a philosophical school conferred elitist status on its holder no matter what his background might have been. An analogy can be made with the leading offices of the Roman Catholic Church where it is possible for the son of a peasant to become a prince of the church.

13. Alvin W. Gouldner, *The Future of Intellectuals and the Rise of the New Class*, 65.

14. Plato, *Ep.*, 7.326b. All translations of Plato's *Epistles* are by G. Morrow. All other translations of Plato, except where noted, are by B. Jowett.

15. Cf. Shils: 'The discovery and the achievement of the optimum balance of civility and intellectual creativity are the tasks of the statesman and the responsible intellectual. The study of these diverse patterns of consensus and dissensus, their institutional and cultural concomitants, and the conditions under which they have emerged and waned are the first items on the agenda of the comparative study of the intellectuals and the powers.' *The Intellectuals*, 21-2.

16. For philosophers in the comedies, see the survey in Rudolf Helm, *Lucian und Menipp*, 371-86; T.B.L. Webster, *Studies in Later Greek Comedy*, 50ff., 110ff. Jacob Burckhardt's comments, however, are quite true: 'Und da die Philosopher einander gegenseitig in ihren Schriften fast moch ärger behandelten, als die Komiker taten, empfinden wir ihnen gegenüber kein grosses Mitleid.' *Griechische Kulturgeschichte*, 265.

17. 'For kings to be philosophers was so far from being a necessity, that it was rather a hindrance: What was really necessary was that they should be willing to hear, and ready to accept the advice of genuine philosophers.' Rose, fr. 70, trans. E. Barker.

18. Michael Howard, 'Conducting the concert of powers', *Times Literary Supplement*, 21 December 1979, 147.

19. G. Murphy and R.O. Ballou (eds.), *William James on Psychical Research*, 310, 320.

20. E.N. Tigerstedt, *Interpreting Plato*, 40.

21. Ibid.

22. M.I. Finley, *The World of Odysseus*, 149. Cf. F.M. Cornford, 'But the true test of an hypothesis, if it cannot be shown to conflict with known truths, is the number of facts that it correlates and explains.' *The Origin of Attic Comedy*, 191. Finley is constructing a variation of the coherence theory of historical narration. For a related account, see Rex Martin, *Historical Explanation*, 215-40.

23. Duane Reed Stuart, 'Author's Lives as Revealed in Their Works: A Critical Resume', in George Depue Hadzsits (ed.), *Classical Studies in Honor of John C. Rolfe*, 285-304. J.A. Fairweather, 'Fiction in the Biographies of Ancient Writers', *Ancient Society*, 5 (1974), 232-6.

24. Finley, *The World of Odysseus*, 146.

25. Max Weber, *The Religion of India*, trans. and ed. Hans H. Gerth and Don Martindale, 351. n.5.

26. W.K.C. Guthrie, *A History of Greek Philosophy*, I, 175. (Hereafter cited as *HGP*.)

27. Bertrand Russell, *A History of Western Philosophy*, 31.

28. See the useful note in F.W. Walbank, *A Historical Commentary on Polybius*, I, 222-4. Also, T.W. Africa, *Science and the State in Greece and Rome*, 29.

29. George Thomson, *Aeschylus and Athens*, 213. See the discussions of Thomson and A.D. Winspear in Alvin W. Gouldner, *Enter Plato*, 130, n.109.

30. Kurt von Fritz, *Pythagorean Politics in Southern Italy*, 96. Cf. also his remark on analogies: 'Analogies are always misleading if taken literally, but they sometimes serve to illustrate a point if considered in the right perspective.' Ibid. Cf. the author's 'Conservative Reaction and One Man Rule in Ancient Greece', in

his *Schriften zur griechischen und römischen Verfassungsgeschichte und Verfassungstheorie*, 229.

31. See James Billington, 'The Intelligentsia and the Religion of Humanity', *American Historical Review*, 807-8.

32. Frank Manuel, *The Prophets of Paris*, 167-8.

33. Cf. Georg G. Iggers, *The Cult of Authority*, 102. 'Like the Greek philosopher, the disciples of Saint-Simon envisaged the possibility of organizing the entire sphere of social and individual activities in accordance with a rational idea. Again, like Plato, that with the wisdom and power of the philosopher-king would go virtue and responsibility.' Iggers goes on to remind us that 'the disciples were not "brown shirts" but intellectuals'. Ibid.

34. Billington, *Fire in the Minds of Men*, 218-19.

35. Ben Knights, *The Idea of the Clerisy in the Nineteenth Century*, 112. For the impact of the Greeks on Coleridge and his contemporaries in general, see also Richard Jenkyns, *The Victorians and Ancient Greece*, and Frank M. Turner, *The Greek Heritage in Victorian Britain*.

36. Knights, *The Idea of the Clerisy*, 41.

37. Quoted in Billington, *Fire in the Minds of Men*, 216. Cf. Manuel, *The Prophets of Paris*, 189-93.

38. The nineteenth-century intellectual movements have been well integrated into the larger political canvas in recent books by Billington and Knights, *The Idea of the Clerisy*. Also J.L. Talmon's two books, *The Origins of Totalitarian Democracy*; *Political Messianism: The Romantic Phase*. Marxism, of course, became the most potent idea of the nineteenth century, but, as Billington correctly notes, it was not until Lenin that the various nineteenth-century revolutionary traditions were brought out of the wilderness and into power. *Fire in the Minds*, 443.

39. For anti-intellectualism in American history, see the important book by Richard Hofstadter, *Anti-Intellectualism in American Life*, especially 3-23.

40. Quoted in Charles Hunter Van Duzer, *Contributions of the Ideologues to French Revolutionary Thought*, 144.

41. Quoted in [Antoine Clare Thibaudeau] *Mémoires sur le Consulat*, 204. The long and the short of it is as George Boas puts it: 'When he saw that his love of ideas might not be compatible with his love of power, his attitude changed.' *French Philosophers of the Romantic Period*, 15. The relationship between Napoleon and the ideologues is given a thorough treatment in S. Moravia, *Il Tramonto dell' illuminismo: filosofia e politica nella società francese*, 293-313; 445ff.

42. The traditions of Plato's sale into slavery are examined by Alice Swift Riginos, *Platonica*, 86-92. The historicity is highly doubtful. See U. Kahrstedt, 'Platons Verkauf in die Sklaverei', *Wurzbürger Jbb*, 2 (1947), 295-300.

43. Paul Gautier, *Madame de Staël et Napoleon*, 50.

44. Max Weber, *The Methodology of the Social Sciences*, 90. See the study by Thomas Burger, *Max Weber's Theory of Concept Formation: History, Laws, and Ideal Types*.

45. Reinhard Bendix and Guenther Roth, *Scholarship and Partisanship: Essays on Max Weber*, 255. The chapter, 'The Genesis of the Typological Approach', was written by Roth.

46. *De orat.*, 3.138-42.

47. Ibid., 3.141. Unless otherwise noted, all translations are either my own or from the Loeb Classical Library.

48. *Adv. Col.*, 1126A-1127E.

49. Ibid., 1126E.

50. Athen., 508d-509c.

51. For the fragments of Demochares' *Oration Against the Philosophers*, see I. Düring, *Herodious the Cratetean*, 149-51. See also U. von Wilamowitz-Moellendorff, *Antigonos von Karystos*, 192, 270.

52. Quoted in Max Beer, *Fifty Years of International Socialism*, 198-9.

53. Eduard Bernstein, *Evolutionary Socialism: A Critique and Affirmation*, trans. Edith C. Harvey, 222. See, in general, Feuer, *Ideology*, 17-68.

54. *Mithr.* 12.28.

55. A Momigliano, *The Development*, 68. The Peripatetic concern with the descriptive anecdote went back to Aristotle. This has been well brought out by George Huxley. Aristotle's 'fondness for scarcely relevant anecdotes takes on a meaning within the unifying scope of his historical thought. Anecdotes may be told for their own sake, and Aristotle tells many just because they take his fancy. But anecdotes are for him an essential part of biography, and so of historiography, because in Aristotle's view the deeds and experiences of individuals are the matter of history — even the deeds of an individual such as Alkibiades, since history deals with the particular, *to kath' ekaston, ti Alkibiades epraksen e ti epathen. Poet.*, 1451b 11.' 'Aristotle's Interest in Biography', *GRBS*, 15, 212-13.

56. Diog. Laert., 2.41. Anecdote 20 in Riginos, *Platonica*, 56-8.

57. For the relations between Josephus and Justus, see Shaye J.D. Cohen, *Josephus in Galilee and Rome*, 15-23, who reviews the *Quellenforschung*. Also, Abraham Schalit, 'Josephus und Justus: Studien zur Vita des Josephus', *Klio*, 26, 67-95; H. Luther, *Josephus und Justus von Tiberias: Ein Beitrag zur Geschichte des jüdischen Aufstandes*, is still of value.

58. *Vita* 9, 39-40. On Justus, besides the works mentioned in n.57, see Tessa Rajak, 'Justus of Tiberias', *CQ* n.s. 23, 345-68, whose opinion is that 'It is clear of course that Justus' digression in itself betrays a desire to parade the author's Greek culture', 364. But everybody digresses in order to trot out their learning. She also feels that a Jew from Tiberias could never be at home in the world of Greek culture. 'Justus', 368. If this were so: Josephus would have alerted us to Justus' insecurity. Josephus had few problems in the wider world. Cf. Emil Schurer, *The History of the Jewish People in the Age of Jesus Christ, 175 BC-AD 135*, rev. and ed. Geza Vermes and Fergus Millar, 34-7. Ben Zion Wacholder, *Eupolemus: A Study of Judaeo-Greek Literature*, 298-306.

59. Xen., *Mem.*, 3.6.1.

60. Fairweather, 'Fiction in the Biographies', 232. Also, Stuart notes the reasoning behind this lay in the ancients' 'assumption that the writings of an author were in no transcendental but in a literal sense expressive of his individuality and his personal experience. A certain character was bound to produce a certain type of work and would be incapable of producing any but this type.' 'Authors' Lives', 301. It therefore follows that Aeschylus first introduced drunken characters upon the stage, according to Chamaeleon of Heraclea, a Peripatetic biographer of writers, because he composed his tragedies while drunk. See Anthony J. Podlecki, 'The Peripatetics as Literary Critics', *Phoenix*, 23 (1969), 123. The so called Peripatetic, Satyrus, in his *Life of Euripides* quotes the important dictum 'as are his characters, so is the man'. Podlecki, 'The Peripatetics', 130.

61. Diog. Laert., 3.20.

62. Ingemar Düring, *Aristotle in the Ancient Biographical Tradition*.

63. Düring, *Aristotle*, 235. The fragments have been collected by Marianus Plezia, *Aristoteles Epistularum Fragmenta Testamento*.

64. Euseb., *Praep. Evang.*, 15.2.11.

65. Diog. Laert., 5.2. The story is upheld by A.H. Chroust, *Aristotle*, I, 138-41, and Olaf Gigon, *Vita Aristoteles Marciana*, Kleine Texte für Vorlesungen and Übungen, 59. Düring, *Aristotle*, 233-6, 339-40, and C.M. Mulvany, 'Notes on the Legend of Aristotle', *CR*, 20 (1926), 162-3, argue against the authenticity.

66. D.L., 5.27, lists nine books of letters which Aristotle addressed to Antipater. See Plezia, *Aristoteles Epistularum*. Chroust notes that after Antipater retook Athens in 322, he executed a number of Aristotle's enemies. *Aristotle*, I, 390, n. 31. Antipater of course was Aristotle's chief executor of his will, D.L., 5.11.

67. 'The younger members of the Isocratean school were traditionally unfriendly towards Aristotle ever since the open fight of the fifties.' Düring, *Aristotle*, I, 386. Düring collects the fragments and comments on them, ibid., 373-95. For Epicurean attacks, see Ettore Bignone, *L'Aristotele perduto e la formazione filosofica di Epicuro*^{2}, I, 1-59.

68. Arnaldo Momigliano, 'Second Thoughts on Greek Biography', in *Quinto contributo alla storia degli studi classici e del mondo antico*, I, 47.

69. M.I. Finley, *Aspects of Antiquity*, 77.

70. For discussion of the historiography of biography in modern times, see Stuart, 'Authors' Lives', 287-300, who looks at the literature up till Friedrich Leo. Momigliano, in *The Development*, 8-22, critically reviews the literature from Bruns and Leo to the present. See also Momigliano's 'Second Thoughts', in *Quinto contributo*.

71. Momigliano, *The Development*, 12.

72. Rudolf Pfeiffer, *A History of Classical Scholarship from the Beginnings to the End of the Hellenistic Age*, 129, 150-51, and P.M. Fraser, *Ptolemaic Alexandria*, I, 453, 515, 781, with important notes in Vol. II for Hermippus and his background. Jørgen Mejer, *Diogenes Laertius and His Hellenistic Background*, 32, n.67, tries to put Hermippus' death scenes within the context of Hermippus' other writings and feels that the death scenes have been overrated. He is correct in maintaining that 'the evidence indicates rather that not Hermippus in particular but the Hellenistic tradition as such, and certainly Diogenes, had this morbid interest'. See also F. Wehrli, *Die Schule des Aristoteles. Supplbd. 1: Hermippos der Kallimacher*, 102-6.

73. Diog. Laert., 1.118.

74. A.A. Long, 'Timon of Phlius: Pyrrhonist and Satirist', *Cambridge Philological Society*, 240 (1978), 81.

75. *De Viris illustribus*, Praef.

76. Athen., 58f; 213f. On Satyrus, see Stephenia West, 'Satyrus: Peripatetic or Alexandrian', *GRBS*, 15 (1974), 279-87. In general Podlecki, 'The Peripatetics as Literary Critics', 127-37.

77. Fraser, *Ptolemaic Alexandria*, I, 454.

78. Index, Herc., col. XI, 1ff, 28 [Mekler] = fr. 89 (Wehrli).

79. Athen., 162c = fr. 91 (Wehrli).

80. Momigliano, *The Development*, 84. Pfeiffer, *History of Classical Scholarship*, 150-51.

81. Fraser, *Ptolemaic Alexandria*, I, 7.

82. Wilamowitz, *Antigonos von Karystos*, 27-129.

83. Wilamowitz, *Antigonos*, 158-63. Esther V. Hansen, *The Attalids of Pergamon*, 397-403.

84. The earlier literature is surveyed by Richard Hope, *The Book of Diogenes Laertius*, 37-97, and A. Delatte, *La Vie de Pythagore de Diogène Laërce*, 16-34. See now M. Gigante, 'Diogene Laerzio, storico e cronista dei filosofi antichi', *Atena e Roma*, n.s., 18 (1973), 105-32, and Mejer's thorough monograph, *Diogenes Laertius and His Hellenistic Background*.

85. Mejer, *Diogenes Laertius*, 50.

86. *Alexander*, 1. For an interpretation of this, see J.R. Hamilton, *Plutarch*, XXXVIII; and A.W. Gomme, *A Historical Commentary on Thucydides*, I, 54-5.

87. The letter's authority is effectively defended by Alberto Grilli, 'Zenone

e Antigono II', *RFIC*, 91 (1963), 287-301.

88. For the general background, B.A. von Groningen, 'General Literary Tendencies in the Second Century AD', *Mnemosyne* 18 (1961), 41-56 is useful if harsh. See also G.W. Bowersock, *Greek Sophists in the Roman Empire*, 11-16; 101-9.

89. Cf. Aelius Aristides, 'Oration on the Four', 46, 404, Dindorf.

90. Bowersock, *Greek Sophists*, 16, and especially E.L. Bowie, 'Greeks and Their Past in the Second Sophistic', in M.I. Finley, *Studies in Ancient Society*, 166-209.

91. Philost., *VS*, 485-86. Typically, for Philostratus, Dias persuaded Philip to lead the expedition. There are no other references to Dias. See Wilmer Cave Wright's Introduction to the Loeb. *Philostratus and Eunapius*, XXIII.

92. *De Stoic. rep.*, 1033B-C.

93. *Adv. Col.*, 1126E; *De Stoic. rep.*, 1033B. On Plutarch see C.P. Jones, *Plutarch and Rome*, 3-64.

94. *Max. cum. princ.*, 777A.

95. Cf. Alan Wardman, *Plutarch's Lives*, 219.

96. *Them.*, 2.5.6. Frank J. Frost, *Plutarch's Themistocles: A Historical Commentary*, 67-8. Also, his article, 'Themistocles and Mnesiphilus', *Historia*, 20 (1971), 21.

97. *Solon*, 3.6.

98. Fairweather, 'Fiction', 261-3; Mejer, *Diogenes Laertius*, 62-75, a good discussion with bibliography.

99. On Plutarch's use of sources, see the discussion in Frost, *Plutarch's Themistocles*, who reviews the historiography and concludes that Plutarch was widely read, 40-59.

100. *Per.*, 4. 4-5, 8.1.

101. *Per.*, 6.1. Cf. *Nic.*, 23.5.

102. *Nic.*, 23.1.

103. *Per.*, 4.1.

104. Wardman, *Plutarch's Lives*, 215-25.

105. Ibid., 219-20.

106. *Dion*, 1.3.

107. *Numa*, 20.8; *Dem. Cic. Comp.*, 3.4.

108. *Cleom.*, 2.2.

109. *Lyc.*, 5.10; *Numa*, 8.2.

110. *Numa*, 20.8.

111. The fragments of Aristotle's writings on the Pythagoreans have been collected by Valentin Rose, *Aristoteles Pseudepigraphus*, 193-210. Pages 211-12 of Rose contain the fragments of Aristotle's work, *On the Philosophy of Archytas*. For an account of the Pythagoreans, based primarily on Aristotle, see J.A. Philip, *Pythagoras and Early Pythagoreanism*. Also W.K.C. Guthrie, 'Aristotle as a Historian of Philosophy', *JHS*, 77 (1957), 35-41. Guthrie is reacting to Harold Cherniss's excessive scepticism of Aristotle's truthworthiness. For example, Cherniss's books, *Aristotle's Criticism of Plato and the Academy*, *Aristotle's Criticism of Presocratic Philosophy* and *The Riddle of the Early Academy*.

112. This is the point of view adopted by Philip, *Pythagoras*; W.K.C. Guthrie, *A History of Greek Philosophy*, I, and Walter Burkert, *Lore and Science in Ancient Pythagoreanism*.

113. Philip, while denying any kind of order or brotherhood, concludes that there may have been Pythagorean political associations in the fifth century. *Pythagoras*, 146. His view is that 'any such institution would be unique in the Greek world before the Christian era', 138. That, however, seems to be just the point with the Pythagoreans. Philip also maintains that Porphyry and Iamblichus

based their descriptions of the Pythagorean order on their own times, 139. Festugière is quoted as having shown this, but Festugière only points out that their descriptions were influenced by contemporary conditions. J.A. Festugière, *La Révélation d'Hermès Trismégiste*, II, 35. Philip's use of the concept of 'brotherhood' seems to be inconsistent as well.

114. See the clear statement of Burkert, *Lore and Science*, 97-109; Kurt von Fritz, *Pythagorean Politics*. For Diogenes Laertius, A. Delatte, *La Vie de Pythagore de Diogène Laërce*.

115. E. Rohde, 'Die Quellen des Iamblichus in seiner Biographie des Pythagoras', in *Kleine Schriften*, II, 102-72 (= *Rhein. Mus.* 26 (1871), 554-76, ibid. 27, 23-61.); A. Delatte, *Essai sur la politique pythagoricienne*; A. Rostagni, 'Pitagora e i Pitagorici in Timeo', in *Scritti Minori*, II, pt. 1, 3-50 (= *Atti Accad. d. Scienze Torino*, 49 (1913-14), 373-95, 554-74.)

116. Von Fritz, *Pythagorean Politics*, 68ff. E.L. Minar, Jr., *Early Pythagorean Politics in Practice and Theory*, independently of von Fritz worked out similar conclusions as to the chronology of the break-up of the Society.

117. Guthrie, *HGP*, I, 171, n.1: '[it is] so exceptionally lucid that it may be taken as a model introduction to source-criticism, whether or not his results are accepted individually.'

118. Ingemar Düring, *Herodicus the Cratetean: A Study in the Anti-Platonic Tradition*, 136.

119. Düring, ibid., 157. Commenting on this, E. Tigerstedt remarks drily: 'This seems a bit hard on the musicians.' *Interpreting Plato*, 121, n. 122.

120. Philip, *Pythagoras*, 14.

121. Arnaldo Momigliano, *The Development of Greek Biography*, 76.

122. See Fritz Wehrli, *Die Schule des Aristoteles*[2], *II: Aristoxenus*, 49, 57-8. Wehrli has collected the fragments (fr. 11-41).

123. D.L., 8.20; *VP*, 36; Iamb. *VP*, 150. Bukert, *Lore and Science*, 107, n.54, 180.

124. D.L., 8.46.

125. Iamb., *VP*, 235-7, and Porphyry, *VP*, 59.

126. Athen., 12.545.

127. Testimonia and comments found in Riginos, *Platonica*, 124-126 (Anecdote 79). For the controversies this story has generated, see Tigerstedt, *Interpreting Plato*, 70-73, with references.

128. Cicero, *Tusc.*, 1.18.41; *Epist. ad Atticum*, 13.32.

129. Werner Jaeger, *Aristotle*, 455-61. Dicaearchus is the champion of the primacy of the practical life, as opposed to the theoretical life. The latter view was held by Theophrastus. For Pythagoras, the most noteworthy exponent of this position was Heraclides of Pontus. See H.B. Gottschalk, *Heraclides of Pontus*, 23-36, for an analysis of the conversation between Pythagoras and Leon of Phlius.

130. Gellius, *N.A.*, 4.11.14; von Fritz, *Pythagorean Politics*, 26-7. Dicaearchus' assertion that Pythagoras had been a harlot in a previous existence is mythological debunking with a vengeance. It may have been intended as a joke about metempsychosis, but the result would have been the same.

131. Von Fritz, *Pythagorean Politics*, 66.

132. Arnaldo Momigliano, *Essays in Ancient and Modern Historiography*, 51, with a bibliographical note, 58-60.

133. For Polybius' polemic against Timaeus, see F.W. Walbank, 'Polemic in Polybius', *JRS*, 52 (1962), 5-12.

134. A. Rostagni, 'Un nuovo capitolo nella storia della Retorica e della Sofistica', in *Scritti Minori*, I, 1-59 (= *Studi Ital. di Filologia Classica*, n.s., 2 (1922), 148-201); de Vogel, *Pythagoras and Early Pythagoreanism*, 58-148. Against the authenticity, see Burkert, *Lore and Science*, 115, n.38; Morrison,

'Pythagoras', 52, Minar, *EPP*, 7 (though he uses the material).
   135. Justin, 20.4, 6-12; D.S., 10.3, 1-3. De Vogel, *Pythagoras*, 60-69.
   136. For the earlier history of the problem, see de Vogel, *Pythagoras*, 141, n.2.
   137. Dindorf, Scholia in Hom. Odyss., 1.9.25.
   138. Rostagni, *Scritti Minori*, I, 14ff.
   139. Ibid., 55.
   140. De Vogel, *Pythagoras*, 227. She notes: 'At the time they were in the news; a generation afterwards, they were in all probability forgotten.' Hence, Aristotle was ignorant of the orations.
   141. De Vogel, ibid., 62.
   142. Pointed out by M.I. Finley, *Ancient Sicily*, 91.
   143. D.S., 16.6.20.
   144. See W.H. Porter, *Plutarch: Life of Dion*, XX.
   145. Riginos, *Platonica*, 204-5. Aristotle mentions Dion in his *Politics*, 1312a 4-6, 33-9; 12b 16-17.
   146. Aristox., *ap.*, Lucian, *Paras.*, 34.
   147. Plato as son of Apollo, Diog. Laert., 3.2. The Apollonian tradition is examined by Riginos, *Platonica*, 9-32.
   148. Guthrie, *HGP*, IV, 10. Cf. Porter, *Plutarch*, XX-XXII.
   149. Glenn R. Morrow, *Plato's Epistles*, 3-16; Paul Friedländer, *Plato*, I, 236-45; Tigerstedt, *Interpreting Plato*, 31-51, 69-74 with notes; Kurt von Fritz, *Platon in Sizilien und das Problem der Philosophenherrschaft*, 8-11, takes the problem briefly from Bentley to the computer. See the interesting article by M. Isnardi Parenti, 'Rilegenda *il Platone* di Ulrich von Wilamowitz-Moellendorff', *Annali della Scuola Normale Superiore di Pisa*, Classe di Lettere e Filosofia, 147-67. Among the more important books to come out recently are, for the authenticity of *Epistle Seven*, von Fritz, *Platon in Sizilien*; against, Ludwig Edelstein, *Plato's Seventh Letter*.
   150. Finley, *History of Sicily*, 92-3.
   151. Ibid., 205. Finley is equally upset with the conclusions that von Fritz draws from his book, namely that the intellectual should remain aloof from politics. Citing Acton and Kant on the corrupting effects of power, von Fritz says, 'Der Korrumpierende Effekt des Besitzes der Gewalt besteht hier in der Uberhebung und "Ungerichtigheit", die sie in der Seele dessen, der sie bestitzt, erzeugt.' *Platon in Sizilien*, 140. See VIII-IX, 139-40.
   152. Cf. also Morrow's remarks, *Plato's Epistles*, 13-16, and, in general, Ronald Syme in *Pseudepigraphica*, I, 1-18.
   153. G.J.D. Aalders in *Pseudepigraphica* I, 181.
   154. Norman Gulley, 'The Authenticity of the Platonic Epistles', in ibid., 105-30; G.J.D. Aalders, 'Political Thought and Political Programs in the Platonic Epistles', in ibid., 147-75.
   155. Konrad Geiser, 'Plato's Enigmatic Lecture "On the Good" ', *Phronesis*, 25 (1980), 5-37; Kurt von Fritz, 'The Philosophical Passage in the Seventh Platonic Letter and the Problem of Plato's "Esoteric" Philosophy' in J.P. Anton and G.L. Kustas (eds.), *Essays in Ancient Greek Philosophy*, 408-47.
   156. J.R. Hamilton, 'The Letters in Plutarch's *Alexander*', *PACA*, 4 (1961), 9. See also the author's *Plutarch Alexander*, IX-X. Lionel Pearson, 'The Diary and Letters of Alexander the Great', *Historia*, 3 (1954/5), 429-55.
   157. Quoted by Friedländer, *Plato*, 236. See also Marian Plezia's commentary on Aristotle's letter to Alexander in 'Lettre d'Aristote à Alexandre sur la politique envers les cités', ed. and trans. Jozef Biolauski, *Archiwum Filologiczne*, 25 (1970), 164.
   158. M.I. Finley, *Aspects of Antiquity*, 80.

159. Tod, 65.
160. The sources have been closely scrutinised by D.E.W. Wormell, 'The Literary Tradition Concerning Hermias of Atarneus', *Yale Classical Studies*, 5 (1935), 57-92. Didymus relied on Hermippus, 'The Literary Tradition', 80. See also Düring, *Aristotle*, 272-83, who collects the sources.
161. Wormell, 'The Literary Tradition', 66-74.
162. Morrow, *Plato's Epistles*, 209, n.1, with bibliography. J. Harward, *The Platonic Epistles*, 183ff., also surveys the earlier literature. Harward believes the Epistle authentic.
163. E. Beckermann and J. Sykutris, 'Speusipps Brief an König Philipp', *Berichte über d. Verh. d. Sach Akad. d. Wissensch.*, 80.
164. On Theopompus' letter, see text and commentary in D.E.W. Wormell, 'The Literary Tradition', 66-74.
165. From Georges Mathieu's Introduction, *Isocrate*, Bude ed., IV: 1962, 183. Cf. Larue Van Hook General Introduction, *Isocrates*, Loeb. Classical Library, III, 367-8 with bibliography in 368, n.a., who is also convinced of the letters' genuineness.
166. 'The Spurned Doxy: An Unnoticed Topos in English Academic Autobiography', *CW*, 73 (1980), 305-6. The reply by Thomas Knowles, 'The Spurned Doxy and the Dead Bride: Some Ramifications for Ancient *Topoi*', *CW*, 73 (1980), 223-5, does not alter Calder's argument.

2. Pythagoras and the Pre-Socratics

1. Dicaearchus, *ap.* D.L., 1.40.
2. Hermippus, *ap.* D.L., 1.42.
3. Dic., *ap.* D.L., 1.41.
4. Hermann Fränkel, *Early Greek Poetry and Philosophy*, 239.
5. D.L., 1.68; Hdt., 7.235.
6. Clem. Alex., *Strom.*, 4.19. Burn thinks he was ruler of Lindas. A.R. Burn, *The Lyric Age of Greece*, 207.
7. D.L., 1.84; cf. 1.88, 'all men are bad'.
8. Burn, *The Lyric Age*, 209.
9. The term is Fränkel's, *Early Greek Poetry*, 240.
10. W.K.C. Guthrie, *The Greeks and Their Gods*[2], 183-4.
11. *Republic*, 4.427b.
12. Similarly, L.S. Feuer has remarked on the conscious or unconscious identification of modern intellectuals with Moses and the Mosaic myth. They see themselves taking up the cause of the exploited, moved by nothing baser than selfless idealism. Suffering exile and imprisonment, the intellectual leads his people to their historic victory. The people, however, are psychologically unprepared to fulfil the great man's vision, and so he reluctantly sets himself up as a benevolent and temporary dictator for the purpose of re-educating them morally for their new life. Before his death, albeit eternally alive in the memories of his grateful people, the leader now the revered lawgiver 'glimpses afar the new existence'. *Ideology and the Ideologist*, 2.
13. On this question, see the important article by Werner Jaeger in *Aristotle*, 426-61.
14. Ibid., 450-61.
15. Ibid., 452.
16. D.L., 1.25. Cf. Guthrie, *HGP*, I, 50-52.

17. Cf. *Rep.*, 508d.
18. *Theaet.*, 174a.
19. Aristotle, *Politics*, 1.4.4-6.
20. Jaeger, *Aristotle*, 461.
21. E. Schrödinger, *Nature and the Greeks*, 51-66.
22. Ibid., 53.
23. Ibid. The emphasis is Schrödinger's.
24. G.L. Huxley, *The Early Ionians*, 103. On page 79, however, he quotes approvingly Demodocus' remark, 'The Milesians are not fools, but they act as if they were.' Diehl. f.1.
25. Heracl. Pont., *ap.* Athen., 12.527A; Hdt., 5. 28-9; Huxley, *The Early Ionians*, 80.
26. Diehl., f. 12, trans. Huxley.
27. Hdt., 1.170; Huxley, *The Early Ionians*, 95.
28. Hdt., 1.75.
29. Burn, *The Lyric Age*, 327.
30. A.D. Winspear, *The Genesis of Plato's Thought*, 112.
31. S.H. Humphreys, *Anthropology and the Greeks*, 222; cf. Fränkel, *Early Greek Poetry*, 342-3. Hdt., 5.36, 125 for Hecataeus' role as adviser.
32. Aelian, *Var. Hist.*, 3.17.
33. John Burnet, *Early Greek Philosophy*, 52, n.2. Anaximander's identity is sceptically treated by Huxley, *The Early Ionians*, 101.
34. Guthrie, *HGP*, I, 413-15.
35. Humphreys, *Anthropology*, 220. As Fränkel notes, 'Solon speaks to the heart of his hearers in order to convince them by logic, vividly, to be sure, but above all rationally.' *Early Greek Poetry*, 219.
36. Thinkers such as Xenophanes and Hesiod had dwelt on political themes. What makes Solon unique was that he threw himself into the political fray, something Xenophanes seemed unwilling to do. As opposed to Hesiod, Solon felt that greed and injustice are intimately associated with the inner life of the *polis*. He writes: 'By my soul I am bidden to teach the Athenian people;/ What great evils and pains lawlessness brings to the state,/ Just as the well lawed state makes all things fitting and even/ It fetters those who would trample on justice and right.' Diehl., f. 3.26, trans. Fränkel. A. Lesky feels that in Solon's recognition of cause and effect within the life of a community, we find the germ of an idea that was to culminate in Plato's *Republic*. *A History of Greek Literature*, 126. Cf. W. Jaeger, 'Solon's Eunomia', in *Five Essays*, 77 ff. The distinction between Solon and Hesiod is minimised by H. Lloyd-Jones, *The Justice of Zeus*, 44.
37. *Phaedr.*, 258c.
38. *Ath. Pol.*, 5-13.
39. Felix Jacoby, *Atthis: The Local Chronicles of Ancient Athens*, 154, Cf. 77, 154-5.
40. *Ath. Pol.*, 9.2.
41. *Pol.*, 11, 9.4. In the *Politics*, Aristotle's aim was to show that Solon desired and founded a mixed constitution by combining the Council of the *Aereopagus*, elective magistracies and popular law courts. On Aristotle and Solon, see James Day and Mortimer Chambers, *Aristotle's History of Athenian Democracy*, 66-93, 97-8.
42. *Aereop.*, 16.
43. *Antid.*, 232.
44. Plut., *Sol.*, 12. 4-5; Arist., *Ath. Pol.*, 1; Neanthes, *ap.* Athen., 13.662C. For Epimenides, see E.R. Dodds, *The Greeks and the Irrational*, 141-3; Erwin Rohde, *Psyche*, 300-303; both with comparative material. The relationship between Epimenides and Solon, found only in Plutarch, is held to be plausible by

Freeman on the grounds that fear of pollution would have been magnified by reverses in war at a time when Solon was prominent in Athens. Kathleen Freeman, *The Work and Life of Solon*, 167. Reviewing the anecdotes, Freeman is of the opinion that 'these stories ... far from proving that Epimenides is a fiction, plainly are grouped about a personality, and indeed, stray only a little way from the facts'. Rohde thunders: 'Because some parts of the story of Epimenides and his life are fabulous, to doubt the truth of his entirely non-fabulous purification from murder is a monstrous inversion of true historical method.' *Psyche*, 320, n.120.

 45. D.L., 1.114. Burnet, *Early Greek Philosophy*, 150-51.
 46. D.L., 1.115, 114.
 47. G.W. Calhoun, *Athenian Clubs in Politics and Litigation*, 7.
 48. Minar, *Early Pythagorean Politics*, 73.
 49. Burn, *The Lyric Age*, 314-18. A. Andrewes, *The Greek Tyrants*, 117-24.
 50. J.A. Philip, *Pythagoras and Early Pythagoreanism*, 185; D.J. de Vogel, *Pythagoras and Early Pythoragoreanism*, 20-24.
 51. Hdt., 4.95; D.L., 8.1. See the collection of sources in R. Cuccioli Melloni, *Ricerche sul Pitagorismo*, I, 40ff., and M. Timpanaro Cardini, *Pitagorici: Testimonianze e Frammenti*, I, 12ff.
 52. Minar, *EPP*, 1.
 53. Ibid., 2-3.
 54. Andrewes, *Greek Tyrants*, 120.
 55. The latest analysis of Greek non-Greek relations is A. Momigliano, *Alien Wisdom: The Limits of Hellenization*, who, however, does not focus on Egypt. On the relationship between Greeks and Egyptians, particularly the Greek image of the Egyptians, see Christian Froidement, *Le mirage Egyptien dans la littérature grecque d'Homère à Aristote*.
 56. Hdt., 2.77; 4.95; Empedocles, *ap.* Por., *VP*, 30; Heracleitus, *ap.* D.L., 8.6.
 57. Isoc., *Bus.*, 28. Froidement, *Le mirage*, 246-50.
 58. Hdt., 2.123.
 59. On this topic, see Walter Federn, 'The Transformations in the Coffin Texts: A New Approach', *JNES*, 19 (1960), 241-57, esp. 243.
 60. Plut., *Quest. conv.*, 8.8.2; Isoc., *Bus.*, 11; Por., *VP*, 11; Iamb., *VP*, 12ff.
 61. For Persia, see Aristoxenus, *ap.* Hippolytus, *Ref.*, 1.2.12, D.L., 8.3, Valer. Max, 8.7.2; other sources in Guthrie *HGP*, I, 253-4. Babylon: Strabo, 9.1.16; Apollonius, *ap.*, Iamb., *VP*, 19, Por., *VP*, 6, Justin, 20.4.3. For travels in general, A. Delatte, *La Vie de Pythagore de Diogène Laërce*, 52-4, and E. Zeller's exhaustive notes in *A History of Greek Philosophy*, I, 324-35. Recently, N. Demand, 'Pythagoras, Son of Mnesarchus', *Phronesis*, 18 (1973), 91-6 has argued that Pythagoras' travels were in the nature of business trips taken on behalf of his father. I do not find her argument persuasive.
 62. Aristox., *ap.* Iamb., *VP*, 147. Cf. W. Burkert, *Lore and Science*, 172.
 63. Aristox, *ap.* Iamb., *VP*, 100, D.L., 8.19. Cf. Ael., *VH*, 12.32.
 64. De Vogel, *Pythagoras*, 3.
 65. Phoenicians: Por., *VP*, 6. Sidon: Iamb., *VP*, 14.
 66. Alexander Polyhistor., *ap.* Clem., *Strom.*, 1. 304B; Eus., *Praep. Ev.*, 10.4.10; J. Ferguson takes the Indian connection seriously. 'There is no reason to doubt the general tradition of a transcendent genius who has moulded his thought to that of India.' *Utopias of the Ancient World*, 46. His attempt to show the Pythagorans as 'the mediating power' between Plato's Republic and Hinduism is not convincing. See his *Moral Values in the Ancient World*, 25-7. Iamb., *VP*, 151, includes the Celts and Iberians.
 67. Josephus, *Con. Ap.*, 1.22. Also Clem., *Strom.*, 5. 560A; Euseb., *Praep.*

Ev., 13.12.1. The subject of Pythagoras' Jewish connections and the legends that arose are extensively treated in Isidore Levy, *La Légende de Pythagore de Grèce en Palestine*, 136ff.

68. Por., *VP*, 11. Zeller's words of caution are quite apt: 'Each later writer has more to tell than his predecessor; and in proportion as the acquaintance of the Greeks with the Oriental civilised nations increases, the extent of the journeys which brought the Samian philosopher to be instructed by them likewise increases. This is the way legends are formed and not historical tradition.' *History of Greek Philosophy*, I, 329-30.

69. Minar, *EPP*, 4.

70. D.L., 8.6. On *historia*, see Aram M. Frenkian, 'Die Historia des Pythagoras', *Maia*, 11 (1959), 243-5.

71. G. Vlastos, 'Theology and Philosophy in Early Greek Thought', in D.J. Furley and R.E. Allen (eds.), *Studies in Pre-Socratic Philosophy*, I, 113.

72. See the discussion and reconstruction of the poem in H. Fränkel, *Early Greek Poetry*, 287-90.

73. Diehl., f. 5, trans. R. Latimore.

74. Diehl., f. 37, trans. Willis Barnstone.

75. Aristox., *ap*. Por., *VP*, 9.

76. Ibid., 21; Iamb., *VP*, 33-4.

77. Guthrie, *HGP*, I, 174.

78. 'He then found his native island under the despotism of Polykrates, which rendered it an unsuitable place either for free sentiments or for marked individuals.' G. Grote, *History of Greece*, IV, 83.

79. Aristox., *ap*. Iamb., *VP*, 20.

80. Quite possibly a number of disciples left with Pythagoras. Cf. Fränkel's speculations, *Early Greek Poetry*, 270.

81. Iamb., *VP*, 20, 25.

82. Hdt., 4.95. See F. Hartog, 'Salmoxis: le Pythagore des Gètes ou l'autre de Pythagore', *Annali della Sc. Norm. di Pisa. Cl. di lett. e. fil.*, 8 (1978), 15-42, gives a basic discussion. M. Eliade, *Zalmoxis: The Vanishing God*, trans. Willard R. Trask is interesting for the Thracian background, but see the warnings of Hartog, 15. On Herodotus and Egyptian religion, see Froidemont, *Le mirage Egyptien*, 187-206. More generally, T.S. Brown, 'Herodotus Speculates on Egypt', *A.J. Phil.*, 86 (1965), 60-76.

83. Burkert, *Lore and Science*, 128.

84. Morrison points out an Ionian precedent in the common meals the *agathoi* gave themselves in their houses where they would have been enlightened or at least entertained by the *sophistes*, 'Pythagoras of Samos', *CQ*, 50 (1956), 140. Also, Hartog, 'Salmoxis', 15-30. M. Detienne emphasises the military character of the meetings, 'C'est parce que ce mage [Salmoxis] les avait convaincus de l'immortalité de l'âme que les Thraces acquièrent la réputation d'un peuple porté plus qu'un autre à l'*andreia*, au courage militaire. L'information de Timée, à travers Justin, que l'arrivée de Pythagore marqua à Crotone un renouveau de traditions militaires n'est certes pas sans fondements.' 'Communications', in *Quinto Convegno di Studi sulla Magna Graecia*, 153. The volume is entitled *Filosofia e Scienze in Magna Graecia*.

85. In their own ways the society doctor and the ascetic philosopher came to minister to the same strata of society. On Democedes, see T.J. Dunbabin, *The Western Greeks*, 370.

86. On the cult of Apollo in Croton and Metapontum, Giulio Gianelli, *Culti e Miti della Magna Graecia*, 151-3; 61-5.

87. Jean Bayet, *Les origines de l'Hercule romain*, 15-16.

88. Burkert, *Lore and Science*, 113. Marcalla was an important cult centre as

well, but it belonged to Croton. 113. Gianelli, *Culti e Miti*, 162-7.

89. Iamb., VP, 152. Bayet, *Les Origines*, 17. M. Detienne, 'Héracles, héros pythagoricien', *Revue de l'Histoire des Religions*, 158 (1960), 19-53.

90. Marcel Detienne, 'La cuisine de Pythagore', *Archives Sociologiques des Religions*, 29 (1970), 147.

91. Dunbabin, *The Western Greeks*, 357.

92. Justin, 20.2. 13-14.

93. Pausanius, 3.19. 11-13; Strabo, 261; D.S., 8.32.

94. Burn, *The Lyric Age*, 375. Dunbabin, *The Western Greeks*, 359.

95. Justin, 20.4.1.

96. The implied statement is that they were sinking to the level of the Sybarites.

97. On alliance coins see Barclay V. Head, *Historia Numorum*, LXIII-LXIV. Dunbabin, *The Western Greeks*, 82-3; Burn, *The Lyric Age*, 384. U. Kahrstedt, 'Zur Geschichte Grossgriechenlands in 5ten Jahrhundert', *Hermes*, 53 (1918), 180.

98. Tim., *ap*. Athen., 12.520a; 521a. Hdt., 5.44, 47; D.S., 12.9; Ps. Her. Pont., *ap*. Athen., 12.521a. Dunbabin, *The Western Greeks*, 78-80.

99. Burn, *The Lyric Age*, 384, n.56; T.S. Brown, *Timaeus of Tauromenium*, 58.

100. Hdt., 5.47.

101. D.S., 12.9. 2-4.

102. D.S., 19.9.4.

103. Iamb., *VP*, 177, cf. 133.

104. 'The worst atrocity wrought by Greeks against a Greek city in that era.' Burkert, *Lore and Science*, 116.

105. Phylarchus, *ap*. Athen., 12.520b, 521d-e; Her. Pont., *ap*. Athen 12.521e-f.

106. Gouldner, *Enter Plato*, 15-16.

107. Minar, *EPP*, 10-11.

108. Ibid., 11-12.

109. A.F.C. Wallace, 'Revitalization Movements', in S.M. Lipset and N.J. Smelser (eds.), *Sociology: The Progress of a Decade*, 211.

110. Guthrie, *The Greeks and Their Gods*, 326-32. Lower-class orientation is maintained by H.J. Rose in his review of Guthrie, in *JHS*, 55 (1935), 260.

111. Tim., *ap*. Iamb., *VP*, 37-57, Dic., *ap*. Por., *VP*, 18. Also, Justin, 20. 4. 6-12 and D.S., 10.3 (both probably derived from Timaeus).

112. Justin, 20.4. 6-7. Pythagoras himself was never seen either laughing or weeping according to Por., *VP*, 35.

113. D.S., 10.3.3. Grote's adjective for Pythagoras' preaching was 'electric'. Even Pythagoras' fourth-century biographers are 'charged' by the tales of the philosopher. Grote, *History of Greece*, IV, 85, 86. Pythagoras' powers of persuasion are clearly revealed in Porphyry's account of how the philosopher persuaded the dictator of Centuripe, Simichus, to relinquish his office and set up a government on Pythagorean lines. Non-Pythagoreans were to hold office; presumably Pythagorean politicians would emerge in the course of time. The wealth of the former dictator was distributed to his sister and others – no doubt select citizens. Simichus thus emerges as a Pythagorean Hermius. Por., *VP*, 22. Von Fritz finds this story closely resembles Plato's and Dion's attempts to convert the younger Dionysius to Platonic principles. The resemblance between Pythagoreanism and the Academy as political activists, although it exists, should not be followed too far. The members of the Academy, as will be seen, acted primarily as individuals motivated less by religion or philosophy than by romanticism in so far as they were motived by ideas at all and nowhere achieved the discipline and unanimity of action that the Italian Greeks did. *Pythagorean Politics*, 101.

114. Iamb., *VP*, 51; Aristox., *ap*. D.L., 8.11.

115. Cf. 'Pythagoras was ... not so much an innovator as a reformer ... The reforms he carried out at Croton may be described as a reform of *nomoi* in the sense of institutions rather than a political constitution ... The Pythagoreans, politically, were for the conservation of the ancestral constitution (*patrios politeia*) against democratic change.' Morrison, 'Pythagoras', 135, 150. From another point of view see Gouldner, who summarises Wallace. Gouldner, *Enter Plato*, 124. Wallace defines revivalistic movement as one which emphasises 'the institutions of customs, values, and even aspects of nature which are thought to have been in the mazeway of previous generations but are not now present'. 'Revitalization Movements', 210. A mazeway in turn is the mental image a person has of society and culture, his body and its behavioural regularities to the end of minimising stress 'at all levels of the system'. The history of Pythagorean activism can be seen as an initially successful attempt at mazeway reformulation, or, in English, a reduction of the tensions which beset individuals – particularly those of the ruling class – followed by renewed and intensified stresses that ultimately destroyed the brotherhood as a political unit along with the empire it had come to control. In this context, it is useful to compare Pythagoras with the Senecan prophet, Handsome Lake, who preached to his dispirited tribe and 'demanded the repression of desire rather than its ritual satisfaction and offered in place of human beings the more abstract images of the Creator and the Punisher, of heaven and hell, and of the prophet as the objects of strivings for dependency'. A.F.C. Wallace, *The Death and Rebirth of the Seneca*, 253.

116. Iamb., *VP*, 53.

117. Aelian, *V.H.*, 2.26.

118. In a crucial passage which possibly comes from Aristotle, Pythagoras takes an arrow from Abaris, travels on it and thus establishes himself as the Hyperborean Apollo. Iamb., *VP*, 140. Discussed by Levy, *Recherches*, 13-19.

119. Aristox., *ap*. Iamb., *VP*, 174. Cf. 203.

120. Ibid., VP, 82, 203.

121. Ibid., 174.

122. Minar, *EPP*, 129.

123. Iamb., *VP*, 85, trans. Dodds.

124. E.R. Dodds, *The Greeks and the Irrational*, 152. For the mind-body dichotomy, see also de Vogel, *Pythagoras*, 181, who, in accordance with her belief that the Pythagoreans were the 'gentlest of people' speaks of the sect's attempts to bring *'philia'* between soul and body'. Minar, *EPP*, 122-31, for a harsher view.

125. Minar, *EPP*, 129. Dodds, *The Greeks*, 152.

126. Detienne, 'La cuisine', 147.

127. Por., *VP*, 18.

128. De Vogel, *Pythagoras*, 105.

129. E. Rohde, *Psyche*, 374; cf. E. Delatte, *Essai*, 4.

130. Weber, *Economy and Society*, II, 241. R. Bendix and G. Roth, *Scholarship and Partisanship*, 170-75, for further elaboration.

131. That there was a strong tradition for Pythagoras' previous lives can be seen through the allusions of the fourth-century comic poet Antiphanes, *ap*. Athen., 4. 108e. Dicaearchus' addition of the prostitute Alco as one of Pythagoras' incarnations showed what he thought of the matter. Burkert, *Lore and Science*, 139.

132. According to Nicomachus, *ap*. Por., *VP*, 27. Aelian, *VH*, 2.26, has it Croton and Metapontum while Philostratus *VA*, 4.10, says Thurii and Metapontum. The tradition was well established.

133. Ael., *VH*, 2.26; D.L., 8.11; Iamb., *VP*, 140.

134. Dic., *ap*. Por., *VP*, 19.23-24; Ael., *VH*, 2.26. 4-17; Iamb., *VP*, 60, 143.

135. Weber, *Economy and Society*, II, 440. This duality comes out in the earlier evidence of Pythagoras, some of which has just been quoted. 'To his admirers he is a man of supernatural gifts and power, to the skeptical a charlatan.' Morrison, 'Pythagoras', 136.

136. Iamb., *VP*, 29-30, trans. E.L. Minar.

137. Justin, 20.4.14. This is expanded on by Dicaearchus in D.L., 8.3; 'He sailed away to Croton in Italy, and there he laid down a constitution for the Italian Greeks, and he and his followers were held in great estimation; for being nearly three hundred in number, so well did they govern the state that its constitution was in effect a true aristocracy.'

138. Isoc., *Bus.*, 29.

139. Minar, 23ff. Cf. Charles Cooley's conception of a 'primary group' in *Social Organization*, 26-7.

140. Connor, *The New Politicians*, 63.

141. Dover, *Greek Homosexuality*, 192-4, for a Spartan example.

142. The tale had wide currency in antiquity. D.S., 10.4.3; Por., *VP*, 59-60; Iamb., *VP*, 234-7. Von Fritz, *Pyth. Pol.*, 24-5. However, even this evidence is rejected by Edelstein as a reconstruction of earlier Pythagorean practices. *The Hippocratic Oath*, 42. He follows E. Frank, *Plato und die sogenannten Pythagoreer*, who is sceptical of any plausible reconstruction, as his title indicates.

143. Burkert, *Lore and Science*, 179-80.

144. H.I. Marrou, *A History of Education in Antiquity*, 77; Pierre Boyance, *Le Culte des Muses*, 233-47.

145. *The Sociology of Georg Simmel*, trans. Kurt Wolff, 355.

146. Iamb., *VP*, 72; D.L., 8.10. E.L. Minar, Jr., 'Pythagorean Communism', *AJPh.*, 75 (1944), 34-46, reviews the evidence.

147. D.L., 8.10.

148. Iamb., *VP*, 239. Cf. Theonor's mission in Plut., *de Genio Socratis*, 582D ff. Theonor notes: 'For if it is a noble act to benefit friends it is no disgrace to be benefited by them.' 582F. As well, there is the story of Thestor of Posidonia and the Etruscan Nausithous. The sources for friendship are collected in de Vogel, *Pythagoras*, 258-61.

149. Iamb., *VP*, 257. Von Fritz, *Pyth. Pol.*, 55-65, for source criticism.

150. Matt., 12:50.

151. Iamb., *VP.*, 133, 177; D.S., 12.9.2.

152. Minar, *EPP*, 12.

153. Weber, *Economy and Society*, I, 437. Dodds notes that for such individuals, 'purity, rather than justice had become the cardinal means to salvation'. *The Greeks and the Irrational*, 154.

154. Weber, *Economy and Society*, I, 348.

155. Tim., *ap.* Athen., 12.518e.

156. Ibid.

157. Hippasos was a heretical Pythagorean whose views gravitated to those held by Heraclitus. He no longer felt bound by the anonymity in which other Pythagoreans wrapped themselves. As often happens, the revelation concerned the Achilles tendon of Pythagorean thinking — the square root of two. Aristotle, *Met.*, 984a. 5. If he was the Hippasos who supported Cylon in his rebellion against the philosophers he broke the solidarity of the order in a very public way. Iamb., *VP*, 257. Burnet calls him the *enfant terrible* of Pythagoreanism. *Early Greek Philosophy*, 106, n.1.

158. Iamb., *VP*, 187. Cf. Winspear, *The Genesis of Plato's Thought*, 85.

159. D.S., 12.9.6. On Milo and Heracles, see Detienne, 'Heracles', 20-22; 'La cuisine', 144-6. The Crotoniates were led by the Pythagoreans, but it was not exclusively a Pythagorean war as Detienne maintains. He thinks all ten thousand

Crotonites were converted Pythagoreans. 'La cuisine', 147.

160. Hdt., 5. 44-5; 6.21. D.S., 12.22.1; cf. esp. Strabo, 6. 263; Dunbabin, *Western Greeks*, 363-4. The Crotoniates were reinforced by the Spartan Dorieus who happened to be in the area with a body of colonists intending to found a colony in Sicily. Hdt., 5. 45. The Crotonites denied this.

161. Cylon is called the governor of Sybaris. Iamb., *VP*, 74. Minar, *EPP*, 69-70. Delatte considers this statement 'une tradition inolée', *Essai*, 229. Dunbabin, *The Western Greeks*, 365-6.

162. Iamb., *VP*, 254-5, trans. J.S. Morrison. Morrison, 'Pythagoras', 147, summarises the earlier source criticisms of the passage and gives references.

163. Iamb., *VP*, 74. Von Fritz agrees that Cylon's animosity was due to his exclusion from the order. It is hard to agree with him, however, when he says that 'in spite of the hierarchic tendencies of the order the strongest opposition came from those among the aristocrats who looked upon themselves as the preservers of the old tradition', *Pyth. Pol.*, 98. Most 'traditionalists' would have sided with the Pythagoreans and Cylon's movement appears to be less a return to old traditions than a play for tyranny.

164. Iamb., *VP*, 258.

165. Ibid., 260.

166. Ibid., 259-60.

167. Rose, fr. 192.

168. Cf. Grote, 'The devoted attachment of Pythagoreans for each other is not less emphatically set forth than their contempt for everyone else.' *History of Greece*, IV, 88. Also page 91.

169. Cf. Aristox., *ap.* D.L., 8.34. Minar, *EPP*, 64. On beans: the most comprehensive study is still A. Delatte, 'Faba', 33-57. For two opposing accounts of the taboo on beans, see Robert S. Brumbaugh and Jessica Schwartz. 'Pythagoras and Beans: A Medical Explanation', *Cl. W.*, 73 (1980), 421-2, and M. Detienne, *Dionysos Slain*, trans. Mireille Muellner and Leonard Muellner, 60-61. In 'La cuisine', Detienne attempts a Levi-Straussian analysis and concludes, 'Le système pythagoricien est ainsi construit sur l'écart de deux termes qui s'opposent entre eux comme deux poles: le positif represente par les aromates, le negatif par la fève.' 154.

170. Iamb., VP, 260.

171. Grote makes the interesting speculation that this refusal had as much to do with religious as with political reasons. Sybaris was kept deserted because the Pythagoreans 'may perhaps have been afraid of the name and recollections of the city'. Grote, *History of Greece*, IV, 97.

172. Minar, *EPP*, 71.

173. Iamb., *VP*, 257.

174. Ibid., 257; cf. 136.

175. Ibid., 261.

176. Ibid.

177. D.L., 8.40; Por., *VP*, 57.

178. For the various traditions concerning Pythagoras' death see Philip, *Pythagoras*, 191-2. In death as in his life, the two opposing traditions were at work trying to mould Pythagoras into their preconceived notions of how a philosopher ought to conduct himself in the conflict of life – 'death in the uprising or withdrawal in the face of it'. See the pertinent summary in Philip, 192.

179. Dion. Hal., *Ant. Rom.*, 20.7; Minar, *EPP*, 71-3; von Fritz, *Pyth. Pol.*, 91.

180. Iamb., *VP*, 280.

181. Max Weber's contention that the interest of intellectuals in salvation and therefore escapist religion usually follows a decline in the political power of a dominant ruling stratum needs to be qualified. According to Weber's view,

intellectuals place optimum value on the intellectual and psychological consequences of their spiritual exercises and tend to downplay the importance of their participation in the political affairs of the mundane world. *Economy and Society*, II, 503-6. After the defeat of Sybaris, however, the Pythagoreans were feeling anything but depoliticised. Although fear of becoming politically obsolete was an important consideration in aristocrats enrolling themselves under a religious prophet's banner, the nobles never felt themselves out of the picture and nothing in the revitalised 'éthique chevaleresque' of Pythagoras' doctrine made them devalue themselves in contrast to the world of their fellow citizens. Detienne, 'Communications', 151.

182. Dunbabin, *Western Greeks*, 369-71, gives a glowing cultural sketch of Magna Graecia during this period. Ciaceri, *Storia della Magna Graecia*, II, 188-206, is even more ecstatic. 'Da quanto si è osservato sin qui appare chiaro che già nel VI secolo a. C. le città greche del mezzogiorno d'Italia avevano raggiunto un grado di civilta si elevato, anche di fronte alla Grecia propria, da potere ben meritare l'appellativo di Magna Graecia. Ma ciò non può, senz'altro, affermarsi.' 186.

183. Paus., 6.13.1; Minar, *EPP*, 42-4.

184. Paus., 6.13.1.

185. Minar, *EPP*, 43.

186. Lewis's turn of phrase, *Ecstatic Religion*, 170. Pythagoreanism at this time corresponded to what Lewis has called a central possession cult. Membership is made up of the dominant strata of society; the cult itself stands in the centre of society and intervenes as agents of justice in human affairs. This community considers itself 'chosen by the gods and personally commissioned by them to exercise divine authority among men ... The spirits communicating through their chosen mediums act as the censors of society.' 170, 137. Highly moralistic, their main concern is that evil deeds not go unpunished. 'The moral character which those who believe in them ascribe to these spirits is ... consistent with their actual social role.' 170. With its emphasis on a controlled form of enthusiasm, Pythagoreanism was a possession religion for gentlemen.

187. U. Kahrstedt, 'Zur Geschichte Grossgriechenlands', 180-87, is still the basic study. The evidence is reviewed in de Vogel, *Pythagoras*, 52-5.

188. Dunbabin, *Western Greeks*, 367-8.

189. Por., *VP*, 21.

190. Minar, *EPP*, 38, 39.

191. Ibid., 39.

192. Ibid., 36-49; von Fritz, *Pyth. Pol.*, 84-6.

193. Kahrstedt, 'Zur Geschichte Grossgriechenlands', 185-6.

194. Polyb., 2.39. 1-4. See F.W. Walbank, *A Historical Commentary on Polybius*, I, 222-4.

195. Iamb., *VP*, 250.

196. Von Fritz, *Pyth. Pol.*, 12.

197. Plut., *Per.*, 4.1; Plato, *Alcib.*, 118c. Also Isocrates, *Antid.*, 235. Detienne, 'Communications', 152.

198. Plut., *Per.*, 4.1; V. Ehrenberg, *Sophocles and Pericles*, 92-3. For Damon and Pythagoreans, see J.S. Morrison, 'The Origins of Plato's Philosopher-Statesman', *CQ*, n.s., 8 (1958), 205.

199. Plut., *Per.*, 4.1; Arist., *Ath. Pol.*, 27.4. Also quoted in *Per.*, 9. 2-3. A.E. Raubitschek, *CM*, 16 (1955), 78-83, maintains that Aristotle confused Damon with Damonides. Ehrenberg, Morrison and Derenne in *supra*, 197, 198, maintain the validity of a Pythagorean Damon.

200. K.J. Dover, 'The Freedom of the Intellectual in Greek Society', *Talanta*, 7 (1976), 30, 52-3. On Aristotle and the anti-Periclean tradition, see Chambers and Day, *Aristotle's History*, 140-47. Aristotle contrasts Pericles unfavourably

with Cimon.

201. Eudore Derenne, *Les Procès d'impiété*, 18, 41. Derenne, following Aristotle rather than Plutarch, ignores Damon. In general, see 13-43. Dover, 'The Freedom', 24ff., esp. 51; G.B. Kerferd, *The Sophistic Movement*, 21-2.
202. Morrison, 'The Origins', 206.
203. Minar, *EPP*, 79.
204. Iamb., *VP*, 262.
205. Ibid.
206. Tim., *ap*. Iamb., *VP*, 263.
207. Minar, *EPP*, 44-9; von Fritz, *Pyth. Pol.*, 95-6.
208. Iamb., *VP*, 267.
209. Ibid., 251.
210. Strabo, 6.280.
211. Ibid., 267. There was Pythagorean activity in Tarentum during Pythagoras' lifetime. Por., *VP*, 56. Aristoxenus, *ap*. Iamb., 249.ff. for Archytas and Lysis at Milo's.
212. Por., *VP*, 56.
213. Arist., *Pol.*, 5.2.8; Dunbabin, *Western Greeks*, 149.
214. Minar, *EPP*, 86-92; Ciaceri, *Storia della Magna Graecia*, II, 284 ff., 446. The compromise won the admiration of Aristotle, *Pol.*, 6.3.5.
215. Minar, *EPP*, 91.
216. Grote, *History of Greece*, IV, 318-20.
217. Hdt., 8.122.
218. Xen., *Resp. Lac.*, 11.3.
219. The common meal raises the question of Spartian influence, though of course communal dining was not limited to Sparta. Justin is the only historian who has Pythagoras visit Sparta and Crete 'in order to acquaint himself with the laws of Minos and Lycurgus which had a great reputation at that time'. Justin, 20.4.4. On the Spartan connection see E.N. Tigerstedt, who believes none of it. *The Legend of Sparta in Antiquity*, I, 230, 514, n.19. On the other hand, M. Detienne in a number of articles has made the close connections between the *synhedrion* and the *syssitia* an important key to the understanding of how the Pythagoreans functioned. See 'Des confrères', 127-31; 'Communications', 149-56; 'La cuisine', 146-8.
220. D.L., 8.62.
221. Ibid., 8.66.
222. Ibid.
223. Ibid., 8.51.72.
224. Weber, *Economy and Society*, II, 425.
225. D.L., 8.77.
226. D.K., 111.9. Cf. Guthrie, *HGP*, II, 246-8; Burkert, *Lore and Science*, 153.
227. Gorgias, of course, is the exception. Not surprisingly, Empedocles was himself an accomplished orator and Aristotle apparently called him the father of rhetoric, *ap*. D.L., 8.57.
228. D.L., 8.59-60; 70. Cf. Burkert, *Lore and Science*, 153-4.

3. Plato and the Academy

1. W.B. Yeats, 'The Statesman's Holiday', in *The Collected Poems*, 389.
2. A. Zwerdling, *Yeats and the Heroic Ideal*, 94.
3. On this, see A. Hamilton, *The Appeal of Fascism: A Study of Intellectuals*

and Fascism: 1919-1945, 276-80.

4. Yeats, 'The Second Coming', in *Collected Poems*, 211.

5. William James, *The Will to Believe and Other Essays in Popular Philosophy*, 211.

6. Dic., *ap*. D.L., 3.4. For the complete list see E. Zeller, *Plato and the Older Academy*, 6, n. 6. Like Isocrates, Plato was reported to have a weak voice; yet, he was willing to go before the *Ecclesia* to defend his supporter, Chabrias. D.L., 3. 23-4. Quite obviously, I do not wish to assert that Plato was incapable of a strenuous mood. The quality, not to speak of the quantity, of his writings, attest to that. With Plato, *theoria* and *praxis* need not be taken as being in opposition with each other; I believe the former to be an over-compensation for his lack of political participation. It must be remembered that Plato saw himself — and was seen by others — as a politician before he became a philosopher. For an opposite point of view, see P. Merlan, 'Form and Content in Plato's Philosophy', *JHI*, 8 (1947), 16 ff. For a discussion of Plato's over-compensation, see Dodds, *Greeks and the Irrational*, 216, who takes his cue from A. Koestler's illuminating essay 'The Yogi and the Commissar', in *The Yogi and the Commissar*, 15-25, 205-32.

7. *Charm.*, 155a.

8. Ibid., 158a.

9. G.C. Field, *Plato and His Contemporaries*, 4. Also, Guthrie, *HGP*, IV, 9-12.

10. On Socrates and *eros*, see Guthrie, *HGP*, III, 69-82; K.J. Dover, *Greek Homosexuality*, 153-65. 'Socrates' here is the Socrates as depicted by Plato and, to a lesser extent, Xenophon.

11. Xen., *Hellen*., 2.3.15-4.19. See also Philost., *VS*, 501-3.

12. *Ep*., 7. 324d. Guthrie comments that in Critias Plato found 'the perfect example of a fine nature ruined by the society of his day, and by sophistic teaching with the emphasis on the attainment of power and indifference to the moral consequences of rhetorical and debating skill'. *HGP*, III, 298.

13. Xen., *Mem*., 3.6. 1-18.

14. Ibid., 1.2.30. Guthrie, *HGP*, III, 70.

15. J. Burnet, *From Thales to Plato*, 168; Guthrie, *HGP*, IV, 11; G. Devereux, 'Greek Pseudo-Homosexuality and the "Greek Miracle" ', *Symbolae Osloensis*, 42 (1967), 78.

16. Diogenes Laertius says that Plato and Socrates first met when Plato was 20. 3.26. He cites no authority for this and Plato may well have been acquainted with Socrates before this. Certainly, Plato had the opportunity for meeting Socrates and Socrates enjoyed the company of young men.

17. Plato, *Symp*., 221c, trans. Michael Joyce.

18. *Apol*., 32c; cf. *Ep*., 7. 324e-325a.

19. *Ep*., 7. 325a.

20. *Apol*., 32b-c; *Ep*., 7. 324c-d. Plato speaks of the democratic regime as being generally detested and his youthful hopes that an unjust reign would be replaced by a just one.

21. Ibid., 325a-b. On Thrasybulus, Xen., *Hellen*., 2.4.2ff.

22. *Ep*., 7. 325b.

23. *Apol*., 31e-32a.

24. *Rep*., 6. 496d.

25. *Ep*., 7. 330d.

26. Ibid., 7. 331a.

27. *Ep*., 5. 322a-b.

28. Ibid., 322b.

29. Diehl., f. 24, trans. W. Barnstone.

Notes

30. Plato uses a number of such similes to defend his political inactivity in Athens. Morrow, *Plato's Epistles*, 137-42. Athenian democracy, however, proved itself to be far more vigorous than its detractors maintained. Democrats may have been led astray on occasion, but their main concern came from oligarchically biased individuals and they had cause to be wary of Plato. For spirited rebuffs of Plato's view, see A.W. Gomme, 'The Athenian Democracy and Its Critics', in *Athenian Democracy*, 41-72; M.I. Finley, 'Plato and Practical Politics', in *Aspects of Antiquity*, 82-8.
31. Aristides was an exception, probably because he was a paragon of honesty. *Gorg.*, 526b. Even here, though, Plato had second thoughts. *Meno*, 94a.
32. *Gorg.*, 515e.
33. Ibid., 519a.
34. Ibid., 521d.
35. Ibid., 522a.
36. Guthrie, *HGP*, IV, 502.
37. Hermodorus, *ap.* D.L., 2.106. Field, *Plato and His Contemporaries*, 12. Guthrie, *HGP*, IV, 14. Zeller, *Plato*, 14-24 with notes. Mekler, *Index Acad. Herc.*, col. 6-9. Plato's travels are chronicled by Zeller, *Plato*, 14-24, and A.S. Riginos, *Platonica*, 61-9.
38. D.L., 3.8. Field, *Plato and His Contemporaries*, 5; Guthrie, *HGP*, IV, 14.
39. Field, *Plato and His Contemporaries*, 6.
40. Ibid.
41. Ibid. Cf. Dunbabin, *The Western Greeks*, 361.
42. Xen., *Hellen.*, 4.4.14.
43. Guthrie, *HGP*, III, 186.
44. Winspear and Silverberg, *Who Was Socrates?*, 62. See Guthrie's comments, *HGP*, III, 94-6.
45. Nepos, *Epam.*, 2. For Lysis, Aristox. *ap.*, Iamb., *VP*, 250; D.L., 8.7; and Nepos, *Epam.*, 2.
46. *Rhet.*, 2.23.11. Probably from Alcidimus.
47. *Crito*, 44b-45c, 53b; *Phaedo*, 99a; Minar, *EPP*, 93. Cf. Morrison, 'The Origins of Plato's Philosopher-Statesman', 202-3.
48. *Ep.*, 7. 325d.
49. Ibid.
50. Ibid., 326b.
51. Ibid., 326b-c.
52. Mekler, *Index Acad. Herc.*, cols. 6-9.
53. Cic., *Rep.*, 1.10. Cf. *Fin.*, 5.29.87; *Tusc. Disp.*, 1.17.39.
54. Morrison, 'The Origins', 211.
55. Nepos, *Dion*, 2. See W.H. Porter, *Plutarch's Life of Dion*, 49-50.
56. Although interested in the Pythagoreans, Dion was never a member of the order. Besides creating a conflict of interests which the elder Dionysius would not appreciate, the order's insistence on things in common may well have made the prince reluctant. For the wealthy Sicilian it was an expensive way to purchase metaphysics. Plato relieved him of such anxieties.
57. Plut., *Dion*, 4. 1-3.
58. Grote discusses the impact with great rhetorical vigour. His contention that the relationship between Dion and Plato 'was not unworthy of being compared with those enthusiastic aspirations which the young Spartan kings Agis and Kleomenes imbibed, a century afterwards, in part from the conversation of the philosopher Sphaerus' is an exaggeration in both instances. Grote, *History of Greece*, IX, 58.
59. *Ep.*, 7. 327a.
60. Ibid.

61. From *The Greek Anthology*, ed. and trans. W.R. Paton, 7.99. Hans Kelsen has seen in this and in a number of Plato's writings strong homosexual connections. 'Platonic Love', *The American Imago*, 3 (1942). For a discussion of Kelsen and Plato, see E.N. Tigerstedt, *Interpreting Plato*, 32-4.

62. J.K. Davies, *Democracy and Classical Greece*, 210. Cf. Kurt von Fritz's statement that 'The oligarchically minded began to look back to the form of government from which oligarchy had sprung in the beginning.' *Schriften zur griechischen und römischen Verfassungsgeschichte und Verfassungstheorie*, 245. Aalders, *Political Thought in Hellenistic Times*, 17-27.

63. See Riginos, *Platonica*, 14-79. Plato's confrontation with Dionysius the Elder was also a test of strength for the two traditions. The pro-Platonic sources used it as a rebuttal to charges that Plato was a parasite at the court of Dionysius. Riginos, 70-85. Grote dislikes the elder Dionysius intensely enough to liken the tyrant to a Frenchman. His comment on the meeting between the sage and tyrant, however, is apt: 'That Dionysius should listen to the discourse of Plato with repugnance, not less decided than that which the Emperor Napoleon was wont to show towards ideologists, was an event naturally to be expected.' Grote, *History of Greece*, IX, 38. The alpha and the omega of the rule of the Dionysii are called, respectively, 'its eighteenth Brumaire' and 'its St Helena'. Grote, *History of Greece*, 98. The Ortygia is the Dionysian Bastile. Grote, *History of Greece*, 119.

64. Plut., *Dion*, 5.4. Cf. Raymond Aron's witty assessment of the interaction of the intellectual and the politician in France. 'The political ambitions of successful French novelists collide with the literary ambitions of French statesmen, who dream of writing novels just as the others dream of being Ministers.' *Opium of the Intellectuals*, 219.

65. Plut., *Dion*, 5.5.

66. Riginos, *Platonica*, 86-92; Porter, 'The Sequel to Plato's First Visit to Sicily', *Hermathena*, 6 (1943), 46 ff.

67. D.L., 3.20.

68. *Ep.*, 7. 331b-c; *Ep.*, 5. 322a-b.

69. Plut., *Ad. princ. iner.*, 779d; Aelian, *VH.*, 12.30.

70. Aelian, *VH*, 2.42; 12.30; D.L., 3.23. Riginos, *Platonica*, 191-2. He did send Aristodymus in his place. Likewise, Menedemus was sent to Pyrrhae and Phormio to Elis. Plut., *Adv. Col.*, 3. 1126c. Similarly, Isocrates and Zeno were quick to recommend trusted associates to go in their place.

71. *Ep.*, 7. 328d.

72. Ibid.

72. *Rep.*, 502b.

74. *Ep.*, 7. 328c. Cf. Grote, *History of Greece*, IX, 68.

75. K. Popper, *The Open Society and Its Enemies*, I, 155. Cf. R.H.S. Crossman, *Plato Today*, 67-8.

76. Isoc., *Ep.*, 1.9.

77. Ibid., 10.

78. *Ep.*, 7. 327e.

79. Plut., *Dion*, 11.2.

80. Ibid., 13. 1-4.

81. Plut., *De adul.*, 52c.

82. Plut., *Dion*, 13. 5-6.

83. M.I. Finley, *Ancient Sicily*, 78.

84. Cf. Davies, *Democracy*, 202-11.

85. *Ep.*, 7. 334c; 324b; 332c; 336a; 351c.

86. *Ep.*, 8. 355e-356e. This combination of a philosophically minded king ruling on the basis of excellent laws is equivalent to the second best method of

government, wrote Plato in the *Statesman*, 301d-e; 300c. As to the best conception of government, see *Republic*, 7. 540ff.; *Statesman*, 293d; *Laws*, 5. 735d-e. Plato talks airily about 'wiping the state clean', and the merits of various forms of purges, but, as Aalders notes, 'Plato in Sicily never envisaged a new start after a radical purging of the citizenry and ..., in political practice, he abhorred violence and bloodshed.' 'Political Thought and Political Programs', 161. Cf. *Ep.*, 7. 327d; 331d; 351c.

87. *Ep.*, 8. 357a-b.
88. Davies, *Democracy*, 207.
89. Isoc., *ad Nic.*, 3.22.
90. In general, Davies, *Democracy*, 198-211. For Dionysius the Elder, H.W. Parke, *Greek Mercenary Soldiers*, 61-72.
91. On this topic see Marcel Piérart, *Platon et la Cité grecque*, 235-58, with references to Plato. Glen Morrow, *Plato's Cretan City*, 179-81.
92. Davies, *Democracy*, 207; Parke, *Greek Mercenary Soldiers*, 114-15. The mercenaries' complaint would have extended to the Younger Dionysius as well. Parke remarks that the 'contrast between Dionysius II's great military forces and the feeble use which he made of them is a commonplace in ancient authors', 114.
93. G.R. Morrow, *Plato's Epistles*, 162.
94. Grote, *History of Greece*, IX, 71-2. Plato was not the only intellectual with such high-handed methods. H.G. Creel notes that Mencius maintained 'that a ruler's tutor stands toward him in the relation of a father or an older brother, and thus of a superior rather than a subject. On the basis of this claim and their own assurance of their worth, some Confucians demanded meticulous attention of the rulers whom they deigned to advise ... In fact, Mencius says that the virtuous rulers of antiquity were not even permitted to visit worthy scholars frequently, unless they showed the very utmost of respect.' *Chinese Thought*, 90.
95. *Ep.*, 3. 315e; 319b: Grote's paraphrase, *History of Greece*, IX, 72. The philosopher's attitude incenses the practical historian: 'if only Plato, during his short-lived spiritual authority at Syracuse, had measured more accurately the practical influence which a philosopher might reasonably hope to exercise over Dionysius'. Grote correctly goes on to point out that much the same charges were made by the tyrant 'upon whom the consequences of the mistake mainly fell'. Grote, *History of Greece*, IX, 74. For Grote's views, see A.D. Momigliano, 'George Grote and the Study of Greek History', in his *Studies in Historiography*, 56-74, and Turner, *The Greek Heritage*.
96. 'It is not the province of the real kingly art to act for itself but rather to control the work of the acts which instruct us in the methods of action. The kingly act controls them according to its power to perceive the right occasions for undertaking and setting in motion the great enterprises of state. The other arts must do what they are told to do by the kingly art.' *Statesman*, 305d, trans. J.B. Skemp; cf. *Laws*, 942a-b.
97. Grote, *History of Greece*, IX, 72-3.
98. Athen., 508d-e.
99. *Ep.*, 6. 322d. Cf. W. Jaeger, *Aristotle*, 113. See also Aalders, 'Political Thought and Political Programs', 162. Aalders makes the point that Plato had in mind a loose federation of Greek cities such as were found in Archaic times between Sparta, Messene and Argos. *Laws*, 683a ff. He would also have been impressed by the confederation of southern Italian cities which came about in the fourth century. Cf. Morrow, *Plat. Ep.*, 154, n.7., who thinks Plato influenced the confederation. Polybius, more correctly, emphasises the role of the Achaeans, 39. 4-7. Von Fritz, *Pyth. Pol.*, 72-3.
100. Plut., *Dion*, 6. 2-5.
101. *Ep.*, 7. 330b.

102. Plut., *Dion*, 9.3.

103. Cf. Aristippus' remark to Plato: 'Our friend [Socrates] at any rate never spoke like that.' Arist., *Rhet.*, 2.23.12. An anecdote concerning the two, if true, may well have taken place before the tyrant. Plato censures Aristippus for extravagant living. The latter then asks his own question: does Plato consider Dionysius to be a good man. On hearing Plato's affirmative reply, the Cyrenaic concludes, 'And yet he lives more extravagantly than I: thus there is no obstacle to living both extravagantly and well.' If the anecdote is complete, then it would not be the first time that Plato decided silence was the best course to follow. D.L., 2.69, 76.

104. Plut., *Dion*, 19.7.
105. Ibid., 19. 6-9.
106. Aristox., *ap*. Athen, 545a-546c.
107. Ibid., 545e-546a.
108. Ibid., 545d.
109. Ibid., 546a-b.
110. Ibid., 546b.
111. *Ep.*, 3. 316a.
112. Plut., *Dion*, 14.4.

113. Ryle, *Plato's Progress*, 70. Ryle provides an extremely hypothetical construction of the events in Sicily. The letters are all forgeries. The forger, however, took notes from Plato's lecture on what was the first version of the *Laws*. Plato delivered it in Athens in 361-360. Also in Syracuse was the young Aristotle. With the air of a triumphant detective, Ryle solemnly exclaims: 'Aristotle and the concocter of the *Letters* were sitting and taking notes on adjacent benches.' Ibid., 100-101. His assessment of Dion is excessively harsh and has little to recommend it. Dion would conquer Sicily with Carthaginian aid and split the island up. He would get Syracuse and the Carthaginians the rest. Ibid., 77-8. That Dion was working throughout with some sort of Carthaginian aid cannot be doubted. On the other hand, Porter, in his haste to exonerate Dion, maintains the episode proves that Dionysius had been carrying on negotiations behind Dion's back. Porter, *Plutarch's Life*, 63.

114. *Ep.*, 7. 320a.
115. *Ep.*, 7. 338c.
116. Ibid.
117. Ibid., 338b.
118. Ibid., 338c.
119. Ibid., 339d-e.
120. Ibid., 339a-b.
121. Ibid., 339b.
122. Ibid., 339a.

123. In her study of the Platonic anecdotal tradition, Riginos notes that there are two opposing traditions concerning Plato. The pro-Plato tradition glorifies, the anti-Plato tradition vilifies the philosopher. Both traditions began in the fourth century BC with Speusippus and Clearchus on the one side, while Aristoxenus and Timaeus were instrumental in forging the anti-Platonic tradition. Elaborations ensued. Riginos, *Platonica*, 199-213. It needs to be emphasised that Plato himself sets the favourable tradition in motion. See also J. Geffcken, 'Anti-platonica', *Hermes*, 64 (1929), 87-109. E. Tigerstedt as an exercise has drawn a composite picture of the philosopher as depicted by the ancient sources opposed to Plato. *Interpreting Plato*, 38-9. The ancients do not leave the moderns behind. Cf. the views of Kelsen or Popper. Also, Benett Simon, *Mind and Madness in Ancient Greece*, 170-79 (for the connoisseur only).

124. Morrow, *Platonic Epistles*, 173.

125. J. Harward, *The Platonic Epistles*, 28.
126. Morrow, *Platonic Epistles*, 98.
127. Plut., *Dion*, 21.5.
128. *Ep.*, 7. 350b.
129. On the Academy, see among other studies C.B. Armstrong, 'Plato's Academy', *Leeds Philosophical and Literary Society: Proceedings* 7 (1953), 89-106. A general overview, Margharita Isnardi, 'Teoria e prassi nel pensiero dell' Accademia antica', *la Parola del Passato*, 11 (1956), 401-33, and the author's 'Studi recenti e problemi aperti sulla structure e la funzione della Prima Accademia Platonica', *Rivista Storica Italiana*, 71 (1959), 271-91. Isnardi attempts to link theory with practice. Claiming that the Academy was geared to action are P.M. Schuhl, 'Platon et l'activité politique de l'Académie', *REG*, 59/60 (1946/47), 44-53, and A.H. Chroust, 'Plato's Academy: The First Organized School of Political Science in Antiquity', *Rev. of Pol.*, 29 (1967), 25-40. Also very useful is Olaf Gigon, 'Platon und politische Wirklichkeit', *Gymnasium*, 69 (1962), 205-19.
130. *Laches*, 179c-d.
131. Ibid., 200c-e.
132. Grote, *Plato and the Other Companions of Socrates*, I, 123-24. D.L., 8.86-87, 89.
133. *Protagoras*, 313d; cf. Kerferd, *The Sophistic Movement*, 25.
134. Athen., 12. 544e, trans. P. Friedländer.
135. Ibid., trans. P. Friedländer.
136. Ibid., 91.
137. *Ep.*, 7. 341c.
138. Paul Friedländer, *Plato*, I, 91.
139. D.L., 3.2. For Plato and Apollo, see the full references with discussion in Riginos, *Platonica*, 8-32.
140. H.I. Marrou, *A History of Education in Antiquity*, 103, with references; Riginos, *Platonica*, 119-23.
141. P. Boyance, *Le culte des Muses chez les Philosophes grecs*, 265-6.
142. Marrou, *History of Education*, 103.
143. Weber, *Economy and Society*, II, 504. It is instructive for purposes of comparison to note the mood of the American intellectuals from the late forties to the mid-fifties. R. Hofstadter, *Anti-Intellectualism in American Life*, has sympathetically described it; L.S. Feuer, *Ideology and the Ideologist*, is critical and describes their rejection by the broad mass of the American populace. 'In their own minds they still were the only ones fit to rule, the only autonomous men, but the masses, the lonely crowd not knowing how lonely and pathetic they were, rejecting the intellectuals in favor of Truman and Eisenhower, had evidently failed in their historic vocation. The intellectuals meanwhile could only retire into the role of cultural critics, until such time as the Lonely Crowd stopped worshipping the Golden Calf.' 124. The terms which Feuer sarcastically utilises, 'the lonely crowd' and 'autonomous man' come from D. Riesman's book, *The Lonely Crowd*. ('A depressing account of what the American character has become ... The most widely read book in the history of sociology.' Hofstadter, 418.) Riesman himself made the cover of *Time* in 1954 and there urged his fellow intellectuals in a Burkhardtian manner to cultivate the 'nerve of failure', turn off their superior social radar and 'develop the ability to make choices out of their own individuality'. *Time*, 27 September 1954, 25. The retreat was not meant to be irreversible. *Time* notes that 'From such models, from men who respect and try to follow day-dreams about their own lives, society may learn again to make social daydreams, those models called utopia.' Plato's rejection was both cultural and political. The difference between his moralising and self-interested stance was minimal. This applies to the aristocratic members of the early Academy as well.

Whereas intellectuals in the Hellenistic and contemporary worlds are often hampered by the split between their self interests and their moralising, the philosophers of the fourth century, as with the authors of the Federalist Papers, knew no such conflict. See Riesman, *The Lonely Crowd*, 172-80.

144. *Chion*, 16.6. All translations of this novel are by I. Düring. This passage would also seem to lend credence to Humphrey's assertion that 'by choosing to speak outside the political context, Greek intellectuals set themselves free to travel'. They also acquired, according to Humphrey, enhanced freedom of speech 'at the price of having their remarks considered irrelevant to political decision making'. So long as Greek intellectuals came from the upper classes, however, they could never be considered politically neutered. Quietists and activists equally attended and were equally welcomed by the schools of Plato, Aristotle and Zeno right down to Roman times. Whatever the Athenian democrats of the fourth century may have thought of the intrinsic merits of the intellectuals' doctrines, they maintained a continuous vigilance of the intellectuals, exactly in the interests of their political decision making. Humphrey's attempts to make the contemplative life the fundamental one for the philosophers as early as the sixth century obscures too much later history. *Anthropology*, 264. According to I. Düring, *Chion* was written by an anonymous author not earlier than the beginning of the first century AD, and the story which underlies it is true, although the author felt free to deck it out with as much imaginative power as he could summon. Düring tentatively suggests that the arguments of Chapters 14-15 would fit well the situation in Rome in the eighties, as judged by a cultivated Greek observer. For Clearchus, substitute Domitian. *Chion of Heraclea: A Novel in Letters*, 14-16, 24.

145. *Chion*, 3.3. The philosopher as warrior, Xenophon, emerges as a fourth-century Godfrey of Bouillon. Düring notes the parallels with Merovingian rulers who also wore their hair long; Xenophon is obviously aping the Spartans. Düring, *Chion of Heraclea*, 85.

146. Ibid., 3.6.

147. Ibid., 5.1. It need not be denied that a revolutionary creed was taught in the Academy, that its members were steeped in it and that they would become the vanguard and leaders of a 'new and purer' Hellenism. Crossman, *Plato Today*, 70. An interesting comparison from a literary and social point of view could be made between *Chion of Heraclea* and the novels of André Malraux. Malraux also takes his intellectuals out of their studies and places them in the middle of a political *agon*. See Victor Brombert, *The Intellectual Hero*, 169-72.

148. Ibid., 14.1; 12.3.

149. Ibid., 17.2. Cf. T.W. Africa's analysis of Thomas More: 'Thomas More and the Spartan Mirage', *Historical Reflections*, 6 (1979), 343-52. More identified with the 'philosopher-king' Agis the way Chion identified with the philosopher-warrior Xenophon.

150. Justin, 16.4.2. For the political and economic background of Heraclea, see S.A. Burstein, *Outpost of Hellenism: The Emergence of Heraclea on the Black Sea*, 44-66.

151. Ibid.

152. *Chion*, 17.1.

153. Burstein, *Outpost*, 56.

154. Memnon, *ap*. Phot., *Bibl.*, 214.

155. Justin, 16.5. 9-10.

156. Ibid., 16.5.13.

157. Isoc., *Ep.*, 7.135.

158. Clearchus and citizenship, Dem., 20.84. For Clearchus' son, Timotheus, Burstein, *Outpost*, 50, 127 n. 32.

159. Ironically, Chion is depicted as putting into practice many of the policies

that the Academic tyrant, Chaeron of Pellene, also employed: the confiscation of estates and the forced marriage of aristocratic women with their slaves. Justin, 16.5 1-4. For Clearchus' assassination, Burstein, *Outpost*, 64-5, who comments 'faced with the failure (of making Clearchus a philosopher-king), he found in Plato's teachings the inspiration to free his city of the tyrant', 64. As Chion's failure shows, however, Plato's teachings seemed to inspire few thoughts on how to handle the events immediately following the political murder.

160. A voluptuary according to Anaximenes, *ap*. Athen., 12.531d. Cf. Davies, *Democracy*, 211.

161. Isoc., *Ep.*, 7.1.
162. Ibid., 7.2.
163. Ibid., 7.4.
164. Ibid., 7.8.
165. Cf. Burstein, *Outpost*, 69.
166. Ibid., 10, 11.
167. Plato, *Laws*, 710c-d.
168. Athen., 11.509a.
169. Ibid., 11.508f.
170. Ibid., 11.509f, cf. Paus., 7.27.2; Athen., 11.508d-509b. Both Chaeron and Timolaus received Macedonian aid. Mimicked by A.H. Chroust who, after giving a list of Plato's disciples and associates, concludes: 'One could justly refer to the Platonic Academy as the 'seedbed' of political tyrants.' 'A Second (and Closer) Look at Plato's Philosophy', *ARSP*, 48 (1962), 486.

171. Plut., *Dion*, 17, 6-10.
172. Ibid., 15.4.
173. Ibid., 17.8.
174. Nepos, *Dion*, 4.4.
175. Plut., *Dion*, 22.2.
176. Porter, *Plutarch's Life*, 19-22.
177. Plut., *Dion*, 50.4.
178. Ibid., 28.3. For an interesting Roman comparison, Philostratus, in his *Lives of the Sophists*, after describing the yeoman service the sophist Dio of Prusa performed in quelling a mutiny which followed the death of Domitian by means of his 'persuasive charm', also pairs the intellectual with a triumphant ruler: 'The Emperor Trajan set Dio by his side on the golden chariot in which the Emperors ride in procession when they celebrate their triumphs in war, and often he would turn to Dio and say: "I do not understand what you are saying, but I love you as I love myself." ' 1.7. The authenticity of the story is doubtful. If the scene did take place, Trajan, who spoke Greek and had a sense of humour, is mocking the loquacity of the sophist. By the time of the Roman Empire, 'gifts, ranks and privileges, were the common currency of exchange between the Emperors and the sophists who spoke before them', notes Fergus Millar in *The Emperor in the Roman World*, 496. However, the dreams of many intellectuals remained fixated on power, though the time for putting them into practice had long slipped by. In the *Life of Apollonius of Tyana*, Philostratus gives us other apocryphal stories of Apollonius and his circle engaging in meaningful discussions with a fascinated and grateful Vespasian. 5.27-61.

179. Plut., *Dion*, 52.3.
180. *Ep.*, 4.320c.
181. Ibid., 320d.
182. Ibid., 321b; cf. Plut., *Dion*, 8.4.
183. Grote, *History of Greece*, IX, 116.
184. *Plut., Dion*, 52.6.
185. Ibid., 37 5-7, 42.6. Significantly, Dion turned to Corinth for counsellors

and auxiliaries partly because Corinth was Syracuse's mother city, but primarily because its oligarchical nature suited his own views. Plut., *Dion*, 53.4; Plato, *Ep.*, 7.334, 336; 8.356.

186. D.S., 16.17.3; Plut., *Dion*, 48.5.

187. Nepos notes, however, that Heracleides was popular even among the aristocrats. *Dion*, 6.

188. Plut., *Dion*, 53.5; 47.3. For Corinth, 53.3.

189. Ibid., 53.5. Cf. Grote, *History of Greece*, IX, 121.

190. Plut., *Dion*, 53.5.

191. Ibid., 54.1. 57.5; Nepos, *Dion*, 9; D.S., 16.31.

192. Plut., *Dion*, 43.1.

193. Ibid., 51.5.

194. Ibid., 55.2. See on this T.W. Africa, 'Psychohistory, Ancient History and Freud: The Descent into Avernus', *Arethusa*, 12 (1979), 13.

195. Ibid., 55. 2-3.

196. Ibid., 55.4.

197. W.D. Westlake, 'Dion: A Study in Liberation', in *Essays in the Greek Historians and Greek History*, 263, is wrong to maintain that Dion died almost willingly. The tragedy of Dion is that he met his death, when it came, not with the placidity of a philosopher but with the terror of a common tyrant. Plut., *Dion*, 57.5.

198. Ibid., 58.1.

199. Grote, *History of Greece*, IX, 128.

200. *Ep.*, 7.324a-c.

201. Cf. Athen., 11.508c.

202. *Ep.*, 8.353c.

203. Ibid., 353d. Cf. N.G.L. Hammond. 'The experiences of Syracuse since the arrival of Dion were repeated in most cities throughout the empire of Dionysius. Liberation meant the end of organized government. Party strife, tyranny, and anarchy ensued ... In 344, when Timoleon came to save Sicily from this fate, grass was growing in the streets of Syracuse.' *A History of Greece*, 519.

204. E. Meyer, *Geschichte des Altertums*, V, 452.

205. Plut., *Adv. Col.*, 1127A.

206. Ibid., 1126C-D.

207. The historian was a student of Isocrates and had personal and political reasons for disliking Hermias. D.E.W. Wormell, 'The Literary Tradition', 68-71.

208. See W. Jaeger, *Aristotle*, 112.

209. Ibid., 112-13.

210. *Ep.*, 6.322e. Jaeger thinks Plato feared the two to be excessively doctrinaire. *Aristotle*, 113.

211. Tod., 165; Jaeger, ibid., 112.

212. Wormell, 'The Literary Tradition', 60.

213. *Ep.*, 6.323b-c.

214. Ibid., 323c.

215. Ibid., 321d; 322a.

216. Ibid., 322d.

217. Jaeger's translation and restoration. *Aristotle*, 114-15. From Didymus, col. 5.52, Diels Schubart.

218. *Aristotle*, 111.

219. *Vita Marc.*, 42. A.H. Chroust, *Aristotle*, I, 119. Düring, *Aristotle*, 459.

220. Jaeger, *Aristotle*, 115.

221. Ibid.

222. Ibid., 120, 289-90.

223. Peter Green, *Alexander of Macedon*, 54.

224. Jaeger, *Aristotle*, 120. Doubted for no good reason by Philip Cawkwell, *Philip of Macedon*, 54.
225. Green, *Alexander*, 54.
226. C. Lord, 'Politics and Philosophy in Aristotle's Politics', *Hermes*, 106 (1978), 354 n. 37.
227. Arist., *Pol.*, 7.6. 2-4.
228. Plut., *Alex.*, 7. Philip had destroyed the city himself.
229. *Pol.*, 2.1.10.
230. For Aristotle's family see Chroust, *Aristotle*, I, 81. For the hymn, see Jaeger, *Aristotle*, 117-19.
231. Green, *Alexander*, 154.
232. *Nic. Eth.*, 10.7.4.
233. T.A. Sinclair, *A History of Greek Political Thought*, 236.
234. On *Ep.*, 3, see P. Merlan, 'Isocrates, Aristotle and Alexander the Great', *Historia*, 3 (1954/55), 60-82.

4. From Polis to Monarchy

1. *Antid.*, 159-61; cf. *Areop.*, 34 ff.
2. For biographical details see Paul Cloché, *Isocrate et son temps*, 5-8; R.C. Jebb, *The Attic Orators from Antiphon to Isaeos*, II, 1-35. Ps. Plut., *Isoc.*, 836E-839D.
3. Jebb, *Attic Orators*, II, 4-5.
4. *Phaedr.*, 278-79e.
5. Cf. G. Norlin's introduction to the Loeb edition of *Isocrates*, XVII-XVIII.
6. Ps. Plut., *Isoc.*, 836E; 838F.
7. *Antid.*, 145, 158.
8. Isocrates harps on this constantly. Among many examples, *Panath.*, 10; *Phil.*, 81; *Epistle*, 1.9; 8.7.
9. He was a slow, cautious worker in general. According to Ps. Plut., *Isoc.*, 837F, the Panathenaic Oration took him 10-15 years to compose. (Among other works no doubt.)
10. *To Phil.*, 82.
11. *Antid.*, 151.
12. Jebb, *Attic Orators*, II, 7-8. Dion. Hal., 18. *Isoc. Paneg.*, 174. Cf. A. Fuks, 'Isocrates and the Social-Economic Situation in Greece', *Ancient Society*, 3 (1972), 24.
13. Morrou, *Education in Antiquity*, 128; 494, n. 11. *Antid.*, 141, 188. R. Johnson, 'Isocrates' Method of Teaching', *AJPh*, 80 (1959), 25-36; 'A Note on the Number of Isocrates' Pupils', *AJPh*, 78 (1957), 297-300.
14. *De orat.*, 2. 94. Cf. M.L.W. Laistner, 'The Influence of Isocrates' Political Doctrines on Fourth Century Men of Affairs', *CW*, 23 (1930), 129-31.
15. *Ep.*, 9. 17.
16. Ibid., 18.
17. *Antid.*, 188.
18. *To Phil.*, 232.
19. W. Jaeger, *Paideia*, III, 86.
20. *Evag.*, 66; 59; D.S., 15.2.4.
21. D.S., 15.9.2.
22. *Evag.*, 78.

23. Ibid., 59, 66.
24. Cf. Davies, *Democracy*, 41.
25. *To Nic.*, 12-13.
26. Ibid., 44.
27. Ibid., 13. Jaeger compares Isocrates with Plato and notes that only urgent and repeated entreaties persuaded Plato to leave for Syracuse (the second and third time), 'but Isocrates invites himself to Cyprus'. *Paideia*, III, 96.
28. *Evag.*, 53.
29. *Paideia*, III, 95.
30. *To Nic.*, 8, 23; *Nic.*, 16-17, 32, 55. Jaeger, *Paideia*, III, 61, 94-5.
31. I. Düring, *Aristotle in the Biographical Tradition*, 311-13, 389-91.
32. *Tusc. Disp.*, 1.4.7.
33. Chroust, *Aristotle*, II, 86-107; I. Düring, *Aristotle's Protrepticus: An Attempt at Reconstruction*, 1964.
34. A.H. Chroust, 'Plato's Academy: The First Organized School of Political Science in Antiquity', *Rev. of Pol.*, 291 (1967), 31. In general, see the author's *Aristotle*, II, 119-25.
35. Chroust, 'Plato's Academy', 31.
36. The two schools were fighting on a number of levels. Not least important was the influence they hoped to attain upon generations of young readers through their works. As well as the Cypriots, they also vied for the allegiance of their contemporaries. Chroust believes, without much support, that, for Aristotle, the reward was permission to offer a course of lectures on rhetoric in the Academy. *Aristotle*, II, 41-2.
37. E.M. Peters, *The Crusades*, 3. For the problem of the image of the Crusades, see Carl Erdeman's important book, *The Origin of the Idea of Crusade*.
38. Ibid., 2, 3.
39. *Antid.*, 80.
40. Jaeger, *Paideia*, III, 53. Cf. H.E.J. Cowdrey on the Crusades: 'The Crusades began at a time of uncertainty and unsettlement in the institutions and ideas of a society undergoing rapid change, which prompted a search for alien elements within and outside it to serve as targets of ideological and physical aggression.' 'The Genesis of the Crusades', in *The Holy War*, 28.
41. *Paneg.*, 173-4.
42. Cowdrey, 'The Genesis', 24.
43. *Paneg.*, 167-8.
44. *Phil.*, 121.
45. Ibid., 120.
46. *Paneg.*, 187.
47. Ibid., 157, 158.
48. Ibid., 181.
49. Ibid., 149, 150. A.H. Munro, in his analysis of Urban's speech notes that 'the crusaders were surprised at the bravery of the Turks when they met the latter in battle'. 'The Speech of Urban II at Clermont', *AHR*, 11 (1905), 238.
50. *Paneg.*, 150, 151.
51. Isocrates embroiders the list more fully. Ibid., 151, 152. *Phil.*, 124.
52. *Paneg.*, 145-9; *Phil*, 90-93.
53. *Paneg.*, 84.
54. Ibid., 182.
55. Ibid., 186.
56. *To Nic.*, 43.
57. *To Phil.*, 151.
58. *Panath.*, 29-32; *Antid.*, 48. *Nic.*, 5-9; *Antid.*, 46-7; *Antid.*, 353. On *logos*, see George Kennedy, *The Art of Persuasion in Greece*, 8.

162 *Notes*

59. *Nic.*, 7, 9. Morrow, *Plato's Epistles*, 122.
60. *Against the Sophists*, 21.
61. Jaeger, *Paideia*, III, 83. A.D. Momigliano, *Filippo il Macedone*, 183-92, has a good overview of Isocrates' aims. As in the fourth century, modern judgement on Isocrates is divided. For example, Minar M. Markle, 'Support of Athenian Intellectuals for Philip: A Study in Isocrates' *Philipus* and Speusippus' *Letter to Philip*', *JHS*, 96 (1976), 80-99, is at pains to show that Isocrates is 'the skilled propagandist – no fool', 82, and constructs arguments of incredible subtlety to prove his point. On the other hand, J. de Romilly, 'Eunomia in Isocrates or the Political Importance of Creating Good Will', *JHS*, 78 (1958), 92-101, purrs: 'Isocrates, it is true, is not very intelligent: but all the same, it must be said: we all take after him in some way or another!' 101. S. Pearlman, 'Isocrates' Philipus – a Reinterpretation', *Historia*, 6 (1957), 306-17, takes a middle course.
62. *Antid.*, 115.
63. Ps. Plut., *Isoc.*, 837C.
64. *Tod.*, 123; cf. *Paneg.*, 126.
65. *Paneg.*, 42.
66. Ibid., 45-50.
67. Ibid., 104-5.
68. *Tod.*, 123.
69. W. Jaeger, 'The Date of Isocrates' *Areopagiticus* and the Athenian Opposition', in *Athenian Studies Presented to William Scott Ferguson*, 439-42.
70. *On the Peace*, 16; 25 ff.; Jaeger, 'The Date', 424-6.
71. *On the Peace*, 19.
72. *Antid.*, 138.
73. *To Phil.*, 119; cf. Xen., *Hellenica*, 6.1.12.
74. *Ep.*, 1. 9-10; *To Phil.*, 81.
75. E.N. Tigerstedt, *The Legend of Sparta*, I, 197-200. C. Mossé, 'Sur un passage de l'Archidamos d'Isocrate', *REA*, 551 (1953), 29-55.
76. Minar M. Markle, 'Support of Athenian Intellectuals', 89-90.
77. Ibid., 93.
78. Reconstructed as far as possible by F. Jacoby, *FGH*, IIB, 115, F 24-246. See Truesdell S. Brown, *The Greek Historians*, 119-24.
79. *Ep. Socr.*, 30.5, trans. J. Wickersham and G. Verbrugghe. Full discussion by Griffith, *History of Macedonia*, II, 514-16, who sneers: 'This is a crook writing, whether for money or merely in order to surpass Isocrates in being of use to Philip.' 515.
80. *GHD*, 1.2-5.23; *Ep. Socr.*, 30.1-5.
81. Ibid., 12.
82. Plato, *Ep.*, 5; Athen., 508e; Dem., *Phil.*, 3. 59ff.
83. A. Lesky, *History of Greek Literature*, 634.
84. See the analysis of T.B.L. Webster, *Studies in Later Greek Comedy*, 37-56.
85. For an excellent and witty fictional account of such phenomena, see Leszek Kolakowski, *The Devil and Scripture*, 47-54.
86. *To Phil.*, 16.
87. Isocrates' suspicions in ibid., 73, 74. The relations between Philip and the Greek intellectuals have been admirably treated in A.D. Momigliano, *Filippo il Macedone*, 127-82.
88. Justin, 8.2.3.
89. Ibid., 8.2.4.
90. *GHD*, 8.3-9.17.
91. Ibid. *To Phil.*, 114-15; Isoc., *Ep.*, 3.5. Cf. Griffith, *History of Macedonia*, II, 515.

92. Theopompus' libels of the Macedonian court are found in Athen., 4. 166f-7c, 6. 260d-1a, Polyb., 8.11.5. See Wormell's comments, 'The Literary Tradition', 71-3.
93. Markle, 'Support', 96-7.
94. Arist., *Pol.*, 3.8.1.
95. Plut., *Alex.*, 4.
96. Rose, fr. 658, trans. P. Green.
97. *Ep.*, 5. 4-5.
98. Plut., *Alex.*, 74. 2-4. Cf. Hamilton, *Plutarch's Alexander*, 205-6.
99. Cf. U. Wilcken, *Alexander the Great*, 80.
100. Strabo, 13.1.2.
101. Ibid., 17.1.43; cf. Plut., *Alex.*, 27. Hamilton, *Plutarch's Alexander*, 68-75.
102. Arrian, 4.10.
103. Am. Mar., 18.3.7.
104. Cf. T.S. Brown, 'Callisthenes and Alexander', *AJPh*, 70 (1949), 235, 318. Plut., *Alex.*, 52.
105. Plut., *Alex.*, 52.
106. Robin Lane Fox, *Alexander the Great*, 324.
107. Cf. Lane Fox, ibid. 'But Anaxarchus would one day die a hero's death, owing nothing to Aristotle's schoolmen, while Callisthenes would be best remembered for hailing his patron as the new son of Zeus.'
108. For this, see among other studies, Brown, 'Callisthenes', 240-46; J.P.V.D. Balsdon, 'The Divinity of Alexander', *Historia*, 1 (1950), 371-82.
109. Brown, 'Callisthenes', 246. Cf. Balsdon, 'Divinity', 378.
110. Plut., *Alex.*, 53.
111. Ibid., 55.
112. D.L., 5.10.
113. Cf. Chroust, *Aristotle*, I, 90.
114. Ibid., 166. Düring sees no political aspect. Aristotle 'was merely one of the old dons of the Academy who returned, a professor among many other foreign professors in Athens'. *Aristotle*, 460. So also Griffith: 'He had better things to do if anyone ever had.' *A History of Macedonia*, II, 520.
115. Chroust, *Aristotle*, I.
116. Sources in Düring, *Aristotle*, 341-2.
117. Sources in Düring, *Herodicus the Cratetean*, 149-51. Düring in *Aristotle* analyses the charges against Aristotle: '(a) certain letters had been found; (b) Aristotle had betrayed Stagira to the Macedonians; (c) after the demolition of Olynthus he had denounced the wealthiest men of Olynthus at the place where the booty was sold', 388.
118. D.L., 5.27. Antipater's high opinion of Aristotle was not just as a thinker. The regent praises Aristotle as a persuasive individual. Plut., *Alcib.* (Comp. 3.) and *Cato*, 29.
119. Cf. Chroust, *Aristotle*, I, 145-54, for the background to the philosopher's expulsion. Chroust waxes indignantly: 'Never loath to deal harshly and unjustly with their benefactors, the Athenians repaid him with flagrant ingratitude. In this, Aristotle, the Macedonian, shared the fate of many of the greatest men in Greek antiquity.' 144; cf. 154. And yet he admitted just two pages earlier, 'The true reason for the final persecution of Aristotle and for his renewed flight from Athens was undoubtedly his political affiliations with Macedonia and, especially, with Antipater, the "Destroyer of Greek freedom".' 142.
120. Jaeger, *Aristotle*, 123. D.L., 5.11.
121. *De cor.*, 280.
122. Düring, *Herodicus*, 138.

123. D.L., 4.9; Plut., *Phoc.*, 27. 1-4.
124. D.S., 18.55. 2-4.
125. Plut., *Phoc.*, 35. 2.
126. Plut., *Phoc.*, 4, 14, 29. The execution of the conservative Phocion was primarily a political affair on the part of Polyperchon's democratic allies.
127. Ibid., 29.
128. Ferguson, *Hellenistic Athens*, 36.
129. D.L., 5.37.
130. Athen., 14. 620b. It should also be noted that Lysimachus had ties with intellectuals. What little we know indicates that 'Onesicritus wrote at his court, and he perhaps joined Cassander in subsidizing the researches of Dicaearchus the Peripatetic ... The tradition that he expelled the philosophers from his kingdom may be untrue, for his finance minister, Mithres, was the close friend of Epicurus and Metrodorus.' W.W. Tarn, in *Cambridge Ancient History*, VII, 90. Lysimachus also supported the Peripatetic Olympiodorus, albeit in a strictly political matter. Ibid., 81, 89.
131. T.S. Brown, 'Euhemerus', 259-60.
132. Ferguson, *Utopias*, 110.
133. Brown, 'Euhemerus', see also Ferguson, ibid.
134. Athen., 3. 98d.
135. W.S. Ferguson, *Hellenistic Athens*, 47, n.3. Theophrastus was the successor to Aristotle's position of head of the Lycaeum. An alien in Athens, he was also the heir to Aristotle's political views and that meant supporting the Macedonian presence and overlordship in Athens. As was the case with Aristotle, Theophrastus engaged in widespread correspondence with monarchs such as Ptolemy and Cassander and he wrote a treatise on royalty and dedicated it to Cassander. D.L., 5.37.
136. Ferguson, *Hellenistic Athens*, 57; Hans-Joachim Gehrke, 'Das Verhältnis von Politik und Philosophie bei Demetrios von Phaleron', *Chiron*, 8 (1978), 171-3, 176-81.
137. Arist., *Pol.*, 4.11.9; 12.8; 6.5.13. Ferguson, *Hellenistic Athens*, 44-5; Gehrke, 'Politik und Philosophie', 151-62, 186-91, has an excellent discussion. For Demetrius as *nomothetes*, see Gehrke, 173-5. Also, 188, n.205 for Gehrke's too brief and cautious assessment of Demetrius as a philosopher in politics.
138. Arist., *Pol.*, 4.12.9; 6.5.13. Gehrke, 'Politik und Philosophie', 162-70.
139. Ferguson, *Hellenistic Athens*, 46.
140. Ibid., 40. Did Theophrastus have his devoted student in mind when in the *Characters* he describes 'The Authoritarian': 'He will go out about midday with his cloak thrown well back, his hair tastefully trimmed, his nails precisely paired, and strut about declaiming statements like this: ... "People who meddle in politics – I can't imagine what they want" ... Or he will tell you how ashamed he feels in the Assembly, when some mean looking, scruffy citizen sits down next to him. "The rich are being bled to death," he says, "with subsidizing the navy, the theatre, the festivals, and everything else. When is it going to end? Democratic agitators – how I detest them!"' If so, then this is satire with a vengeance. *Characters*, 16. 4-6. Trans. P. Vellacott.
141. D.S., 20.46; Plut., *Demetr.*, 10.12. Cf. Athen., 15. 697a.
142. E. Derenne, *Les procès d'impiété intentés aux philosophes à Athenes aux Ve-IVe siècles*, 213, 259.
143. Pollux, 9.42; D.L., 5.38; Athen., 13. 610f. The stage for this action had once again been set by comedy. There is a fragment of Alexis' *Hippeus* that echoes the popular reaction against the philosophers, in this instance Xenocrates: 'Is this the Academy of Xenocrates? May the gods bless Demetrios and the law givers for sending those who claim to give young men the power of argument the

hell out of Attica.' See T.B.L. Webster, *Studies in Later Greek Comedy*, 105.

144. Polyb., 12.13.9 ff. Ferguson's paraphrase. In his attack on philosophers, Demochares would have felt at home with Louis Bromfield's definition of an 'egghead' written in 1952, a time when American intellectuals were coming into increased attack. 'Egghead: A person of spurious intellectual pretensions, often a professor or the protégé of a professor. Fundamentally superficial. Over-emotional and feminine in reactions to any problem. Supercilious and surfeited with conceit and contempt for the experience of more sound and able men. Essentially confused in thought and immersed in a mixture of sentimentality and violent evangelism. A doctrinaire supporter of Middle-European socialism as opposed to Greco-French-American ideas of democracy and liberalism.' Quoted in R. Hofstadter, *Anti-Intellectualism in American Life*, 9. The anti-intellectualism of the fifties was not limited to the United States. In another context, V. Brombert speaks of the anti-intellectual reaction in French literature. *Intellectual Hero*, 204-21.

145. Ferguson, *Hellenistic Athens*, 106.

146. D.L., 5.38. Grote, who thinks Demochares 'deserves to be commemorated as the last known spokesman of free Athenian citizenship', is taken aback by this action of his hero. 'It is remarkable that Demochares stood forward as one of its [Sophocles' law] advocates', *History of Greece*, X, 312-14.

147. Derenne, *Procès d'impiété*, 258-9. Also Dover, 'The Freedom of the Intellectual', 24-54.

148. Ibid., 259-60. Hippias of Rhegium and Aristodemus are cited as examples. 'Nous pourrions citer d'autres savants et philosophes qui auraient pu être accusés d'impiété pour leurs doctrines et que cependant on laissa en paix.' 260.

149. Düring, *Herodicus*, 147.

150. Ibid.

151. W.W. Tarn, *Antigonos Gonatas*, 27.

152. Ibid., 28.

153. Tarn, *CAH*, VII, 81, 86, 89. For Lyco and his peers, see the remarks of A. Momigliano, *Essays in Ancient and Modern Historiography*, 44-6.

154. D.L., 5.66.

155. Timon, *ap*. Athen., 6.251c.

156. D.L., 2.110.

157. Polyb., 5.93.8. F.W. Walbank, *A Historical Commentary on Polybius*, I, 624.

158. D.L., 4. 38-9.

159. Tarn, *Antigonos Gonatas*, 27, 334.

160. No bolder than Tarn, who asserts 'in the darkest hours of Macedonian rule, Arkesilaos' class-room was one of the places in which still glowed the spark of liberty, waiting to burst into flame'. Ibid., 355.

161. Polyb., 10.22.2; Plut., *Philop*., 1; Paus. 8.49.2. Tarn, *Antigonos Gonatas*, 334, 357-9. M. Cary, *A History of the Greek World*, 138-41.

162. Plut., *Philop*., 1, M. Errington, *Philopoemen*, 13, notes that Philopeomen's training was primarily practical and quotes Polybius, 10.22.4, that Philopoemen 'soon came to excel all his contemporaries in endurance and courage both in hunting and in war'.

163. Polyb., 3.58. 3-4.

164. Tarn, *Antigonos Gonatas*, 29-30.

165. G.J.D. Aalders, *Political Thought in Hellenistic Times*, 2.

166. Ibid., 40-41.

167. Ibid., 43.

168. Plut., *De tranq. am*., 465ff.; Philodemus, *Rhet*., 1. 136ff.

169. Aalders, *Political Thought*, 45; P.T. Fraser, *Ptolemaic Alexandria*, I, 416 and notes. Cineas: Plut., *Pyrrhus*, 14. 1. ff.

166   *Notes*

170. Pointed out by Ludwig Edelstein, *The Meaning of Stoicism*, 85.
171. On Zeno's *Politeia*, see the important article by H.C. Baldry, 'Zeno's Ideal State', *JHS*, 79 (1959), 3-15. Also M.I. Finley, 'Utopianism Ancient and Modern', in *The Use and Abuse of History*, 188.
172. Finley, 'Utopianism Ancient and Modern', 188. Cf. M.I. Rostovtzeff, *The Social and Economic History of the Hellenistic World*, Vol. II, 1129-33; Aalders, *Political Thought*, 84.
173. *De Stoicorum repugnantis*. Plutarch uses many of the same rhetorical devices he had employed in *Adversus Colatus*. According to Plutarch, the primary vice of the Stoics is hypocrisy.
174. D.L., 7.122.
175. T.W. Africa, *Phylarchus and the Spartan Revolution*, 17. Also, Aalders, *Political Thought*, 75-93; Margaret E. Reesor, *The Political Theory of the Old and Middle Stoa*, 9-26.
176. D.L., 2.110.
177. Tarn, *Antigonos Gonatas*, 21-7, maximises the role of Menedemus whom he calls approvingly 'that rare thing, a philosopher at home in the work-a-day world'. 26. T. Gomperz, *Greek Thinkers*, II, 206-7, is equally ecstatic. See also Wilamowits, *Antigonos von Karystos*, 86-95.
178. Carystus, *ap.* D.L., 2.143.
179. William James, *Pragmatism*, 19. This also seems to be one of the guiding principles of Guthrie's history of Greek philosophy. See, for example, *HGP*, I, 117.
180. James, *Pragmatism*, 19.
181. E.C. Whitmont, *The Symbolic Quest*, 60; E.F. Edinger, *Ego and Archetype*, 174.
182. D.L., 7. 13-14.
183. Ibid., 7.13.
184. Aelian, *VH*, 2.20. Cf. Tarn, *Antigonos Gonatas*, 247-54, who correctly brings out the importance of Antigonus' mother, Phila, in the formation of such an ideal.
185. D.L., 7.6.
186. Ibid., 7.9.
187. D.L., 7.36. Also, Tigerstedt, *The Legend*, II, 47-8.
188. In Nicola Festa, *I frammenti degli Stoici antichi*, II, 60, n. 5a; 64-8.
189. D.L., 7.36.
190. Plut., *Arat.*, 23; Mekler, *Ind. Stoic. Herc.*, col. 15.
191. *De Amicitia*, 11.37.
192. See discussions of T.W. Africa, ibid., 16-17, and Tigerstedt, *The Legend*, II, 73 with notes.
193. Tigerstedt, *The Legend*, II, 69-70.
194. D.R. Dudley, 'Blossius of Cumae', *JRS*, 31 (1941), 94-5.
195. *De Am.*, 11.37.
196. Ibid.
197. Ibid.
198. Val. Max, 4.7.1; Plut., *Tib. Gracchus*, 8.17.
199. J.B. Becker, 'The Influence of Roman Stoicism Upon the Gracchi Economic Land Reforms', *La Parola del Passato*, 19 (1964), 125-34. Aalders, *Political Thought*, 79, n. 9, has further references.
200. *De Am.*, 11.37; Val. Max, 4.7.1.
201. *De Am.*, 11.37. There is an allusion here to an earlier speech Tiberius made where he stated that the rival tribune Octavius, who had annulled a piece of popular legislation, was more culpable than a tribune who might order the destruction of the Capitol. *Tib. Gracchus*, 8.15. See Henry C. Boren, *The Gracchi*, 73.

202. *Tib. Gracchus*, 2.20.
203. Boren, *The Gracchi*, speculates that 'Blossius was released, perhaps from sheer admiration for his courage'. 73. However, the Romans never hesitated to execute a brave enemy.
204. On Aristonicus: V. Vávrinek, 'La révolte d'Aristonicos', *Rozpravy Ceskoslovenské Akadémie Véd*, 67 (1957), no. 2; John Ferguson, *Utopias of the Classical World*, 138-45; T.W. Africa, 'Aristonicus, Blossius, and the City of the Sun', *International Review of Social History*, 6 (1961), 110-24. Africa, 116, provides a succinct historiographical background.
205. Strabo, 13.4.2.
206. *Utopias of the Classical World*, 142.
207. Eutropius, 4.20.
208. The citizens of Pergamum were sufficiently alarmed by Aristonicus' propaganda that they passed a liberal piece of legislation extending the franchise to resident aliens and most of the royal slaves. W. Dittenberger, *OGIS*, 338.
209. Strabo, 14.1.38, trans. John Ferguson.
210. Cic., *de Am.*, 11.37.
211. Toynbee, *A Study of History*, Vol. 5, 179-80.
212. *Hannibal's Legacy*, Vol. 2, 606; Ferguson, *Utopias*, 144.
213. Bidez, 'La Cité du Monde', 280.

5. Epilogue

1. D.L., 2.78-9.
2. This is not to deny that intellectuals exerted no influence or scored no success at all. They may have been instrumental in setting up certain laws. In the case of Isocrates, his 'Asian policy' was adhered to and Alexander resettled mercenaries in Asia Minor. *Phil.*, 86ff. Green, *Alexander*, 47-50.
3. E. Shils, *The Intellectuals and the Powers*, 55.
4. K. Mannheim, *Ideology and Utopia*, 155-61.
5. Aron, *The Opium*, 213.
6. L. Kolakowski, *Marxism and Beyond*, 55-6. The view of the intellectual as a jester has been applauded by poets and sociologists such as Günter Grass and Rolf Dahrendorf. See the latter's 'The Intellectual and Society: The Social Function of the Fool in the Twentieth Century', in *On Intellectuals: Theoretical Studies and Case Studies*, ed. P. Rieff. H.B. Acton, *The Idea of a Spiritual Power*, regards the idea with Platonic distaste.
7. Isaiah Berlin, *The Hedgehog and the Fox*, 1-2.

BIBLIOGRAPHY

The following ancient texts were taken from The *Loeb Classical Library* Texts and English Translations. London and Cambridge, Mass.: William Heinemann Ltd and Harvard University Press, various dates: Appian, Aristotle, Athenaeus, Cicero, Diodorus Siculus, Diogenes Laertius, Herodotus, Isocrates, Josephus, Pausanius, Philostratus, Plutarch, Polybius, Xenophon.

Aalders, G.J.D., 'Political Thought and Political Programs in the Platonic Epistles', 147-75, in *Entretiens sur l'antiquité classique: Pseudepigrapha*, I, Geneva: Vandoeuvres, 1971.
— *Political Thought in Hellenistic Times*, Amsterdam: Adolf M. Hakkert, 1975.
Adkins, A.W.H., *Moral Values and Political Behaviour in Ancient Greece from Homer to the End of the Fifth Century*, New York: W.W. Norton & Company, 1972.
Africa, Thomas W., 'Aristonicus, Blossius, and the City of the Sun', *International Review of Social History*, 6 (1961), 110-24.
— *Phylarchus and the Spartan Revolution*, Berkeley and Los Angeles: University of California Press, 1961.
— 'Psychohistory, Ancient History and Freud: The Descent into Avernus', *Arethusa*, 12 (1979), 5-33.
— *Science and the State in Greece and Rome*, New York: John Wiley & Sons, 1967.
Andrewes, A., *The Greek Tyrants*, New York: Harper Torchbooks, 1963.
Armstrong, C.B., 'Plato's Academy.' *Leeds Philosophical and Literary Society: Proceedings* 7 (1953), 89-106.
Arnheim, M.T.W., *Aristocracy in Greek Society*, Ithaca: Cornell University Press, 1977.
Aron, Raymond, *Politics and History*, edited and translated by Miriam Bernheim Conant, New York: The Free Press, 1978.
— *The Opium of the Intellectuals*, translated by Terence Kilmartin, New York: The Norton Library, 1962.
Baldry, H.C., 'Zeno's Ideal State', *Journal of Hellenic Studies*, 79 (1959), 3-15.
Balsdon, J.P.V.D., 'The Divinity of Alexander', *Historia*, 1 (1950), 3/1-82.
Barker, Ernest, *Greek Political Theory*, London: University Paperbacks, 1960.
Barnstone, Willis (trans.), *Greek Lyric Poetry*, New York: Schocken Books, 1972.
Bayet, Jean, *Les origines de l'Hercule romain*, Paris: E. De Boccard Editeur, 1926.
Beck, Frederick A.G., *Greek Education*, London: Methuen & Co. Ltd, 1964.
Becker, J.B., 'The Influence of Roman Stoicism upon the Gracchi Economic Land Reforms', *La Parola del Passato*, 19 (1964), 125-34.
Beer, Max, *Fifty Years of International Socialism*, New York: Macmillan, 1935.
Bendix, Reinhard and Roth, Guenther, *Scholarship and Partisanship: Essays on Max Weber*, Berkeley and Los Angeles: University of California Press, 1971.
Berlin, Isaiah, *The Hedgehog and the Fox*, New York: Simon & Schuster, 1953.
Bernstein, Eduard, *Evolutionary Socialism: A Critique and Affirmation*, translated by Edith C. Harvey, New York: Schocken Books, 1961.
Bickermann, E. and Sykutris, Joh., 'Speusipps Brief an König Philip', *Berichte über die Verhandlungen der Sachsiche der Wissenschaften zu Leipzig*, Philologische-historische Klasse, 80 (1928), 1-86.

Bidez, J., 'La Cité du Monde et la Cité du Soleil chez les Stoiciens', *Bulletin de l'Académie Royale de Belgique*, Lettres, 18 (1932), 244-94.
Bignone, Ettore, *L'Aristotele perduto e la formazione filosofica di Epicuro*, 2 vols, 2nd. rev. ed, Florence: La Nuova Italia Editrice, 1973.
Billington, James, *Fire in the Minds of Men: Origins of the Revolutionary Faith*, New York: Basic Books, 1980.
— 'The Intelligentsia and the Religion of Humanity', *American Historical Review*, 65 (1960), 807-21.
Bluck, R.S., 'Plato's Biography: The Seventh Letter', *Philosophical Review*, 58 (1949), 503-9.
Boas, George, 'Fact and Legend in the Biography of Plato', *Philosophical Review*, 57 (1948), 439-57.
— *French Philosophers of the Romantic Period*, Baltimore: The Johns Hopkins Press, 1925.
Boren, Henry, C., *The Gracchi*, New York: Twayne Publishers, 1968.
Bowersock, Glen, *Greek Sophists in the Roman Empire*, Oxford: Clarendon Press, 1969.
Bowie, E.L., 'Greeks and Their Past in the Second Sophistic', 166-209, in M.I. Finley (ed.), *Studies in Ancient Society*.
Boyance, Pierre, *Le culte des Muses chez les philosophes grecs: études d'histoire et de psychologie religieuse*, Paris: E. De Boccard Editeur, 1937.
Brombert, Victor, *The Intellectual Hero: Studies in the French Novel 1880-1955*, Philadelphia: Lippincott, 1961.
Brown, Truesdell, S., 'Callisthenes and Alexander', *American Journal of Philology*, 70 (1949), 225-48.
— 'Euhemerus and the Historians', *Harvard Theological Review*, 29 (1946), 259-74.
— 'Herodotus Speculates on Egypt', *American Journal of Philology*, 86 (1965), 60-76.
— *The Greek Historians*, Lexington, Ky.: D.C. Heath & Co., 1973.
— *Timaeus of Tauromenium*, Berkeley and Los Angeles: University of California Press, 1958.
Brumbaugh, Robert S. and Jessica Schwartz, 'Pythagoras and Beans: A Medical Explanation', *Classical World*, 73 (1980), 421-2.
Burckhardt, Jacob D., *Griechische Kulturgeschichte*, edited by Rudolf Max, Stuttgart: Kroner, 1948.
Burger, Thomas, *Max Weber's Theory of Concept Formation: History, Laws, and Ideal Types*, Durham, NC: Duke University Press, 1976.
Burkert, Walter, *Lore and Science in Ancient Pythagoreanism*, translated by Edwin L. Minar, Jr., Cambridge, Mass.: Harvard University Press, 1972.
Burn, A.R., *The Lyric Age of Greece*, London: Edward Arnold, 1960.
Burnet, John, *Early Greek Philosophy*, 4th ed., London: Adam & Charles Black, 1930.
— *Greek Philosophy: Thales to Plato*, London: Macmillan & Co. Ltd, 1964.
Burstein, S.M., *Outpost to Hellenism: The Emergence of Heraclea on the Black Sea*, Berkeley and Los Angeles: University of California Press, 1976.
Calder, W.M., 'The Spurned Doxy: An Unnoticed *Topoi* in English Academic Autobiography', *Classical World*, 73 (1980), 305-6.
Calhoun, George Miller, *Athenian Clubs in Politics and Litigation*, Austin, Texas: University of Texas Bulletin No. 262, reprint, 1913.
Cameron, Alister, *The Pythagorean Background of the Theory of Recollection*, Menasha, Wisconsin: George Banta Publishing Company, 1938.
Cary, Max, *A History of the Greek World from 323 to 146 BC*, 2nd rev. ed., London: Methuen & Co. Ltd, 1959.

Cawkwell, George, *Philip of Macedon*, London: Faber & Faber, 1978.
Cherniss, Harold, *Aristotle's Criticism of Plato and the Academy*, New York: Russell & Russell, 1962.
Chroust, A.H., *Aristotle*, 2 vols, London: Routledge & Kegan Paul Ltd, 1973.
— 'Plato's Academy: The First Organized School of Political Science in Antiquity', *Review of Politics*, 29 (1967), 25-40.
— 'A Second (and Closer) Look at Plato's Political Philosophy', *Archiv für Rechts- und Sozialphilosophie*, 48 (1962), 449-86.
Ciaceri, Emanuele, *Storia della Magna Graecia*, 3 vols, 2nd rev. ed., Milan: Città di Castello, 1928.
Clark, Stephen L.R., *Aristotle's Man*, Oxford: Clarendon Press, 1975.
Cloché, Paul, *Isocrate et son temps*, Paris: Les Belles Lettres, 1963.
Cohen, Shaye J.D., *Josèphus in Galilee and Rome*, Leiden: E.J. Brill, 1979.
Connor, W. Robert, *The Politicians of Fifth Century Athens*, Princeton: Princeton University Press, 1971.
Cook, S.A., Adcock, F.E. and Charlesworth, M. (eds.), *Cambridge Ancient History*, Vol. VII, Cambridge: Cambridge University Press, 1969.
Cooley, Charles, *Social Organization: A Study of the Larger Mind*, Introduction by Philip Rieff, New York: Schocken Books, 1967.
Cornford, F.M., *From Religion to Philosophy: A Study in the Origins of Western Speculation*, New York: Harper Torchbooks, 1957.
— *The Origin of Attic Comedy*, Garden City, NY: Anchor Books, 1961.
Coser, Lewis A., *Men of Ideas*, New York: The Free Press, 1970.
Cowdrey, H.E.J., 'The Genesis of the Crusades: The Springs of Western Ideas of Holy War', 9-32, in Thomas Patrick Murphy (ed.), *The Holy War*, Columbus: Ohio State University Press, 1976.
Creel, H.G., *Chinese Thought*, London: University Paperbacks, 1962.
Crossman, R.H.S., *Plato Today*, 2nd rev. ed., London: Unwin Books, 1971.
Dahrendorf, Rolf, *Society and Democracy in Germany*, Garden City, NY: Doubleday & Co. Inc., 1967.
Davies, J.K., *Democracy and Classical Greece*, London: Harvester Press, 1978.
Day, James and Chambers, Mortimer, *Aristotle's History of Athenian Democracy*, Berkeley and Los Angeles: University of California Press, 1962.
De Huszar, George B. (ed.), *The Intellectuals: A Controversial Portrait*, Glencoe, Illinois: The Free Press, 1960.
Delatte, Armand, *La Vie de Pythagore de Diogène Laërce*, Académie Royale des Sciences et Belles Lettres de Bruxelles, Classe Mémoires, Ser. 2, Tome 17 2nd, 1922.
—*Essai sur la politique pythagoricienne*, Liège: Imp. H. Vaillant-Carmanne, 1922.
Demand, N., 'Pythagoras, Son of Mnesarchus', *Phronesis*, 18 (1973), 91-6.
Derenne, Eudore, *Les procès d'impiété intentés aux philosophes à Athenes au Vme au IVme siècles avant J-C*, Paris: Eduard Champion, 1930.
Detienne, Marcel, ['Communications'] in *Filosofia e scienze in Magna Graecia: Atti del quinto convegno di studi sulla Magna Graecia*, Naples: L'Arte Tipografica (1966), 149-56.
— 'Des confréries de guerriers à la société pythagoricienne', *Revue de l'Histoire des Religions*, 163 (1963), 127-31.
— 'La cuisine de Pythagore', *Archives Sociologiques des Religions*, 29 (1970), 141-62.
—*Dionysos Slain*, translated by Mireille Muellner and Leonard Muellner, Baltimore: The Johns Hopkins University Press, 1979.
— 'Héraclès héros pythagoricien', *Revue de l'Histoire des Religions*, 158 (1960), 19-53.

— *La Notion de Daimon dans le Pythagorisme ancien*, Paris: Les Belles Lettres, 1963.
Devereux, Georges, 'Greek Pseudo-Homosexuality and the "Greek Miracle" ', *Symbolae Osloensis*, 42 (1967), 69-92.
De Vogel, C.J. (ed.), *Greek Philosophy, A Collection of Texts: Selected and Supplied with Some Notes and Explanations*, 3 vols, Leiden: E.J. Brill, 1950-59.
— *Pythagoras and Early Pythagoreanism*, Assen: Van Gorcum & Co., 1966.
Dittenberger, Wilhelm, *Orientis Gracii Inscriptiones Selectae*, Vol. I, Leipzig: S. Hirzel, 1903.
Dodds, E.R., *The Greeks and the Irrational*, Berkeley and Los Angeles: University of California Press, 1951.
Dover, K.J., 'The Freedom of the Intellectual in Greek Society', *Talanta*, 7 (1976), 24-54.
— *Greek Homosexuality*, London: Duckworth, 1978.
Dudley, Donald R., *A History of Cynicism from Diogenes to the 6th Century AD*, London: Methuen & Co. Ltd, 1937.
— 'Blossius of Cumae', *Journal of Roman Studies*, 31 (1941), 94-9.
Dunbabin, T.J., *The Western Greeks: The History of Sicily and South Italy from the Foundations of the Greek Colonies to 480 BC*, Oxford: Clarendon Press, 1948.
Düring, Ingemar, *Aristotle in the Ancient Biographical Tradition*, Studia Graeca et Latina Gothoburgensia 5, Goteborg: Goteborgs Universitets Arsskrift, 1957.
— (ed. and trans.), *Chion of Heraclea: A Novel in Letters*, Goteborg: Acta Universitatis Gotoburgensis, Goteborgs Hogskolas Arsskrift 57, 1951.
— *Herodicus the Cratetean: A Study in the Anti-Platonic Tradition*, Stockholm: Wahlstron & Widstrand, 1941.
Edelstein, Ludwig, *Plato's Seventh Letter*, Leiden: E.J. Brill, 1966.
— (trans.), *The Hippocratic Oath*, Baltimore: The Johns Hopkins Press, 1943.
Edinger, Edward F., *Ego and Archetype*, Baltimore: Penguin Books, 1973.
Ehrenberg, Victor, *Sophocles and Pericles*, Oxford: Basil Blackwell, 1954.
Eliade, Mircea, *Zalmoxis: The Vanishing God*, translated by Willard R. Trask, Chicago: University of Chicago Press, 1972.
Erdmann, Carl, *The Origin of the Idea of the Crusade*, translated by Marshall W. Baldwin and Walter Goffart, Princeton: Princeton University Press, 1977.
Errington, R.M., *Philopoemen*, Oxford: Clarendon Press, 1969.
Fairweather, J.A., 'Fiction in the Biographies of Ancient Writers', *Ancient Society*, 5 (1974), 231-75.
Federn, Walter, 'The Transformations in the Coffin Texts: A New Approach', *Journal of Near Eastern Studies*, 19 (1960), 241-57.
Ferguson, John, *The Heritage of Hellenism*, New York: Science History Publications, 1973.
— *Moral Values in the Ancient World*, London: Methuen & Co. Ltd, 1958.
— *Utopias of the Ancient World*, Ithaca, NY: Cornell University Press, 1975.
Ferguson, William Scott, *Hellenistic Athens: An Historical Essay*, London: Macmillan & Co., Ltd, 1911.
Festa, Nicole (ed. and trans.), *I frammenti degli Stoici antichi*, 2 vols., Bari: Gius. Laterza & Figli, 1932-5.
Festugière, A.J.M., ' "De Vita Pythagorica" de Jamblique', *Revue des Etudes Grecques*, 50 (1937), 437-61.
— *La Révélation d'Hermès Trismégiste*, Vol. II, Paris: Librarie Lecoffre, 1949.
Feuer, Lewis S., *Ideology and the Ideologists*, New York: Harper & Row, 1975.
— 'The Political Linguistics of Intellectual: 1898-1918', *Survey*, 78 (1971), 156-83.

Field, G.C., *Plato and His Contemporaries*, 3rd ed., London: Methuen, 1967.
Finley, M.I., *Aspects of Antiquity*, New York: Viking Press, 1968.
— *A History of Sicily: Ancient Sicily to the Arab Conquest*, rev. ed., London: Chatto & Windus, 1979.
— (ed.), *Studies in Ancient Society*, London: Routledge & Kegan Paul Ltd, 1974.
— 'Utopianism Ancient and Modern', 178-92, in *The Use and Abuse of History*, New York: Viking Press, 1975.
— *The World of Odysseus*, 2nd rev. ed., New York: Viking Press, 1918.
Frank, E., *Plato und die sogenannten Pythagoreer*, 2nd ed., Darmstadt: Wissenschaftliche Buchgesellschaft, 1962.
Frankel, Hermann, *Early Greek Poetry and Philosophy*, translated by Moses Hadas and James Willis, New York: Harcourt Brace Jovanovich, 1975.
Fraser, P.M., *Ptolemic Alexandria*, 3 vols., Oxford: Clarendon Press, 1972.
Freeman, Kathleen, *The Work and Life of Solon*, Cardiff: University of Wales Press Board, 1926.
Frenkian, Aram M., 'Die Historia des Pythagoras', *Maia*, 11 (1959), 243-5.
Friedlander, Paul, *Plato*, Vol. I, 2nd rev. ed., translated by Hans Meyerhoff, Princeton: Princeton University Press, 1969.
Fritz, Kurt von, 'The Historian Theopompos: His Political Convictions and His Concept of Historiography', *American Historical Review*, 46 (1941), 765-87.
— 'The Philosophical Passage in the Seventh Platonic Letter and the Problem of Plato's "Esoteric" Philosophy', 408-47, in J.P. Anton and G.L. Kustas (eds.), *Essays in Ancient Greek Philosophy*, Albany: State University of New York Press, 1971.
— *Platon in Sizilien und das Problem der Philosophenherrschaft*, Berlin: Walter de Gruyter & Co., 1968.
— *Pythagorean Politics in Southern Italy*, New York: Columbia University Press, 1940.
— *Schriften zur griechischen und römischen Verfassungsgeschichte und Verfassungstheorie*, Berlin: Walter de Gruyter & Co., 1976.
Froidement, Christian, *Le mirage Egyptien dans la littérature grecque d'Homère à Aristote*, Paris: Imprimerie Louis-Jean, 1971.
Frost, Frank, *Plutarch's Themistocles: A Historical Commentary*, Princeton: Princeton University Press, 1980.
— 'Themistocles and Mnesiphilus', *Historia*, 20 (1971), 20-25.
Fuks, A., 'Isocrates and the Social-Economic Situation in Greece', *Ancient Society*, 3 (1972), 17-44.
Gaiser, Konrad, 'Plato's Enigmatic Lecture "On the Good"', *Phronesis*, 25 (1980), 5-37.
Gautier, Paul, *Madame de Staël et Napoléon*, Paris: Plon, 1903.
Geffcken, J., 'Antiplatonica', *Hermes*, 64 (1929), 87-109.
Gehrke, Hans-Joachim, 'Das Verhältnis von Politik und Philosophie im Wirken des Demetrios von Phaleron', *Chiron*, 8 (1978), 149-93.
Gella, Aleksander, *The Intelligentsia and the Intellectuals: Theory, Method and Case Study*, Sage Studies in International Sociology 5, Beverly Hills, California: Sage Publications Inc., 1976.
Gianelli, Giulio, *Culti e miti della Magna Graecia*, 2nd ed., Florence: Samson Editore, 1963.
Gicante, M., 'Diogene Laerzio, storico e cronistica dei filosofi antichi', *Atena e Roma*, n.s., 18 (1973), 105-32.
Gigon, Olaf, 'Platon und politische Wirklichkeit', *Gymnasium*, 69 (1962), 205-19.
— (ed.), *Vita Aristoteles Marciana*, Kleine Texte für Vorlesungen und Ubungen 59, Berlin: Walter de Gruyter & Co., 1962.

Gomme, A.W., *Athenian Democracy*, Oxford: Basil Blackwell, 1966.
— *A Historical Commentary on Thucydides*, Vol. I, Oxford: Clarendon Press, 1950.
Gomperz, T., *Greek Thinkers*, Vol. 2, edited and translated by C.G. Berry, London: John Murray, 1905.
Gottschalk, H.B., *Heraclides of Pontus*, Oxford: Clarendon Press, 1980.
Gouldner, Alvin W., *Enter Plato: Classical Greece and the Origins of Social Theory*, New York: Basic Books, 1965.
— *The Future of Intellectuals and the Rise of the New Class*, London: Heinemann, 1971.
Green, Peter, *Alexander the Great*, rev. ed., Harmondsworth: Penguin Books, 1974.
Grilli, Alberto, 'Zenone e Antigono II', *Rivista di Filologia e di Instruzione Classica*, 91 (1963), 287-301.
Groningen, B.A. von, 'General Literary Tendencies in the Second Century AD', *Mnemosyne*, 18 (1965), 41-56.
Grote, George, *A History of Greece*, new edition, 10 vols., London: John Murray, 1888.
— *Plato and the Other Companions of Socrates*, 3 vols., 3rd ed., London: John Murray, 1875.
Gulley, Norman, 'The Authenticity of the Platonic Epistles', 105-30, in *Entretiens sur l'antiquité classique: Pseudepigrapha I*.
Guthrie, W.K.C., 'Aristotle as a Historian of Philosophy', *Journal of Hellenic Studies*, 77 (1957), 35-41.
— *The Greeks and Their Gods*, Boston: Beacon Press, 1955.
— *A History of Greek Philosophy*, Vols., I-V. Cambridge: Cambridge University Press, 1962-78.
— *Orpheus and Greek Religion*, London: Methuen & Co. Ltd, 1935.
Hamilton, Alastair, *The Appeal of Fascism: A Study of Intellectuals and Fascism: 1919-1945*, London: A. Blond, 1971.
Hamilton, J.R., 'The Letters in Plutarch's Alexander', *Proceedings of the African Classical Association*, 4 (1961), 9-20.
— *Plutarch's Alexander: A Commentary*, Oxford: Clarendon Press, 1969.
Hammond, N.G.L. and Griffith, G.T., *A History of Macedonia*, Vol. 2, Oxford: Clarendon Press, 1979.
Hansen, Esther V., *The Attalids of Pergamon*, 2nd ed., Ithaca: Cornell University Press, 1971.
Hartog, F., 'Salmoxis: le Pythagore des Gètes ou l'autre de Pythagore', *Annali della Scuola Normale di Pisa*, Classe di Lettere e Filosofia, 8 (1978), 15-42.
Harward, J. (ed. and trans.), *The Platonic Epistles*, Cambridge: Cambridge University Press, 1932.
Head, Barclay V., *Historia Numorum: A Manual of Greek Numismatics*, 1911, reprint, Chicago: Argonaut Inc., Publishers, 1967.
Helm, Rudolf, *Lucian und Menipp*, Leipzig and Berlin: B.G. Teubner, 1906.
Hengel, Martin, *Judaism and Hellenism*, 3 vols, translated by John Bowden, London: SCM Press, 1974.
Hofstadter, Richard, *Anti-Intellectualism in American Life*, New York: Alfred A. Knopf, 1963.
Hope, Richard, *The Book of Diogenes Laertius*, New York: Columbia University Press, 1930.
Howard, Michael, 'Conducting the Concert of Powers', *Times Literary Supplement*, 21 December 1979, 147-8.
Humphreys, S.C., *Anthropology and the Greeks*, London: Routledge & Kegan

Paul, 1978.
Huxley, George L., *The Early Ionians*, London: Faber & Faber, 1966.
— 'Aristotle's Interest in Biography', *Greek, Roman and Byzantine Studies*, 15 (1974), 203-13.
Iggers, George G., *The Cult of Authority*, The Hague: M. Nijhoff, 1958.
Jacoby, Felix, *Atthis: The Local Chronicles of Ancient Athens*, Oxford: Clarendon Press, 1949.
— *Die Fragmente der griechischen Historiker*, 3 vols. in many parts, Leiden: E.J. Brill, 1940-55.
— 'Some Remarks on Ion of Chios', *Classical Quarterly* (1947), 1-13.
Jaeger, Werner, *Aristotle: Fundamentals of the History of His Development*, 2nd. ed., translated by Richard Robinson, London: Oxford University Press, 1962.
— 'The Date of Isocrates' *Areopagiticus* and the Athenian Opposition', 409-50, in *Athenian Studies Presented to William Scott Ferguson*, Cambridge, Mass.: Harvard University Press, 1940.
— *Five Essays*, translated by Adele M. Fiske, Montreal: M. Casalini, 1966.
— *Paideia: The Ideals of Greek Culture*, 3 vols., 2nd ed., translated by Gilbert Highet, New York: Oxford University Press, 1945.
James, William, *The Will to Believe and Other Essays in Popular Philosophy*, new ed., London: Longmans, Green, 1937.
— *Pragmatism*, New York: Longmans, Green, 1943.
Jebb, R.C., *The Attic Orators from Antiphon to Isaeos*, 2 vols., London: Macmillan & Co., 1876.
Jenkyns, Richard, *The Victorians and Ancient Greece*, Cambridge, Mass.: Harvard University Press, 1980.
Johnson, R., 'Isocrates' Method of Teaching', *American Journal of Philology*, 80 (1959), 25-36.
— 'A Note on the Number of Isocrates' Pupils', *American Journal of Philology*, 78 (1957), 297-300.
Joly, Robert, *Le thème philosophique des genres de vie de l'antiquité classique*, Académie Royale de Belgique, Classe des lettres et des sciences morales et politiques, Mémoires 2e Série, Vol. 29, fasc. 3.
Jones, C.P., *Plutarch and Rome*, Oxford: Clarendon Press, 1971.
Jowett, Benjamin (trans.), *The Dialogues of Plato*, 4 vols., 4th rev. ed., Oxford: Clarendon Press, 1953.
Kahrstedt, U., 'Platons Verkauf in die Sklaverei', *Würzburger Jahrberichte*, 2 (1947), 295-300.
— 'Zur Geschichte Grossgriechenlands im 5. Jahrhundert', *Hermes*, 53 (1918), 180-87.
Kelsen, Hans, 'Platonic Love', *The American Imago*, 3 (1942), 3-110.
— 'Platonic Justice', *Ethics*, 48 (1937-8), 367-400.
Kerferd, G.B., *The Sophistic Movement*, Cambridge: Cambridge University Press, 1981.
Kennedy, George, *The Art of Persuasion in Greece*, Princeton: Princeton University Press, 1963.
Kirk, G.S. and Raven, J.E. (eds.), *The Presocratic Philosophers*, Cambridge: Cambridge University Press, 1963.
Knights, Ben, *The Idea of the Clerisy in the Nineteenth Century*, Cambridge: Cambridge University Press, 1978.
Knowles, Thomas, 'The Spurned Doxy and the Dead Bride: Some Ramifications for Ancient *Topoi*', *Classical World*, 73 (1980), 223-5.
Koestler, Arthur, *The Yogi and the Commissar*, New York: Macmillan Co., 1967.

Kolakowski, Leszek, *The Devil and Scripture*, translated by Nicholas Bethel and Celina Wieniewska, London: Oxford University Press, 1973.
— *Marxism and Beyond*, translated by Jane Zielonko Peel, London: Pall Mall Press, 1969.
Laistner, M.L.W., 'The Influence of Isocrates' Political Doctrines on Fourth Century Men of Affairs', *Classical World*, 23 (1930), 129-31.
Lane Fox, Robin, *Alexander the Great*, New York: The Dial Press, 1974.
Lattimore, Richard (trans.), *Greek Lyrics*, 2nd rev. ed., Chicago: University of Chicago Press, 1960.
Lesky, Albin, *A History of Greek Literature*, 2nd ed., translated by James Willis and Cornelis de Heer, London: Methuen & Co. Ltd, 1966.
Levy, Isidore, *La légende de Pythagore de Grèce en Palestine*, Paris: Librarie Ancienne Honore Champion, 1927.
— *Recherches sur les sources de la légende de Pythagore*, Paris: Editions Ernest Leroux, 1926.
Lewis, I.M., *Ecstatic Religion: An Anthropological Study of Spirit Possession and Shamanism*, Harmondsworth: Penguin Books, 1971.
Lipset, Seymor Martin and Basu, Asoke, 'Intellectual Types and Political Roles', 433-70, in Lewis A. Coser (ed.), *The Idea of Social Structure: Papers in Honor of Robert K. Merton*, New York: Harcourt Brace Jovanovich, 1975.
Lloyd-Jones, Hugh, *The Justice of Zeus*, Berkeley and Los Angeles: University of California Press, 1960.
Long, A.A., 'Timon of Phlius: Pyrrhonist and Satirist', *Cambridge Philological Society: Proceedings*, 204 (1978), 68-91.
Lord, C., 'Politics and Philosophy in Aristotle's "Politics" ', *Hermes*, 106 (1978), 337-58.
Luther, H., *Josephus and Justus von Tiberias: Ein Beitrag zur Geschichte des jüdischen Aufstandes*, Halle: Wischau & Burkhardt, 1910.
Lynch, John Patrick, *Aristotle's School*, Berkeley and Los Angeles: University of California Press, 1972.
Mannheim, Karl, *Ideology and Utopia: An Introduction to the Sociology of Knowledge*, translated by Louis Wirth and Edward Shils, New York: Harcourt, Brace & World, 1970.
Manuel, Frank, *The Prophets of Paris*, Cambridge, Mass.: Harvard University Press, 1962.
Markle, Minar M., 'Support of Athenian Intellectuals for Philip: A Study in Isocrates' *Philippus* and Speusippus' *Letter to Philip*', *Journal of Hellenistic Studies*, 96 (1976): 80-99.
Marrou, H.I., *A History of Education in Antiquity*, 3rd ed., translated by George Lamb, New York: Mentor Books, 1964.
Martin, Rex, *Historical Explanation*, Ithaca: Cornell University Press, 1977.
Mekler, Segofredus (ed.), *Academicorum Philosophorum Index Herculanensis*, Berlin: Apud Weidmannos, 1902.
Merlan, P., 'Form and Content in Plato's Philosophy', *Journal of the History of Ideas*, 8 (1947), 406-30.
— 'Isocrates, Aristotle and Alexander the Great', *Historia*, 3 (1954-55), 60-82.
Mejer, Jørgen, *Diogenes Laertius and His Hellenistic Background*, Hermes Einzelschriften, vol. 40, Wiesbaden: Franz Steiner Verlag, 1978.
Melloni, Rita Cuccioli, *Ricerche sul Pitagorismo*, Vol. 1, Bologna: Editirice Compositori, 1969.
Meyer, E., *Geschichte des Altertums*, Vol. 5, 1913, reprint, Darmstadt: Wissenschaftliche Buchgesellschaft, 1975.
Millar, Fergus, *The Emperor in the Roman World*, London: Duckworth, 1977.
Minar, Edwin L., Jr., *Early Pythagorean Politics in Practice and Theory*, Baltimore:

Waverly Press Inc., 1942.
— 'Pythagorean Communism', *Transactions and Proceedings of the American Philological Association*, 75 (1944), 34-46.
Momigliano, Arnaldo, *Alien Wisdom: The Limits of Hellenization*, Cambridge: Cambridge University Press, 1975.
— *The Development of Greek Biography*, Cambridge, Mass.: Harvard University Press, 1971.
— *Essays in Ancient and Modern Historiography*, Oxford: Basil Blackwell, 1977.
— *Filippo il Macedone*, Florence: Felice le Monnier, 1934.
— 'Second Thoughts on Greek Biography', 33-47, in *Quinto contributo alla storia degli studi classici e del mondo antico*, Vol. I, Rome: Edizioni di storia e letteratura, 1975.
— *Studies in Historiography*, London: Weidenfeld & Nicolson, 1966.
Moravia, S., *Il Tramonto dell' illuminismo filosofia e politica nella società francese 1770-1810*, Bari: Laterza, 1968.
Morrison, J.S., 'The Origins of Plato's Philosopher-Statesman', *Classical Quarterly*, n.s., 8 (1958), 198-218.
— 'Pythagoras of Samos', *Classical Quarterly*, n.s., 6 (1956), 135-56.
Morrow, Glen R., *Plato's Cretan City*, Princeton, NJ: Princeton University Press, 1960.
— (trans.), *Plato's Epistles*, Indianapolis: Bobbs-Merrill, 1962.
Mossé, Claude, *Athens in Decline 404-86 BC*, translated by Jean Stewart, London: Routledge & Kegan Paul, 1973.
— *La fin de la démocratie Athénienne*, Paris: Presses Universitaires de France, 1962.
— 'Sur un passage de l'Archimados d'Isocrate', *Revue des Etudes Anciennes*, 551 (1953), 29-55.
Mulvany, C.M., 'Notes on the Legend of Aristotle', *Classical Review*, 20 (1926), 155-63.
Munro, A.H., 'The Speech of Urban II at Clermont', *American Historical Review*, II (1905), 221-42.
Murphy, G. and Ballou (eds.), *William James on Psychical Research*, London: Chatto & Windus, 1961.
Murray, Gilbert, *Greek Studies*, Oxford: Clarendon Press, 1946.
Nicholas, Ray, *Treason, Tradition and the Intellectual: Julien Benda and Political Discourse*, Lawrence, Kansas: The Regents Press of Kansas, 1978.
Oldfather, W.A., 'Pythagoras on Individual Differences and the Authoritarian Principle', *Classical Journal*, 33 (1937/8), 537-9.
Parente, M. Isnardi, 'Rilegendo *il Platone* di Ulrich von Wilamonitz-Moellendorf', *Annali della Scuola Normale Superiore di Pisa*, Classe di Lettere e Filosofia, 3 (1973), 147-67.
— 'Studi recenti e problemi aperti sulla structura e la funzione della Prima Accademia Platonica', *Rivista Storica Italiana*, 71 (1959), 271-91.
— 'Teoria e prassi nel pensiero dell' Accademia antica', *La Parola del Passato*, 11 (1956), 401-33.
Parke, H.W., *Greek Mercenary Soldiers: From the Earliest Times to the Battle of Ipsus*, Oxford: Clarendon Press, 1933.
Pearleman, S., 'Isocrates' *Philippus* – a Reinterpretation', *Historia*, 6 (1957), 306-17.
— 'Panhellenism, the Polis and Imperialism', *Historia*, 15 (1976), 1-30.
Pearson, Lionel, 'The Diary and Letters of Alexander the Great', *Historia*, 3 (1954/5), 429-55.
Peters, Edward M. (ed.), *The First Crusade: The Chronicle of Fulcher of Chartres and Other Source Materials*, Philadelphia: University of Pennsylvania Press,

1971.

Pierart, Marcel, *Platon et la Cité grecque: théorie et réalité dans la constitution des 'Lois'*, Académie Royale de Belgique, Mémoires de la classe des lettres, Collection in 8º-2e série, Vol. 62, fasc. 3, 1974.

Pfeiffer, Rudolf, *A History of Classical Scholarship: From the Beginnings to the End of the Hellenistic Age*, Oxford: Clarendon Press, 1968.

Philip, J.A., *Pythagoras and Early Pythagoreanism*, Toronto: University of Toronto Press, 1966.

Plezia, Marian (ed. and trans.), 'Lettre d'Aristote à Alexandre sur la politique envers les cités', *Archiwum Filologiczne*, 25 (1970).

—— (ed.), *Aristoteles Epistularum Fragmenta Testamento*, Warsaw: Panstwowe Wydawn, Naukowe, 1961.

Podlecki, Anthony J., 'The Peripatetics as Literary Critics', *Phoenix*, 23 (1969), 114-37.

Popper, Karl, *The Open Society and Its Enemies*, Vol. I, 4th ed., London: Routledge & Kegan Paul, 1962.

Porter, W.H., *Plutarch: Life of Dion; With Introduction and Notes*, Dublin: Hodges, Figgis & Co. Ltd, 1952.

—— 'The Sequel to Plato's First Visit to Sicily', *Hermathena*, 61 (1943), 46-55.

Rajak, Tessa, 'Justus of Tiberias', *Classical Quarterly*, 23 (1973), 345-68.

Reesor, Margaret E., *The Political Theory of the Old and Middle Stoa*, New York: J.J. Augustin Publisher, 1951.

Rhode, Erwin, *Kleine Schriften*, Vol. 1, Tübingen and Leipzig: J.L.B. Mohr, 1901.

—— *Psyche*, 8th ed., translated by W.B. Hillis, London: Kegan Paul, Trench, Trubner & Co. Ltd, 1925.

Rieff, Philip (ed.), *On Intellectuals: Theoretical Studies, Case Studies*, Garden City, NY: Doubleday & Company Inc., 1969.

Riesman, David, *The Lonely Crowd*, abridged ed., New Haven: Yale University Press, 1971.

Riginos, Alice Swift, *Platonica: The Anecdotes Concerning the Life and Writings of Plato*, Leiden: E.J. Brill, 1976.

Romilly, J. de, 'Eunoia in Isocrates or the Political Importance of Creating Good Will', *Journal of Hellenic Studies*, 78 (1958), 92-101.

Rose, Valentin (ed.), *Aristoteles Pseudepigraphus*, 1863, reprint, Hildesheim: Georg Olms Verlag, 1971.

Rostagni, A., 'Un nuovo capitolo nella storia della retorica e della Sofistica', in *Scritti Minori*, Vol. 1, Torino: Bottega d'Erasmo, 1955.

—— 'Pitagora e i Pitagorici in Timeo', in *Scritti Minori*, Vol. 2, 1.

Rostovtsev, M.A., *The Social and Economic History of the Hellenistic World*, Vol. II, Oxford: Clarendon Press, 1961.

Roth, Guenther and Schluchter, Wolfgang, *Max Weber's Vision of History: Ethics and Methods*, Berkeley and Los Angeles: University of California Press, 1979.

Russell, Bertrand, *A History of Western Philosophy*, London: Allen & Unwin, 1974.

Ryle, Gilbert, *Plato's Progress*, Cambridge: Cambridge University Press, 1966.

Schalit, Abraham, 'Josephus und Justus: Studien zur Vita des Josephus', *Klio*, 26 (1933), 67-95.

Schrödinger, Ervin, *Nature and the Greeks*, Cambridge: Cambridge University Press, 1954.

Schuhl, P.M., 'Platon et l'activité politique de l'Académie', *Revue des Etudes Grecques*, 59/60 (1946/7), 44-53.

Schurer, Emil, *The History of the Jewish People in the Age of Jesus Christ 175 BC-AD 135*, revised and edited by Geza Vermes and Fergus Millar, Vol. 1,

Edinburgh: T. & T. Clark Ltd, 1973.
Seel, Otto (ed.), *M. Iuniani Iustini: Epitoma Historiarum Philippicarum Pompei Trogi*, Stuttgart: B.G. Teubner, 1972.
Shils, Edward, *The Calling of Sociology and Other Essays on the Pursuit of Learning*, Chicago: University of Chicago Press, 1980.
— *Center and Periphery: Essays in Macrosociology*, Chicago: University of Chicago Press, 1975.
— *The Intellectuals and the Powers and Other Essays*, Chicago: University of Chicago Press, 1972.
Simmel, Georg, *The Sociology of Georg Simmel*, edited and translated by Kurt H. Wolff, Glencoe, Illinois: The Free Press, 1950.
Sinclair, T.A., *A History of Greek Political Thought*, London: Routledge & Kegan Paul Ltd, 1961.
Stuart, Duane Reed, 'Authors' Lives as Revealed in Their Works: A Critical Resumé', 285-304, in George Hadzsits (ed.), *Classical Studies in Honor of John C. Rolfe*, Philadelphia: University of Pennsylvania Press, 1931.
— *Epochs of Greek and Roman Biography*, Berkeley: University of California Press, 1928.
Talmon, J.L., *Political Messianism: The Romantic Phase*, London: Secker & Warburg, 1960.
— *The Origins of Totalitarian Democracy*, London: Secker & Warburg, 1952.
Tarn, W.W., 'Alexander the Great and the Unity of Mankind', *Proceedings of the British Academy*, 19 (1933), 123-66.
— *Antigonos Gonatas*, Oxford: Clarendon Press, 1969.
Thibaudeau, Antoine Claire, *Mémoires sur le Consulat. 1799 à 1804: par un ancien conseiller d'état*, Paris: Ponthieu, 1827.
Thomson, George, *Aeschylus and Athens*, 3rd ed., New York: Grosset & Dunlap, 1968.
Tigerstedt, E.N., *Interpreting Plato*, Stockholm: Almqvist Wiksen International, 1977.
— *The Legend of Sparta in Classical Antiquity*, 2 vols., Stockholm: Almqvist & Wiksell, 1956-74.
Timpanaro Cardini, Maria (ed.), 3 vols., *Pitagorici: Testimonianze e Frammenti*, Florence: La Nuova Italia, 1958.
Tod, Marcus N., *A Selection of Greek Historical Inscriptions*, Vol. 2, Oxford: Clarendon Press, 1948.
Toynbee, Arnold J., *Hannibal's Legacy*, Vol. 2, London: Oxford University Press, 1965.
— *A Study of History*, Vol. 5, London: Oxford University Press, 1939.
Turner, Frank M., *The Greek Heritage in Victorian Britain*, New Haven: Yale University Press, 1981.
Van Duzer, Charles Hunter, *Contribution of the Ideologues to French Revolutionary Thought*, Baltimore: The Johns Hopkins Press, 1935.
Vavrinek, V., 'La révolte d'Aristonicos', *Rozpravy Ceskoslovenské, Akademie Véd*, 67, No. 2 (1957), 1-75.
Vlastos, Gregory, 'Theology and Philosophy in Early Greek Thought', 92-109, in David J. Furley and R.E. Allen (eds.), *Studies in Presocratic Philosophy*, Vol. I, New York: Humanities Press, 1970.
Von Albrecht, Michael (ed.), *Iamblichos: Pythagoras: Legende, Lehre, Lebensgestaltung*, Zurich and Stuttgart: Artemis Verlag, 1963.
— 'Das Menschenbild in Iamblichs Darstellung der pythagoreischen Lebensform', *Antike und Abenland*, 12 (1966), 51-63.
Wacholder, Ben Zion, *Eupolemus: A Study of Judaeo-Greek Literature*, Cincinnati: Hebrew Union College, Jewish Institute of Religion, 1974.

Walbank, F.W., *A Historical Commentary on Polybius*, Vol. 1, Oxford: Clarendon Press, 1957.
— 'Polemics in Polybius', *Journal of Roman Studies*, 52 (1962), 5-12.
Wallace, A.F.C., 'Revitalization Movements', 207-20, in S.M. Lipset and N.J. Smelser (eds.), *Sociology: The Progress of a Decade*, Englewood Cliffs, NJ: Prentice-Hall, Inc., 1961.
— *The Death and Rebirth of the Seneca*, New York: Alfred A. Knopf, 1970.
Wardman, Alan, *Plutarch's Lives*, London: Paul Elek, 1974.
Weber, Max, *Economy and Society*, edited by Guenther Roth and Claus Wittich, 3 vols., New York: Bedminster Press, 1968.
— *The Methodology of the Social Sciences*, translated and edited by Edward A. Shils and Henry A. Frich, New York: The Free Press, 1949.
— *The Religion of India*, translated and edited by Hans H. Gerth and Don Martindale, New York: The Free Press, 1958.
Webster, T.B.L., *Studies in Later Greek Comedy*, 2nd ed., Manchester: Manchester University Press, 1970.
Wehrli, Fritz R., *Die Schule des Aristoteles*, Vol. 2: *Aristoxenus*, 2nd ed., Basel and Stuttgart: Schwabe & Co. Verlag, 1967.
— *Die Schule des Aristoteles*, Supplement 1 (1974), *Hermippos der Kallimacheer*.
West, Stephanie, 'Satyrus: Peripatetic or Alexandrian', *Greek, Roman, and Byzantine Studies*, 15 (1974), 279-87.
Westlake, H.D., 'Dion: A Study in Liberation', 251-64, in *Essays on the Greek Historians and Greek History*, New York: Barnes & Noble Inc., 1969.
Whitmont, Edward, *The Symbolic Quest*, New York: Harper Colophon Books, 1973.
Wickersham, John and Verbrugghe, Gerald (eds.), *Greek Historical Documents: The Fourth Century*, Toronto: Hakkert, 1973.
Wilamowitz-Moellendorf, Ulrich von, *Antigonos von Karystos*, Berlin: Weidmannsche Buchhandlung, 1881.
Wilcken, Ulrich, *Alexander the Great*, translated by G.C. Richards, New York: W.W. Norton, 1967.
Wilcox, Stanley, 'Criticism of Isocrates and His *Philosophia*', *Transactions of the American Philological Society*, 74 (1943), 113-33.
Wild, John, *Plato's Modern Enemies and the Theory of Natural Law*, Chicago: University of Chicago Press, 1953.
Will, Edouard, *Histoire politique du monde hellénistique*, 2 vols., Nancy: Imp. Berger-Levrault, 1966-7.
Winspear, A.D., *The Genesis of Plato's Thought*, 2nd rev. ed., New York: Russell & Russell, 1956.
Winspear, A.D. and Silverberg, T., *Who Was Socrates?*, 2nd. ed., New York: Russell & Russell, 1960.
Wormell, D.E.W., 'The Literary Tradition Concerning Hermius of Atarneus', *Yale Classical Studies*, 5 (1935), 57-92.
Yeats, W.B., *The Collected Poems*, 2nd ed., London: Macmillan & Co. Ltd, 1955.
Zeller, Eduard, *Plato and the Older Academy*, 3rd. ed., translated by Sarah Frances Alleyne and Alfred Goodwin, London: Longmans, Green & Co., 1888.
Znaniecki, Florian, *The Social Role of the Man of Knowledge*, New York: Columbia University Press, 1940.
Zwerdling, A., *Yeats and the Heroic Ideal*, New York: New York University Press, 1965.

INDEX

Aalders, G.J.D. 27, 123
Academy 26, 73, 101, 104, 111, 116-17, 121
   as elite group 2, 9, 83-6
   political activities 10, 28, 75, 78, 86-95, 97, 103, 122
   see also Aristotle, Isocrates, Pythagoreans
Adkins, A.W.H. 34
Aeschines 75
Africa, T.W. 124, 126
Alexander the Great 11, 98, 111-16, 118, 130
Alexarchus 118
Anacreon 39-40
Anaxagoras 20, 59, 120
Anaxarchus 112-14
Anaximander 33, 39
Anaximenes of Lampascus 115
Anaximines of Miletus 39
Androtion 109
Antigonus II Gonatus 18-19, 124-6, 131
Antigonus III Doson 121
Antigonus of Carystus 16-18
Antipater 15, 95, 98, 111-12, 114-18
Antipater of Magnesia 109-10
Antisthenes 25
Apollo 26, 30-1, 42-3, 46, 49, 85
Appian 12-13
Arcesilaus 121
Archedemus 82-3
Archidamus III 109
Archytas 23, 57, 59-60, 62, 71-2, 80-3
Aristippus 75, 79-81, 83, 130-2
Ariston of Athens 13
Ariston of Ceos 121
Aristonicus 124, 128-9
Aristonymus 93
Aristophones 25
Aristotle 3, 5, 78, 109, 116, 118, 123
   as source 12, 22, 24, 26, 28, 34-5, 46, 54, 58
   relations with Alexander 112-16
      with Athens 1, 15, 95, 115-16
      with Hermias 95-6
      with Isocrates 98, 100, 102-3
      with Philip 97-8, 111
      with Plato and the Academy 66, 96-8, 103
Aristoxenus 18, 22-4, 26, 31, 36, 39-41, 47, 50, 56, 69
Arnheim, M.T.W. 3
Aron, Raymond 131
Arrian 113
Athens: relations with philosophers 116-21
   see also Aristotle, Isocrates, Plato

Bayet, Jean 42
Beckermann, E. 29
Benda, Julien 1
Bernstein, Eduard 13
Bidez, J. 126, 129
Blossius 124, 126-9
Boeckh, August 28
Brown, Truesdale 114
Burn, A.R. 33
Burkert, W. 51
Burnet, John 33
Calder, W.M. 29
Callipus 26, 88, 90, 92, 96
Callisthenes 28, 95, 112-15
Callistratus 107
Cassander 112, 117-19, 121
Chabrias 101, 117
Chaeron 17, 89, 131
Charmides 64-6
Chilon 30
Chion 86-8
Chion of Heraclea 86, 88
Chroust, A.H. 103
Chrysippus 124
Cicero 12, 71, 103, 127
Cineas 123
Clearchus 86-9
Cleobulus 30
Cleomenes III 126-7
Cleomnis 88
Coleridge, Samuel Taylor 9
Comte, Auguste 8
Corsicus 28, 78, 93-5
Crates 123

Critias 64-6
Cylon 53-7

Damon of Athens 21, 58-9
Damon of Syracuse 23, 50
Davies, J.K. 73, 76
Delatte, A. 22, 24
Demetrius of Phaleron 116-20
Demetrius I Poliorcetes 119-20
Democedes 42, 55
Demochares 10, 12-13, 15, 89, 115-16, 119-20
Demophames 122
Demosthenes 10, 115-16, 121
Derenne, Eudore 120
Detienne, Marcel 42, 147
Devereux, G. 65
Dias 19
Dicaearchus 22, 24-5, 30-2, 36
Didymus 28-9, 94
Diodorus Siculus 25, 45
Diogenes Laertius 13, 17-18, 31, 125, 130
Dion 20-1, 25-6, 71-81, 83, 88-93, 96, 108
Dionysius I 25-6, 60, 72-3, 76-7, 81, 87, 101-2, 109
Dionysius II 23, 25, 50, 72, 75-81, 90, 94, 125, 130-1
Dodds, E.R. 47
Dudley, D.R. 127
Dunbabin, T.J. 57
Düring, Ingemar 15, 22-3, 131

Ecdemos 122
Eisner, Kurt 13
Egypt 38-40
Empedocles 61-2
Epaminondas 20, 70, 87
Ephorus 25
Epicureans 12, 19, 93, 123-4
Epicurus 12, 123
Epimenides 30, 35, 62
Ephippos 84
Erastus 28, 78, 93-5
Euaeon 89
Eucleides 69-70
Eudoxus 84-5, 93
Euhemerus 118, 129
Euphantus 121, 125
Euphraeus 78, 110
Euripides 3
Evagoras 101-2

Fairweather, Janet 7, 14

Ferguson, John 118, 128
Ferguson, William 117
Feuer, Lewis 120
Fichte, Johann Gottlieb 8
Field, G.C. 69-70
Finley, M.I. 7, 27, 76, 124
Fränkel, H. 30
Friedländer, Paul 27
Fritz, Kurt von 8, 22, 24, 27-8, 58

Gaiser, Konrad 28
Gautier, Paul 11
Gorgias 25, 62, 99
Gouldner, A.W. 4
Gracchus, Tiberius 126-7, 129
Green, Peter 96-7
Grote, George 10, 40, 60, 78, 84
Gulley, Norman 27
Guthrie, W.K.C. 8, 26, 40, 68

Hagmonides 117
Hamilton, J.R. 28
Harward, J. 82
Hecataeus 33
Hegesippus 109
Helicon 79
Heracleides Lembus 16
Heracleides of Syracuse 83, 91-2
Heracleides Ponticus 26, 32, 87
Heracles 42, 53
Heraclitus 33, 39
Hermias 28, 78, 93-8, 108-9, 116
Hermippus 16-17
Hermodorus 26
Herodotus 33, 38-9, 41, 61, 73
Himareus 115
Hippasos 53, 60, 147n157
Howard, Michael 5
Humphreys, S.C. 33-4
Huxley, G.L. 32

Iamblichus 22, 24-5, 44-5, 53, 57
Iambulus 129
Ibycus 39
intellectuals:
    comparative analysis 7-13
    definition 1-4, 165n144
intellectuals, Greek:
    as elite 2-5, 8-9, 63, 132, 133n12
    see also Academy, Pythagoreans
    attitude towards power 4, 21, 31-2, 75, 78, 89, 101, 108, 110, 125, 129, 148n181

see also Aristotle, Isocrates,
  Plato, Zeno
 attitude towards war 52-3, 103-4
 legitimising functions of 80, 102,
  110-11, 130
 rivalry among 5, 31, 75, 79-80,
  88, 98, 109-11, 130, 161n36
Isocrates 8, 12
 as source 29, 35, 38, 49, 99-111
  passim
 Panhellenic ideal 8, 99, 103-6,
  109, 111
 personality of 100, 105-6
 relations with Athens 63, 99-100,
  102, 107-8
  with Plato and the Academy
   75, 88, 100-3, 109
  with rulers 100-3, 106-9
  with students 77, 88-9, 94,
   100-3, 107-8
 see also Pythagoras

Jaeger, W. 32, 95, 104, 107
James, William 6, 64, 125
Jason of Pherae 108-9
Josephus 13, 39
Justin-Trogus 25, 45, 88
Justus 13-15

Kahrstedt, U. 57-8
Kissinger, Henry 5
Knights, Ben 9
Kolakowski, Leszek 131

Long, A.A. 17
Lyceum 115, 117, 122
Lycon 121
Lycurgus 21, 34, 61, 91
Lysis 70

Mannheim, Karl 3, 131
Manuel, Frank 8
Markle, M.M. 111
Marrow, Glen 106
Mathieu, Georges 29
Mejer, Jørgen 18
Memnon 87
Menedemus of Eretria 16, 18, 125-6
Menedemus of Pyrrha 93, 131
mercenaries 61, 77, 81, 83, 90-2,
  102, 105
Meyer, Edward 27, 93
Milo 42, 52, 58, 59
Minar, E.L. 36-7, 40, 45, 47, 57-9

Mnesiphilus 20, 59
Momigliano, Arnaldo 16-17, 23
Morrison, J.S. 59, 72
Mosaic dream 120, 129, 141n12

Napoleon 9-11
Nepos, Cornelius 25, 72
Nicanor 117
Nichols, Ray 1
Nicocles 77, 88, 102-3
Ninon 53-6
Numa 21

Ollier, F. 126
Olympiodorus 121
Orphism 45, 47, 61

Parmenides 70
Pearson, Lionel 28
Perdiccas 78, 94, 110
Periander 30
Pericles 20-1, 58-9, 68
Peripatetics 116-17, 121
Persaeus 17, 124-6
Persia 38-9, 96, 102-5
Pfeiffer, Rudolf 17
Pherecydes 16, 30
Philip II 10-11, 29, 96-8, 101, 103,
  105-6, 109-11
Philip, J.A. 23
Philistus 75-6, 78-80, 83, 91
Philodemus 71
Philolaus 71-2
Philonides of Laodicea 123
Philonides of Thebes 126
Philopoemen 122
philosopher-king 4, 68, 71, 75, 122
Philostratus 19
Phintias 23, 50
Phocion 101, 117
Phocylides 33
Phormio 131
Pittacus 30
Plato 4-5, 31, 90-1, 95, 108, 110,
  116, 123, 129
 as source 26-8, 32, 34-5, 63-94
  passim
 in Athenian politics 64-9, 73-4
 in Sicily 71-83
 personality of 36, 64, 151n6
 political reticence of 64-8, 74-5
 relations with Archytas 60, 71-2,
  81-3
  with Aristotle 66, 96

with Dion 72-8, 81, 90-1
with Dionysius II 75-9, 81-3,
   125, 130-1
with family 64-6
with Isocrates 88, 105
with Pythagoreans 70-2, 75,
   82, 85
with students 74-5, 85-6, 93-4,
   100
sources for 6, 13-15, 25-8, 82,
   153n63
see also Pythagoras
Plutarch 12-13, 18-22, 28, 34, 58,
   72-3, 76, 79, 90, 93, 114, 122,
   124, 126-7
Polyarchus 23, 80-1
Polybius 58, 119, 122
Polycrates 37-40
Popper, Karl 74
Porphyry 22, 39, 57
Prorus 51
Prytanis 121
Pyrilampes 65-6
Pyrrhus 123-4
Pythagoras 8, 31, 100
   and Pythagoreans, sources for
      22-5, 36-7
   compared with Isocrates 105
      with Plato 85
   death of 55, 57
   in Croton 45-9
   in Samos 37-42
   personality and description of 34,
      36, 38, 40-1, 47-9, 60, 145n113
   puritanical views 46-7
   status of 1, 46
Pythagoreans 50-2, 61-2, 146n115
   as elite group 2, 9, 36, 49-50,
      53-4, 57, 84, 149n186
   as politicians 10, 36, 53-9
   compared with Academy 145n113
Python of Byzantium 109

Reyband, Louis 10
Riginos, Alice Swift 14-15
Rohde, Erwin 22, 48
Rostagni, A. 22, 24-5
Ryle, Gilbert 80

Saint-Simonians 8-10
Salmoxis 41
Satyrus 16-17
Schrödinger, Ervin 32
Seven Sages 30-2

Shils, Edward 2
Silverberg, T. 70
Simmel, Georg 51
Sinclair, T.A. 98
Socrates 20, 41, 64-71, 84-5, 99,
   115, 131
Solon 20, 30, 34-6, 62, 64, 68, 118,
   120, 142n36
Sophists 84
Sophocles of Sunium 12, 89, 119-21
Sources:
   anecdotal 13-17, 19, 23-4
   epistles 13, 26-8
   Hellenistic 16-19
   problems with 6, 12-29 *passim*
   see also Aristotle, Isocrates, Plato,
      Pythagoras
Speusippus 26, 28-9, 67, 85, 90,
   95-6, 109-11, 116
Sphaerus 21, 124, 126, 129
Stilpo 119
Stoics 19, 123-4, 126
   in politics 124-9
Strabo 129
Straton 121
Stuart, D.R. 7
Sybaris 42-4, 51-3, 55-6
Sykutris, J. 29

Tarn, W.W. 121-2, 126
Telys 43-4, 52
Thales 30-3, 39
Themison 78, 94, 103
Themistius 96
Themistocles 20, 59
Theodorus 70, 119
Theodotes 83
Theophrastus 31, 95, 97-8, 115,
   117-18, 120-1, 164n135, 164n140
Theopompus 13, 25, 28-9, 78, 93,
   102, 109-11
Theramenes 99-100
Thesleff, H. 27
Thomson, George 8
Tigerstedt, E.N. 6, 27
Timaeus 22, 24-6, 36, 43, 45, 49,
   51-4, 62, 71, 92
Timolaus 89, 131
Timon 17
Timonides 26, 90-1
Timotheus 87-9, 94, 101-2, 107-8
Toynbee, A.J. 129

Urban II 104

Valerius Maximus 127
Vogel, C.J. de 24-5, 48

Wallace, A.F.C. 45
Wardman, Alan 21
Weber, Max 2, 7-11, 48-9, 62, 86
Wilamowitz, Ulrich von 27
Winspear, A.D. 33, 70

Xenocrates 95, 115-17
Xenophanes 33
Xenophon 61, 65, 86, 105, 157n145

Yeats 63

Zeno of Citium 19, 123-6, 131
Zeno of Elea 57, 70
Znaniecki, Florian 2